Hindu Writings

A SHORT INTRODUCTION TO THE MAJOR SOURCES

OTHER BOOKS IN THIS SERIES

Buddhism: A Short Introduction, Klaus K. Klostermaier, ISBN 1–85168–186–8
Buddhism: A Short History, Edward Conze, ISBN 1–86168–221–X
Hinduism: A Short History, Klaus K. Klostermaier, ISBN 1–85168–213–9
Hinduism: A Short Introduction, Klaus K. Klostermaier, ISBN 1–85168–220–1
Islam: A Short History, William Montgomery Watt, ISBN 1–85168–205–8
A Short Introduction to Islamic Philosophy, Theology and Mysticism, Majid Fakhry, ISBN 1–85168–134–5
Muhammad: A Short Biography, Martin Forward, ISBN 1–85168–131–0
Jesus Christ: A Short Biography, Martin Forward, ISBN 1–85168–172–8
Christianity: A Short Introduction, Keith Ward, ISBN 1–85168–229–5
Judaism: A Short History, Lavinia and Dan Cohn-Sherbok, ISBN 1–85168–206–6
Judaism: A Short Introduction, Lavinia and Dan Cohn-Sherbok, ISBN 1–85168–207–4
A Short Reader in Judaism, Lavinia and Dan Cohn-Sherbok, ISBN 1–85168–112–4
A Short Introduction to the Old Testament Prophets, E. W. Heaton, ISBN 1–85168–114–0
Sufism: A Short Introduction, William C. Chittick, ISBN 1–85168–211–2
The Bahá'í Faith: A Short History, Peter Smith, ISBN 1–85168–208–2
The Bahá'í Faith: A Short Introduction, Moojan Momen, ISBN 1–85168–209–0
Confucianism: A Short Introduction, John and Evelyn Berthrong, ISBN 1–85168–236–8

RELATED TITLES PUBLISHED BY ONEWORLD

A Concise Encyclopedia of Hinduism, Klaus K. Klostermaier, ISBN 1–85168–175–2
The Bhagavad Gita: A Verse Translation, Geoffrey Parrinder, ISBN 1–85168–117–5
Hindu and Muslim Mysticism, R.C. Zaehner, ISBN 1–85168–046–2

Hindu Writings

A SHORT INTRODUCTION TO THE MAJOR SOURCES

Compiled and annotated by
Klaus K. Klostermaier

ONEWORLD
OXFORD

HINDU WRITINGS: A SHORT INTRODUCTION TO THE MAJOR SOURCES

Oneworld Publications
(Sales and Editorial)
185 Banbury Road
Oxford OX2 7AR
England
http://www.oneworld-publications.com

Oneworld Publications
(US Marketing Office)
160 N. Washington St.
4th Floor, Boston
MA 02114
USA

A CIP record for this title is available
from the British Library

ISBN 1–85168–230–9

Cover design by Design Deluxe
Typeset by LaserScript Limited, Mitcham, UK
Printed and bound by Clays Ltd, St Ives plc

CONTENTS

FOREWORD

Hindu Writings: A Short Introduction to the Major Sources has been conceived as companion to *Hinduism: A Short History* (Oneworld, 2000) and *Hinduism: A Short Introduction* (Oneworld, 1998) providing fairly extensive textual documentation for the narrative. The brief introductions and the comments accompanying the texts are meant to contextualize the quotes and to explain names and words that are essential for an understanding of the issues.

Full references have been given for those quotes that are translations from Indic languages. The endnotes identify existing translations (in English) of the complete sources referred to. While these translations (and others in other languages) were consulted, they were modified on the basis of the original texts. An attempt was made to avoid all archaisms and complicated sentence constructions, in order to make the texts as accessible as possible for the interested non-specialist today. Where an existing translation was adopted as found in the original referred to, this has been explicitly acknowledged. Texts originally written in English have been reproduced without any changes in style or the transliteration of Indic words.

As the readers of *Hinduism: A Short History* will know, the essentials of Hinduism are not fully circumscribed by ancient Hindu scriptures (large as these may be) but include also Hindu customs and practices as well as historical developments through the ages. Hinduism has always been, and still is, in the making. Sources from our own time have been included to demonstrate this continuing growth of Hinduism and the changes that are taking place as a consequence of constant reinterpretations of the ancient sources, and in response to challenges and stimuli from outside.

Klaus K. Klostermaier
Winnipeg, November 1999

INTRODUCTION

Hinduism is unlike any of the other major historic religions. It does not trace its teachings to the authoritative words of an identifiable founder nor its origin to a specific date in history. Nor does it consider a single scripture as the source of its teachings. Some Hindus presume their tradition to derive from a primeval revelation of the Supreme to privileged sages; others consider it beginningless *sanātana dharma*, the eternal law that governs everything independently of any divine or human agency. Hinduism also never rejected a parent tradition from which it would separate as a rebel child, as all other major living religions have done. For most of their history Hindus did not find it necessary to define "the essentials of Hinduism" or prove Hinduism different from other religions.

Traditional Hinduism has preserved surprisingly much of the character of an autochthonous native tradition, maintaining the holistic, all-embracing approach typical of these. There is no hard and fast distinction between the sacred and the secular, no strict separation of religious ritual from essential daily activities, no real difference or tension between religion and culture.

The various branches of what became known as Hinduism do not have a common creed and they do not demand from their followers any declaration of a Hindu faith. Until recently one could not become a Hindu, unless one was born into a Hindu family; and one could not cease to be a Hindu, if one was born a Hindu, unless one committed a serious breach of traditional law that was punishable by expulsion from one's caste.

As far as membership of the Hindu community was concerned, it did not matter what one thought or believed as long as one observed the laws of one's caste and participated in the traditional rituals which were also part and parcel of traditional Indian culture. On the other hand, many of the *saṃpradāyas*, specific worship traditions within Hinduism, drew very close and narrow boundaries. Those who wished to be members had to obey a very strict regimen with regard to diet, lifestyle, reading, and worship; they must not accept the teachings of any other *saṃpradāya*, not even read books or listen to sermons from them.

Left to itself, the large, ancient, wise Hindu civilization quietly appropriated whatever was brought into it from the outside, absorbed it, transformed it, and made it its own. That process of assimilation was first disturbed in a major way by the massive onslaught of Islamic conquerors from the tenth century C.E. onwards. The Muslims came to conquer India and to convert the native "idolaters" to their own religion. The rigid monotheism of Islam, the exclusivity claim of Mohammed's revelation, and the rejection of the caste system proved irreconcilable with the native, religio-cultural traditions of India.

While Islam could claim partial success – for over half a millennium most of India was under Muslim rule and a third of the population accepted Islam – it generated a resistance among Hindus who began to realize an identity of their own based on their native "Hindu" traditions. Not by accident, from the eleventh century onwards, *nibandhas* were composed: encyclopedic works that collected Hindu legal traditions, information about Hindu holy places, and the Hindu rituals and customs of all *saṃpradāyas*. Hindus became aware of Hinduism as distinct from Islam. Islamic hostility towards "idolatry" further served to underscore the differences between Hindu traditions and other religions.

The second major disturbance was created by Western European powers from 1498 C.E. onwards. While the main interest of the Portuguese, Dutch, Danish, French, and English – all of whom established colonies in India – was trade, they were soon persuaded by the ecclesiastical powers of their home-countries that they also had a duty to spread their Christian faith among the "heathen."

By demanding from the citizens of Goa, the first European colony on Indian soil, either to convert to the Catholic Church or to emigrate, the Portuguese established a hard and fast line between Christianity and Hinduism and also made sure that future relations between the two religions were based on hostility and exclusivity. Like Islam, Christianity became a foreign invader and remained a foreign, religio-cultural presence in India. It also provoked a reaction and a resistance among Hindus that became quite articulate from the end of the nineteenth century onwards.

The global designation "Hinduism" is apt to disguise the great diversity of Indian religious traditions. Till very recently "Hindus" defined their religious identities by using specific appellations like Vaiṣṇava, Śaiva, Śākta, Smārta, etc., and several modern movements, like the Ramakrishna Mission and the International Society for Krishna Consciousness, emphatically denied being "Hindu" so as not to be identified with other branches of Hinduism that held beliefs contrary to their own.

BASIC HINDU SOURCE LITERATURE

The total mass of writings considered Hindu Scriptures, i.e. books that are religiously authoritative and believed to have been inspired by a superhuman agency, far exceeds any scriptural tradition of any other religion. While much of it is accepted as divinely revealed only by believers in particular communities, there is a large corpus of books called Vedas that is accepted by all Hindus as "sacred."

Before the term "Hinduism" was introduced, Hindus called their religion *vaidika dharma*, the Vedic law, indicating a common source to the diverse Hindu worship traditions (*saṃpradāyas*). The term Veda, "(sacred) knowledge," is used in a narrower and a wider sense, as explained in the next section (*śruti* and *smṛti*). Although the writing down of sacred texts was apparently forbidden for a long time, their collection, memorization, and recitation was central to ancient Indian traditions.

The language of the Vedas (in the narrower sense) is an archaic Sanskṛt, "the refined language" that became the language of Hindu holy books and philosophical expositions, a language that remained in the possession of the Hindu elite and that was less and less understood by the people at large. The ordinary people spoke a variety of Prākṛts, "natural languages," that have much of their vocabulary rooted in Sanskṛt but with a much simplified grammar and often a different pronunciation. The heterodox movements chose Prākṛts as their sacred languages:

the Jain canon is written in Ardhamāgadhī and the (Theravāda) Buddhists chose Pālī for their scriptures and their scholarly works. The medieval preachers of religions of devotion (*bhakti*) used the vernaculars of the areas they lived in: Tamil, Avadhī, Brajbhāṣa, Bengālī, Mahraṭṭī, Gujaratī etc., languages also used today by the popular Hindu teachers. Sanskṛt, however, has retained its importance as the language of Hindu scholarship and ritual.

Śruti *and* Smṛti

Authoritative Hindu religious literature is divided into two main categories: *śruti* (literally: "that which has been heard") and *smṛti* (literally: "that which has been remembered.") *Śruti* has the connotation of "revelation," "truth" in an unquestionable sense, norms of belief and practice. *Smṛti* bases its authority on the standing of the writer to which it is attributed, authoritative only to the extent to which it conforms to *śruti*. It offers a certain freedom of choice between conflicting opinions and allows interpretation that is more than the mere establishing of the one correct meaning of words and sentences.

Śruti, according to Hindu orthodoxy, is identical with the Veda (literally "knowledge") in its wider sense which comprises:

1. The Veda in the narrower sense, i.e. the four *saṃhitās* (literally, "collections" (of hymns)):
   - a) *Ṛg-Veda* (Veda of hymns, or verses)
   - b) *Yajur-Veda* (Veda of rituals)
   - c) *Sāma-Veda* (Veda of melodies)
   - d) *Atharva-Veda* (Veda of incantations and spells)
2. The *Brāhmaṇas*, large texts explanatory of the rituals associated with each of the four *saṃhitās* as follows:
   - a) *Ṛg-Veda*: i) *Aitareya (Āśvalāyaṇa)*
     ii) *Kauśītaki (Sāṁkhāyaṇa)*
   - b) *Yajur-Veda*: i) *Taittirīya*
     ii) *Śathapatha*
   - c) Eight *Sāma-Veda* of which the most important:
     i) *Prauḍha (Pañcaviṃśa)*
     ii) *Tāṇḍya*
     iii) *Ṣadviṃśa*
   - d) *Atharva-Veda*: *Gopatha*

3. *Āraṇyakas*, literally "forest treatises," i.e. teachings no longer relating to sacrifice and ritual, namely:

a) *Bṛhad*
b) *Taittirīya*
c) *Aitareya*
d) *Kauṣītaki*

Some of the *Āraṇyakas* are combined with the *Upaniṣads*.

4. *Upaniṣads*, also called "Vedānta," "end of the Veda," esoteric texts designed to teach the means of liberation from rebirth and all suffering. There is a very large number of these, of which 108 are usually enumerated as "genuine." There are ten to twelve so-called "major *Upaniṣads*," that have been commented upon by classical authors. There is a large number of so-called "sectarian Upaniṣads," compendia of Vaiṣṇava, Śaiva, and Śākta teachings and practices, and others.

Smṛti or "tradition" comprises a very large number of heterogeneous works, classified as follows:

1. *Smṛtis*, codes of law, often introduced by creation-narratives and concluded by advice on how to reach salvation. They are fairly numerous, but some have acquired an authority that stands out, such as *Manu-Smṛti*, attributed to Manu, the forefather of all humans now living, *Yājñavalkya-Smṛti*, attributed to an important Vedic sage, *Viṣṇu-Smṛti*, and many others. Given the importance of custom and law in Hinduism, these works rank very high in the list of authoritative Hindu literature.
2. *Itihāsa*, "history," comprising the two ancient Indian epics: *Rāmāyaṇa*, ascribed to Vālmīki, and *Mahābhārata* (including *Bhagavadgītā*), ascribed to Vyāsa.
3. *Purāṇas*, "ancient (books)," texts that provide information about the creation of the universe, about genealogies of patriarchs and kings, rules of life, and mythologies of the major deities they are dealing with. They are subdivided into eighteen *Mahā-Purāṇas*, "Great Purāṇas," classified according to the deity they are devoted to, and a large number of *Upa-Purāṇas*, "Lesser Purāṇas."
   a) The *Mahā-Purāṇas* comprise:
      - Six Vaiṣṇava (*sattva*) Purāṇas: *Viṣṇu-Purāṇa; Nāradīya-Purāṇa; Bhāgavata-Purāṇa; Garuḍa-Purāṇa; Padma-Purāṇa; Varāha-Purāṇa*

- Six Śaiva (*rājasa*) Purāṇas: *Matsya-Purāṇa; Kūrma-Purāṇa; Liṅga-Purāṇa; Śiva-Purāṇa; Skanda-Purāṇa; Agni-Purāṇa*
- Six Brahma (*tāmasa*) Purāṇas: *Brahma-Purāṇa; Brahmāṇḍa-Purāṇa; Brahmavaivārta-Purāṇa; Mārkaṇḍeya-Purāṇa; Bhaviṣya-Purāṇa; Vāmana-Purāṇa*

b) *Upa-Purāṇas*: a large number, many of which fall into the above pattern of *Mahā-Purāṇas*.

The ascription to either category is not undisputed. Thus, for example, the Śāktas consider the *(Mahā)-Devī Bhāgavata Purāṇa* a "Mahā-Purāṇa," while others classify it as an "Upa-Purāṇa."

In general, the members of a particular *saṃpradāya* would consider the Purāṇa that they adopt as theirs as *śruti*, "revelation," with the same authority as that of the Vedas.

c) There are also numerous *Sthala-Purāṇas*, associated with major temples, which are works that describe the history of a particular holy place (*sthala*), embellishing it with numerous miraculous events associated with the image and its worship.

The Sūtras

At a certain point in time, when memorizing the increasingly voluminous primary literature apparently became next to impossible, short compendia, *sūtras* (literally "threads") were composed that presented the essentials of each discipline in a succinct and reliable manner. In the course of time, virtually all subjects of traditional learning received their *sūtras*. Thus we have *Śrauta-Śutras*, summarizing the rules applying to public sacrifices, *Gṛhya-Sūtras*, providing a summary of domestic rites, *Kalpa-Sūtras*, compendia of other rituals, *Dharma-Sūtras*, manuals of religious and secular law, and *Śulva-Sūtras*, providing elementary geometry and rules of construction for fire-altars and so forth.

When the Veda became difficult to understand owing to its archaic language and the distance in time between its authors and its later students, *Vedāṅgas*, books teaching auxiliary sciences connected with Veda-study, were provided. These include *Śikṣā* (phonetics), *Chaṇḍas* (metre), *Vyākaraṇa* (grammar), *Nirukta* (etymology), *Jyotiṣa* (astronomy), and *Kalpa* (ritual).

While training in the Vedas was mandatory for brahmins in order to enable them to fulfill their priestly duties, very often they were also taught secular subjects, termed *Upa-Vedas* (sciences not connected with Veda-study). The traditional subjects were *Āyur-Veda* (medicine), *Gandharva-Veda* (music and dancing), *Dhanur-Veda* (archery), and *Sthāpatya-Veda* (architecture).

Sectarian Literature

In addition to this vast body of writing, which forms the common heritage of Hinduism, there is an extensive sectarian literature, which advocates tenets that are exclusive to certain *saṃpradāyas* and are not shared by other Hindus. Thus, there are numerous *Saṃhitās*, Vaiṣṇava writings, *Āgamas*, Śaivite works, and *Tantras*, Śākta books. The followers of these *saṃpradāyas* hold these works to be revealed (*śruti*) and equal in authority to the Veda. While offering some philosophical reflections on the nature of God, the world, and living beings from the specific theological perspective which the particular community advocates, the texts are mostly concerned with ritual and with regulations of the life of the devotees. Some are manuals of worship as it is performed in major temples. Thus the *Parameśvara Saṃhitā* codifies the worship of the great Viṣṇu sanctuary at Śrīraṅgam, Southern India; while the *Somaśambhu-paddhati* details the daily ritual in Southern Indian Śiva temples.

While the classification of Hindu scriptures is fairly universally accepted, both the relative and the absolute dating of individual works is controversial. As regards relative dating, there are Hindu scholars who assume that the *Atharvavdea* is older than the *Ṛgveda* and there is a fairly strong Hindu tradition that insists that the Purāṇas are as old as the Vedas, antedating the epics. With regard to absolute dating, the gap between those who accept the Āryan-invasion theory, conceived by European scholars in the late nineteenth century, and those who reject it, is enormous: the dates for the composition of the *Ṛgveda*, given by representatives of the two schools of thought, differ by as much as three thousand years.

Non-Sanskṛt Hindu literature

The entire mass of literature mentioned so far is written in Sanskṛt, one of the oldest of the known Indo-European languages. Parallel to it, a large religious literature also developed in Indian vernaculars. Its authors were usually non-brahmins who wished to communicate with the ordinary people in their own languages. Non-Sanskṛt Hindu literature has been produced in virtually all the major Indian vernaculars and in many smaller dialects as well.

There is an ancient rivalry between North and South in India that also extends to language and scriptures. While the North insists on the primacy of Sanskṛt scriptures and considers Sanskṛt the only sacred language proper, the South claims that Tamil is older than Sanskṛt and that certain Tamil writings are on an equal footing with Sanskṛt *śruti*. This linguistic-cum-religious issue came to the fore in medieval Tamilnadu: the *ācāryas* of Śrīraṅgam had the Tamil hymns of the Āḷvārs recited in temple-worship, side by side with Sanskṛt hymns.

With the development of popular *bhakti* movements, which replaced much of traditional Brahminism and its ritual, compositions in the vernaculars of India also became part of religious ritual. Tulsīdās's *Rāmcaritmānas*, and the Avadhī (Eastern Hindī) re-creation of the *Rāmāyaṇa*, all but eclipsed Vālmīki's Sanskṛt original in Northern India, and the inspired poetry of singers in many tongues became the preferred hymns sung by groups of devotees meeting for *bhajan* singing. The religious literature created by hundreds of saint-singers is enormous.

In addition, contemporary leaders and poets contribute to the volume. The devotees of a particular *guru* usually consider his or her words inspired. Thus the recorded conversations of acknowledged saints like Ramakrishna Paramahamsa, Ramana Maharṣi, Ānandamayī Mā, and many others, are treated as "gospels" by their followers and reverently read out in religious gatherings. There is, quite literally, no end to the production of Hindu religious literature in a great many different languages, and there is no possibility that any single person could read all of it.

THE GODS AND GODDESSES OF HINDUISM

Hinduism is characterized on the one hand by the worship of an immense variety of gods and goddesses, and on the other by the insistence that there is only one Supreme Being.

Already in the Vedas we encounter a large number of *devas*, the recipients of praise and sacrifice: Agni, Indra, Vāk, Aditi, Rudra, Mitra,

Varuṇa – to name only a few. We also see the *ṛṣis* address in turn each of these as the highest, the most powerful, the god of gods. Max Müller coined the term "henotheism" to differentiate Vedic religion both from popular "polytheism" and from (biblical) "monotheism." The *Ṛgveda* itself contains an oft-quoted verse that Indra is known by many names but that the sages know that he is One. The *Upaniṣads* see in the many different Vedic gods only symbols and manifestations of *brahman*, an immaterial highest principle, the unborn and indestructible ground of the universe.

With the development of the Epics and Purāṇas the worship of many gods and their numerous manifestations became the prevalent form of religion. Some of the names of gods mentioned in the Vedas, such as Viṣṇu, Śiva, Sūrya, emerged as prominent and became the focus of large communities of worshippers that tended to regard their god as the Supreme Being, while other gods were assigned lesser roles. For Vaiṣṇavas, Viṣṇu is the Supreme God; for Śaivites, Śiva; for Śāktas, Devī. Accordingly, the roles of creator, sustainer, and saviour are ascribed to each of them. They also appear in numerous manifestations that often became the object of independent worship. The best-known are the ten *avatāras* (descents) of Viṣṇu, of whom Rāma and Kṛṣṇa are the most prominent in today's Hinduism.

Philosophically it was always clear to Hindus that there could only be one Supreme Being. To circumvent the sectarian quarrels between Vaiṣṇavas and Śaivites, Śāktas, and followers of other traditions, Śaṅkara, the great, early-medieval Hindu reformer, described *brahman*, the Supreme Being of the *Upaniṣads*, as non-personal, not qualified by any attributes, not identifiable by name, without history or mythology, and not requiring particular forms of external worship; only to be reached in the depth of one's own consciousness through meditation. To satisfy ordinary believers, he introduced the *pañcāyatana pūjā* in which obeisance is rendered to Śiva, Viṣṇu, Devī, Sūrya, and Gaṇeśa collectively.

Another popular expression of the Oneness of God, in spite of the manifoldness of divine manifestations, is the well-known *trimūrti*, the "Hindu Trinity" of Brahmā, Viṣṇu and Śiva. Individually they represent the divine power of creation, sustenance, and dissolution of the world; collectively they are the Supreme Being.

In Sanskṛt the word *brahman* designates the absolute principle of philosophy, a sacred text, a hymn of praise, a class of writings, the soul, the personal creator-god of religion, and the members of the highest caste (and some other things). In English there is a convention to spell the latter *brahmin*, the personal god *Brahmā*, and to use the term "*brahman*" exclusively for the purely spiritual principle of the Upaniṣads. Things are, however, complicated by the insistence of Vaiṣṇavas that Viṣṇu is identical to *brahman* (no longer seen as impersonal, but as a person); of Śaivas that Śiva is identical to *brahman*; and by Śāktas that Devī is identical to *brahman* (conceived as a composite of matter and spirit).

While there are many genealogies (*vaṃśa*) of gods offered in texts like the *Bṛhaddevatā* and various Purāṇas, there is no commonly accepted Hindu pantheon, in which fixed places are definitely assigned to all the Hindu gods. Each major branch of Hinduism has it own way of arranging the multitude of gods and goddesses in such a way as to assure the prominence of the one god who is the focus of worship in this particular tradition.

The sources quoted will offer parallel texts for the three mainstream Hindu traditions of Vaiṣṇavism, Śaivism and Śāktism. There are many others that are not included here, but which have considerable followings.

THE FOUR WORLD-AGES

Hindus assume that the present universe is just one of many that have preceded it and that will follow. They began early to calculate with immense numbers when dealing with the age of our cosmos. While various sources use different terminologies and measures, many of the texts quoted use expressions like *kalpa* and *yuga*. A *kalpa*, also called a day of Brahmā, lasts 4,320,000,000 human years. We are now living in the Śrīśvetavarāhakalpa. It is followed by a night of Brahmā of equal length, when the universe is dormant. Each *kalpa* consists of 1000 *Mahā-yugas*, world-ages. Each *Mahā-yuga* is subdivided into four periods. At the beginning is a golden age, the *Kṛta-yuga*, lasting 1,728 000 years, in which everybody follows the full *dharma* and people lead long and happy lives. It is followed by a silver age, the *Tretā-yuga*, lasting 1,296,000 years, in which signs of slight deterioration become visible. Together with the diminishing of virtue, life is shortened and less happy than before. Then comes *Dvāpara-yuga*, lasting 846,000 years, in which *dharma*, symbolized by a cow, is moving on only two feet instead of four and people's lives become shorter and more difficult. The last of the world ages is *Kali-yuga*, "the age of strife," lasting 432,000 years, full of misery and wickedness. At present we are living in a *Kali-yuga* which began with the Mahābhārata war (3002 B.C.E.) and which is to end with the apparition of the *Kalki-avatāra* who brings about a final confrontation between the good and the wicked.

1 THE VEDIC INDRA RELIGION

Vedic religion was centered around sacrifices (*yajña*) that were offered to a great many different gods (*deva/devatā*) to obtain everything necessary for life in the world here and beyond.

INDRA IN THE *ṚGVEDA*

Indra is the *deva* to whom most of the hymns of the *Ṛgveda* are addressed. A wealth of epithets express his importance and describe his nature. No single trait figures more prominently than his being *Vṛtrahan*, the slayer of *Vṛtra*.

> I now will proclaim the first of the valiant deeds of Indra, the wielder of the *vajra*: he killed the Great Snake, released the waters and ruptured the mountain barriers.
>
> He killed the Great Snake, that lay on the mountains; Tvaṣṭṛ had fashioned the *vajra*. The waters rushed to the sea like cows with calves.
>
> Like a bull he lapped up the *soma*, emptied the three sacrificial vessels; the Great One took the *vajra* and killed the Firstborn of the Great Snake.
>
> Indra, after you had slain the Firstborn of the Great Snake and overcome the tricks of the magicians, you gave life to sun and dawn and sky: no one was left to oppose you.
>
> Indra, with his great and deadly *vajra* smashed to pieces Vṛtra, the worst of all evildoers. Like a tree felled by the ax lies the Great Snake low on the earth.
>
> Indra is king of all that moves and that does not move, of wild and domestic animals, the *vajra* wielder. He rules as sovereign over all people.[1]

The etymology of the name "Indra" is uncertain. Connected with the phenomena of storm and rain as well as war and conquest, Indra represents power and victory. His greatest victory is the vanquishing of Vṛtra.

Regarding the identity of Vṛtra, the ancient sources are of divided opinion. So are modern interpreters. Some see in Vṛtra a demon, others a rain cloud. The former appears to agree better with the texts. Vṛtra represents everything that is oppressive, fearsome, unhealthy, repugnant. The Vedic Vṛtra has his counterparts in mysterious, usually malevolent spirits, believed in by many mountain people who live in environments that are threatened by all kinds of catastrophic events.

The *vajra*, often translated as "thunderbolt," is a magical weapon the identity of which is not easy to establish. It almost certainly has nothing to do with the natural phenomenon of lightning: in the *Śatapatha Brāhmaṇa* the *vajra* with which Vṛtra is to be killed is formed from the bones of the sage Dadhīca. In later tantric Hinduism the *vajra* is the "diamond" symbol used in worship and identified with the ultimate wisdom that penetrates everything.

The term "*ahi*" has been rendered as "dragon" by other translators. However, there is no dragon-myth tradition in India, and "*ahi*" is a generic term for snakes. The Vedic Vṛtra is not exhibiting the typical features of dragons, as described in other mythologies.

There has been a long scholarly debate about the nature of soma, the juice, possibly fermented, pressed from the stalks of the soma plant, identified by some with the fly agaric, and by others with hemp. Soma was a necessary ingredient in Vedic sacrifice and the entire ninth book of the *Ṛgveda* consists of hymns to soma. It appears to have had an intoxicating and exhilarating effect.

Maghavan, "The Great One," is an attribute of the highest god and a title later also bestowed on Viṣṇu and Śiva.

INDRA IN THE *BṚHADDEVATĀ*

The *Bṛhaddevatā*, an early work that systematizes and summarizes the content of the Vedic hymns, adds, in its account of Indra's battle with Vṛtra, some interesting elements not mentioned in the *Ṛgveda* that apparently belonged to a floating, popular Indra saga:

> Soma, oppressed by fear of Vṛtra, fled from the gods and betook himself to a river named Aṃśūmatī in the country of the Kurus. He approached, with Bṛhaspati only, the slayer of Vṛtra, being about to fight in company with the greatly rejoicing Maruts, armed with various weapons. Soma, seeing them approaching stood in array with his forces, thinking Vṛtra was approaching him with a hostile host, intent on slaying him. To him, arrayed and ready with his bow, Bṛhaspati spoke: "This is the Lord of Maruts, O Soma, come back to the gods, O Lord." Hearing the speech of the preceptor of the gods, which was unavailing because he believed it was Vṛtra, he replied: "No!" So the mighty Śakra, taking him by force, went to the gods in heaven. The celestials [then] drank him in due form. And having drunk him they slew in battle nine times ninety demons ... Having tormented these three worlds Vṛtra remained unassailable by reason of his fury. Him Indra could not slay. Going to Viṣṇu he said "I wish to slay Vṛtra; stride forth today and stand at my side. May Dyaus make room for my outstretched bolt." Saying "Yes," Viṣṇu did so, and Dyaus gave him an opening.[2]

In the system of gods, according to *Bṛhaddevatā* I, 121, Indra is the name for the manifestations in the middle-sphere.

> In Indra are contained Parjanya, Rudra, Vāyu, Bṛhaspati, Varuṇa, Ka, Mṛtyu, and the god Brāhmaṇaspati. Manyu, Viśvakarman, Mitra, Kṣetrapati, Yama, Tārṣkya, Vāstoṣpati and also Sarasvat, Apām napāt and Dadhikra, Suparṇa, Purūravās, ṛta, Asunīti, Vena, in his sphere is also Aditi; and Tvaṣṭṛ and Savitṛ, Vāta as well as Vācaspati, Dhātṛ and also Prajāpati, and those who are called the Atharvāns; and so also the Falcon and Agni, and who is called Ilā, Vidhātṛ, Indu, Ahirbudhnya, Soma, Ahi ...[3]

INDRA IN THE *BRĀHMAṆAS*

The *Brāhmaṇas* also contain detailed descriptions of the Vedic rituals, fairly full accounts of the myths that are often only alluded to in the Vedic hymns. Thus the *Śatapatha Brāhmaṇa* combines with Indra's Vṛtra-slaying another story about his killing of Tvaṣṭṛ's three-headed son Viśvarūpa.

> Tvaṣṭṛ had a three-headed, six-eyed son. He had three mouths; and because he was thus shaped his name was Viśvarūpa ["Universal Form"]. One of his mouths was soma-drinking, one spirit-drinking, and one was for other kinds of food. Indra hated him and cut off these heads of his.
>
> Now from the one which was soma-drinking, a hazel-cock sprang forth; whence the latter is of brownish color, for king Soma is brown.

From the one which was spirit-drinking a sparrow came forth; whence the latter talks as if stammering, for he who drinks spirits, talks as if he stammered.

Then from the one which served for other kinds of food a partridge sprang, whence the latter is much variegated in color: on its wings, namely, butter-drops, as it were, have dropped in one place, and honey-mead drops in another, for suchlike, as it were, was the food which he consumed with that [mouth].

Tvaṣṭṛ was furious: "Has he indeed slain my son?" he exclaimed. He brought soma-juice from which Indra was excluded; and just as the soma-juice on being produced had Indra excluded from it so it remained when it was offered up.

Indra ... though uninvited consumed what pure soma was in the tub ...

Tvaṣṭṛ was furious ... and what was left of the soma he let flow into the fire saying: "Grow you, having Indra for your foe." ... It became possessed of Agni and Soma, of all sciences, all glory, all nourishment, all prosperity.

And since it so developed whilst rolling onwards, it became Vṛtra; and since he sprang forth footless he was a serpent. Danu and Danāyū received him like mother and father, whence they call him Dānava.

And because Tvaṣṭṛ said: "Grow you having Indra for your foe!" therefore Indra slew him. Had he said "Grow, the foe [slayer] of Indra," he would certainly have forthwith slain Indra.[4]

Tvaṣṭṛ's intention had been to create a being that was an "Indra-defeater." Due to faulty accenting it became a being "to be defeated by Indra." The story probably was also intended to inculcate in the brahmins officiating at a sacrifice a sense of strict discipline, illustrating the catastrophic consequences of any lapses, and be it just a single wrong accent in a *mantra*.

INDRA IN THE *UPANIṢADS*

With the *Upaniṣads* a profound change occurs in the Vedic tradition. Together with the diminishing role of the *yajña* Indra's position also becomes reduced. Vedic sacrifices are now considered "useless rafts" for the crossing of the ocean of *saṃsāra*, and Indra, as sovereign of the world perceived by the senses, becomes unimportant for a spirituality that seeks the world-transcendent *brahman*. As far as ultimate liberation from rebirth is concerned, Indra is no better off than any ordinary mortal.

The *Chāndogya Upaniṣad* narrates how Indra gained enlightenment under the human *guru* Prajāpati:

> The Self which is free from evil, ageless, deathless, sorrowless, hungerless, thirstless, whose desire is the Real, whose conception is the Real – He should be searched out, Him one should desire to understand. He obtains all worlds and desires who has found out and who understands that Self.[5]

Thus spoke Prajāpati. Both the *devas* and the *asuras* heard it. Then they said:

> Come, let us search out that Self, through whom one obtains all worlds and all desires. Then Indra from among the *devas* and Vairocana from among the *asuras* went forth and presented themselves to Prajāpati, fuel in hand.[6]

The two lived as *brahmacāris* with Prajāpati for thirty-two years. Then Prajāpati asked them: "Desiring what have you been living?" The two repeat the description of the Self which Prajāpati had given at the outset. Prajāpati now imparts his teaching:

> "The person that is seen in the eye, that is the self," he said. "That is the immortal, the fearless, that is *brahman*." "But, Sir, he who is perceived in water and in a mirror, who is he?" He replied, "The same one, indeed is perceived in all these. Look at yourself in a pan of water and whatever you do not understand of the self, tell me." The two looked in a pan of water. Then Prajāpati said to the two, "What do you see?" Then the two said, "We both see the self thus altogether. A picture even to the very hairs and nails." Then Prajāpati said to the two, "After you have well adorned yourselves, put on your best clothes, make yourself tidy, look into a pan of water. Then the two adorned themselves well, put on their best clothes, made themselves tidy and looked into a pan of water. Then Prajāpati said to the two, "What do you see?" The two said, "Just as we are, Sir, well adorned, with our best clothes and tidy, thus we see both these." "That is the self," said he, "that is the immortal, the fearless, that is *brahman*." They both went away with a tranquil heart. Then Prajāpati looked at them and said: "They go away without having perceived, without having known the self. Whosoever will follow such a doctrine, be they *devas* or *asuras* they shall perish." Then Vairocana with a tranquil heart went to the *asuras* and declared that doctrine, "One's bodily self is to be made happy here, one's bodily self is to be served. He who makes his own self happy here and he who serves his own self, he obtains both worlds, this one and the next."[7]

While Vairocana is satisfied with this information, Indra is not. He returns to Prajāpati for a further sixty-nine years of studenthood. At the end of it Indra receives the true teaching about the true Self that transcends his own realm:

> This body, verily is mortal. It has been appropriated by death. But it is the standing-ground of that bodiless, deathless Self. One who is in a body has been appropriated by pleasure and pain. There is no freedom from pleasure and pain for one who is in a body. One who is bodiless, is untouched by pleasure and pain.[8]

INDRA IN THE EPICS AND *PURĀṆAS*

In the Epics and the *Purāṇas* there are numerous references to Indra and especially to his slaying of Vṛtra. In the *Mahābhārata* there are altogether five versions of the Indra–Vṛtra myth. The *Bhāgavata Purāṇa* narrates at extraordinary length the Indra–Vṛtra story, giving it a sectarian Vaiṣṇava twist, but repeating also many elements of the ancient Vedic myth.

Indra had offended Bṛhaspati, the divine preceptor, by not rising from his seat when Bṛhaspati entered, and Bṛhaspati deserted the gods. The *asuras* then immediately took up arms against the *devas*. The badly beaten *devas* approached Brahmā for help. Brahmā advised the gods to ask Viśvarūpa, "son of Tvaṣṭṛ, a Brahmin, a *tapasvin*, self-controlled," to become their *guru*. Viśvarūpa accepted.

> Viśvarūpa snatched by means of a prayer addressed to Lord Viṣṇu the fortune of the *asuras* and restored it to the great Indra. Viśvarūpa, nobleminded, taught to Indra the prayer protected by which that mighty god with a thousand eyes was able to conquer the demon hosts.
>
> Viśvarūpa had three heads: with one he drank soma, with the second he drank liquor, and with the third he ate food. He faithfully performed the sacrifices to the gods since the gods were his fathers. But he secretly offered a share to the *asuras* . . . for he had his sympathies with the *asuras* because of the affection his mother [Rācanā] bore to them.[9]

Indra gets angry at this and cuts off his heads. The first head turns into the *kapiñjala*, the second into the sparrow, and the third into the partridge. Indra accepts the sin of Brahmanicide, remains with it for a year, and then divides it into four parts among the earth, water, trees, and women, together with a boon.

Tvaṣṭṛ, whose son had been killed, pours oblations into the sacred fire in order to obtain another son who would kill Indra:

> Now from the *anvāhāryapacana* rose a demon of terrible aspect who looked like Death appearing at the time of universal dissolution for the destruction of the worlds. He rapidly grew to the extent of an arrow's throw on every side from day to day, presented the appearance of a burnt

> hill, and possessed the glow of a mass of evening clouds. With a beard and moustache and hair red as heated copper and eyes as fierce as the midday sun, he danced as if holding the vault of heaven on the end of his brilliant trident, gave a loud roar, and shook the earth with his feet. Terribly afraid, all creatures ran to and fro, as they saw him respiring again and again with his extensive gaping mouth, containing fearful teeth, and deep as a cavern, which seemed to imbibe the firmament, lick the stars with the tongue, and devour the three worlds. That sinful and ferocious demon was rightly named Vṛtra, inasmuch as these worlds were enveloped by that darkness appearing in the form of Tvaṣṭṛ's offspring. Rushing against him with their troops, the generals of the gods asailed him, each with his hosts of celestial missiles and weapons; he, however, swallowed them all.[10]

The humiliated gods this time approach Viṣṇu, addressing him with a long prayer. Viṣṇu, pleased, advises the gods to go to Dadhyañc (Dadhīca), the original possessor of the *Nārāyaṇa Kavaca*, and ask his body from him. From its limbs the divine artisan Viśvakarman should make a weapon "by means of which and strengthened with my power you will be able to sever the head of Vṛtra. When he is slain you will regain your glory." He concludes: "Enemies can never destroy those who are devoted to me."[11]

The *Bhāgavata Purāṇa* locates the Indra–Vṛtra battle on the banks of the Narbadā River at the beginning of the *Tretā yuga* "during the very first round of the four *yugas*." Two formidable armies meet: the *asuras* make no impression on the *devas* and flee, leaving Vṛtra alone. Vṛtra appears composed, calm, and virtuous, following the rules of scripture, preaching *Yoga* to his fellow-*asuras* and Viṣṇubhakti to Indra. He curses Indra as a Brahmin-murderer and killer of his *guru*, and he prays to Viṣṇu to be reborn as a servant of his servants. Vṛtra and Indra begin to fight.

Vṛtra appears clearly superior to Indra and several times Indra is almost slain. It is only Viṣṇu's boon which preserves Indra. Vṛtra swallows Indra. Indra comes out, ripping open Vṛtra's belly, lopping off his arms and his head. But it appears as if willed by Vṛtra himself, whose soul entered and merged into Viṣṇu in a resplendent form.

> Though revolving quickly, and cutting on all sides, the thunderbolt felled the neck of Vṛtra in as many days as are taken by the northward and southward marches of heavenly bodies at the time appointed for the death of the demon. At that time drums sounded with a loud noise, and

> *Gandharvas* and *Siddhas* along with hosts of eminent sages, joyously showered flowers on him, glorifying him with sacred hymns celebrating the prowess of the slayer of Vṛtra.[12]

Indra is guilty of Brahmin murder; though the *devas* are relieved and happy, Indra must be sad. The sin pursues Indra

> in human form, resembling a Pariah-woman suffering from consumption, clad in blood-stained clothes, her limbs trembling due to old age, throwing about her gray hair crying, "Stop, stop" and befouling the road with her breath that stinks like fish.[13]

Indra hides in the fibres of a lotus stalk in Mānasarovara for a thousand years, during which time Nahuṣa rules in his stead. Indra's sin is "neutralized through meditation on Śrī Hari" and he returns to heaven. "The sin, that had been deprived of its force by Śrī Rudra, could not assail him, protected by Goddess Lakṣmī."[14] The Brahmins then prepare a horse-sacrifice in honour of Lord Viṣṇu and thus they exterminate the sin of Vṛtra-killing.

THE VEDIC *YAJÑA*

The *yajña*, the sacrifice, was the central ritual of Vedic religion, and the main function of the Vedic scriptures is to provide the *mantras* (texts) and ritual detail for the sacrifice. The very existence of the universe and everything it contained was ascribed to the performance of a primeval sacrifice in which the *puruṣa*, the primeval being, was offered up and dismembered.

> *Puruṣa* with thousands of heads, thousands of eyes, thousands of feet, is enveloping the earth on all sides, protruding beyond it by two hand-widths.
>
> *Puruṣa* is all that is, all that was and all that shall be. He is Lord of immortality and of all that grow strong by food. Such is his greatness; *Puruṣa* is even greater than that.
>
> All beings are one fourth of him; three-fourths, immortal, are in heaven. Three-fourths of *Puruṣa* ascended to heaven, one fourth remained here and spread out on all sides over what eats and does not eat.
>
> From him *Virāṭ* was born; from *Virāṭ*, *Puruṣa*. As soon as he was born he divided himself up into the earth and various bodies.
>
> The gods offered *Puruṣa* in a sacrifice: spring was the butter, summer was the fuel, and autumn was the libation. They besprinkled *Puruṣa* as a

> victim on the sacred grass. With that all the gods and the sages sacrificed.
>
> From that holocaust, butter mixed with curds was collected and the creatures that dwell in the air, in the forest and in the villages were made from it.
>
> From that holocaust were born the *ṛks* and the *sāmans*, the verse-metres and the ritual formulas. From it horses were born and all animals with two rows of teeth, cows as well as goats and sheep.
>
> When they dismembered *Puruṣa*, how many parts did they obtain? What was his mouth, his arms, his thighs, his feet?
>
> The *brahmin* was his mouth; the *kṣatriya* was made of his two arms; the *vaiśya* came from his two thighs; the *śūdra* was born from his two feet.
>
> The moon came out from his mind, from his eye the sun, from his mouth Indra and Agni, from his breath Vāyu. From his navel came the mid-region, from his head the sky, from his two feet the earth, from his ear the four quarters. Thus the world was made.
>
> Seven were the enclosing sticks, twenty-one sticks made the fuel when the *devas* performing the *yajña* bound *Puruṣa* like a sacrificial animal.
>
> With the *yajña* the *devas* sacrificed the *yajña*. These were the primeval customs whereby those heroes attained the heaven where the ancient Sādhyās and the *devas* are living.[15]

The *puruṣa-sūkta* became a key text in the history of Hinduism. It not only served as the scriptural basis for the caste-division but also underscored the centrality of the sacrifice and the crucial role of the brahmins who alone were authorized to offer sacrifices. It is also referred to as the source of the belief, so central to Vaiṣṇavism, that the whole visible universe is God's body. The word *puruṣa* means human being, specifically a male, and scholars are debating whether the hymn alludes to a real human sacrifice, the most powerful type of *yajña*.

The famous *aśvamedha*, the horse-sacrifice referred to in one of the above texts (see p. 19), was probably originally a fertility rite; later it was reinterpreted as a purificatory act to cleanse the sacrificer from sins, and a means to obtain one's desires. It was the concluding part of the most solemn of Vedic rituals, the *Rājasūya*, at the time of the installation of a new king. In one hymn the dying horse is addressed in this way:

> Truly at this moment you do not die, nor are you harmed, because you go by auspicious paths to the gods. May this horse bring to us all-sustaining wealth, an abundance of cows, excellent horses, and male offspring; may the spirited steed bring us freedom from wickedness; may this horse, offered in oblation, obtain for us bodily vigour.[16]

A very important ingredient of many sacrifices was soma. It is identified in the Veda with the moon, and called *amṛta*, "nectar," the means to obtain immortality (*Ṛgveda* IX, 70, 2). "Now this king Soma, the food of the gods, is no other than the moon . . . an offering in honor of the Vṛtra-slayer then is the full-moon sacrifice. Vṛtra, assuredly is no other than the moon."[17]

According to an ancient tradition an eagle brought soma to Indra – the gods gained immortality by drinking soma. In later mythology *amṛta* is described as having been obtained from the churning of the milk-ocean. Soma is called "child of heaven," "milk of heaven," "lord of heaven;" it is supposed to possess healing powers, to drive away blindness and lameness; it is called "king and father of the gods," "king of gods and mortals." In one hymn we read: "We have drunk soma, we have become immortal; we have gone to the light, we have found the gods. What can hostility now do to us, and what the malice of mortal men, immortal one?"[18]

OTHER FEATURES OF VEDIC RELIGION

While Indra-worship is very prominent in the *Ṛgveda* there are features of Vedic religion that appear unassociated with it. *Ṛta*, "law," "order," is one example. Some other gods, especially Mitra and Varuṇa, are called the "guardians" of *ṛta*. Therefore, the sinner who has transgressed the law has recourse to Varuṇa to ask for forgiveness. Agni is also called the "charioteer of *ṛta*." In one place even the origin of the world is ascribed to *ṛta*. The sacrifice makes the power of *ṛta* available to men.

> Plentiful waters belong to *ṛta*, the thought of *ṛta* destroys crooked acts, the brilliant and rousing hymn of praise to *ṛta* pierces the benumbed ears of men. The props of *ṛta* are firm, its manifestations are lovely and many of the sake of the body. Through *ṛta* they desire food. The cows entered the worship by *ṛta*. He who wins over *ṛta* acquires it. To *ṛta* belongs heaven and earth. To *ṛta* the two cows yield milk.[19]

While Vedic religion and Indra-worship were largely superseded by puranic *pūjā* and the formation of large communities of adherents of Viṣṇu and Śiva, it never disappeared completely. It retained its place in the administration of the *saṃskāras* (Hindu "sacraments") and it experienced a revival in the nineteenth-century Ārya-Samāj, whose founder demanded a return to the Vedas and to Vedic fire sacrifice. In today's India, Vedic *yajñas* are quite frequently performed at particular occasions and are believed to counteract evil influences of all kinds.

2 VAIṢṆAVISM

Vaiṣṇavas, Hindus who worship Viṣṇu as Highest God, Lord and Saviour, form the most numerous religious community in today's India numbering several hundred million followers. They are divided into a large number of teaching traditions (*saṃpradāyas*) established by historic personalities. They, too, claim to be "Vedic" and maintain that their teachings represent but an unfolding of Vedic religion.

VIṢṆU IN THE *VEDAS*

Only five hymns out of the 1,028 in the *Ṛgveda* are addressed to Viṣṇu, and only in a few other instances is Viṣṇu mentioned in other hymns. The most popular theme connected with Viṣṇu from the earliest times is his feat of covering with three strides earth, ether, and heaven – the sun's course from morning through midday to evening.

> One who in search of blessings takes his gift and prayer to far-striding Viṣṇu will soon obtain riches.
>
> One who worships him with his whole heart wins himself a great benefactor.
>
> Viṣṇu, be propitious to us!
>
> Three times this god strode forth in all his splendor over the earth.
>
> Viṣṇu is the foremost, stronger than the others: glorious is his name, who lives forever.
>
> Viṣṇu strode across this earth with mighty steps, ready to give it as a home to humankind.

In him the simple people trust and they feel safe with him; he, the nobly born, has given them spacious dwellings.[1]

The *Ṛgveda Saṁhitā* mentions this "mighty deed of Viṣṇu" several times. It deals especially with the "third step," "the highest step," which is beyond the reach of mortals and which is said to be "the well-loved mansion, where men devoted to the gods are happy."[2]

The *Bṛhaddevatā* treats the name Viṣṇu as one of the names of the Sun: "Because the three regions shine with brilliance as his footsteps, therefore Medhātithi pronounced him *Viṣṇu trivikrama*."

The same work derives the etymology of Viṣṇu from the root *viṣ* (following the *Nirukta*) and explains Viṣṇu as "pervasion" applied to the Sun "who is everything and is contained in everything."[3]

The "Hymn to *Ka*" in the *Ṛgveda* relates most of the essential elements of Vaiṣṇavism. *Ka* is one of the names of *Viṣṇu*.

> In the beginning rose Hiraṇyagarbha, born only Lord of all created beings. He settles and holds up this earth and heaven.
>
> Giver of vital breath, of power and vigor, whose commandments all the gods acknowledge, the Lord of Death, whose shadow is life immortal.
>
> He is Lord of men and cattle. His, through his might, are these snow covered mountains, and men call sea and *rasa* his posession.
>
> By him the heavens are strong and the earth is steadfast, by him the regions in mid-air were measured.
>
> What time the mighty waters came, containing the universal germ, producing Agni, thence sprang the gods' one spirit into being.
>
> He is the God of gods and none besides him. Never may he harm us who is the earth's begetter, nor he whose laws are sure, the heaven's creator. He who brought forth the great and lucid waters.[4]

Though the *Ṛgveda* itself does not explicitly mention Viṣṇu in the famous *puruṣa-sūkta*, mentioned on p. 19, Vaiṣṇava tradition accepts it as relating to Viṣṇu – this is also corroborated by some interpretations in Vedic works. One of the most often used names of Viṣṇu is *puruṣottama*.

The *Śatapatha Brāhmaṇa* amplifies that notion:

> All the worlds have I placed within mine own self and mine own self have I placed within all the worlds; all the gods have I placed within mine own self and mine own self have I placed within all the gods; all the Vedas have I placed within mine own self, and mine own self have I placed within the vital airs. For imperishable indeed are worlds, imperishable the gods, imperishable the Vedas, imperishable the vital airs, imperishable is the All:

> and verily whosoever knows this, passes from the perishable unto the imperishable, conquers recurrent death and attains the full measure of life.[5]

VIṢṆU IN EPICS AND *PURĀṆAS*

The *Viṣṇu Purāṇa* is one of the oldest and one of the most authoritative among the *Mahā-purāṇas*. It describes the creation, maintenance and dissolution of the universe as the work of Viṣṇu, it contains the ethical rules to be followed by Vaiṣṇavas and it supports faith in Viṣṇu with the help of stories of famous Viṣṇu *bhaktas* such as Prahlāda. It ends by eulogizing itself and Viṣṇu, to whom it is devoted:

> Whoever listens to this great mystery, which removes the curse of Kali, shall be freed from all sins. Who hears it every day fulfills the daily obligations towards ancestors, gods and humans. The merit that one gains from donating a brown cow – great and difficult to attain – accrues from listening to ten chapters of this Purāṇa. Someone who hears the entire Purāṇa, contemplating in the mind Acyuta [a name of Viṣṇu], who is all things, and of whom all things are made, who is the sustenance of the whole world, the receptacle of spirit, who is knowledge and that which is known, who is without beginning and end, and the benefactor of the gods, obtains assuredly the reward that results from uninterrupted Aśvamedha sacrifices.
>
> One who reads and retains with faith this Purāṇa, which describes in the beginning, middle and end the glorious Acyuta, the lord of the universe in every stage, the master of all that is, that moves and does not move, composed of spiritual knowledge, acquires such purity as exists not in any world, the eternal state of perfection which is Hari [another name of Viṣṇu]. One who fixes the mind on Viṣṇu does not go to hell.
>
> May that unborn, eternal Hari, whose form is manifold, and whose essence is composed of both matter and spirit, bestow upon all humankind that blessed state which knows neither birth nor decay.[6]

There are some ancient stories connected with Viṣṇu that are found in virtually all Vaiṣṇava scriptures.

Viṣṇu Trivikrama

The "three steps of Viṣṇu" described in the following text have often been understood as a symbol for the course of the sun: sunrise – midday – sunset. The identification of Viṣṇu with the sun has a long history. In the *trivikrama* story, Viṣṇu's *vāmana* (dwarf) *avatāra* defeats the *asura* (demon) Bali and asserts his universal rule. Bali, in spite of being a "demon," is always described as a virtuous king, whom Viṣṇu redeems:

> Now the most glorious Lord Viṣṇu took his descent through Aditi and, assuming the form of the divine Dwarf, sought the presence of Bali. Asking for ground that could be covered by three strides and accepting the offer of land, the Lord, who owns all the three worlds, devoted as he was to the welfare of his creation, covered the three worlds in three strides, and subduing Bali restored them to the great Indra. The Lord, possessed of extraordinary glory, placed all the three worlds once more under the sway of Indra.[7]

The *Bhāgavata Purāṇa* connects with this myth an apparition of the *Virāṭ* form of Viṣṇu.

> With a single stride he measured the earth which belonged to Bali and covered the sky with his person and the quarters with his arms. To him, as he took a second stride, heaven proved of no account, so that indeed not an atom was left for the third. Extending higher and higher, the foot of the Cosmic Person presently reached beyond Maharloka and Jñānaloka as well as beyond Tapoloka.[8]

Nārāyaṇa

Nārāyaṇa, explained as "the (final) abode (*ayaṇa*) of (all) people (*nāra*)" is one of the oldest and most revered names of Viṣṇu. In all likelihood there existed in ancient times an independent community of Nārāyaṇa worshippers, which later merged with the Vaiṣṇavas. The famous Nārāyaṇanīya section of the *Śāntiparvan* in the *Mahābhārata* is the earliest and longest account of the Nārāyaṇa religion.

> Towards the north, in the Ocean of Milk, there is a large island named Śvetadvīpa (The White Island). The learned say that its distance from Meru is greater than 32000 *yojanas*. The inhabitants of that realm have no sense-perception. They live without taking food of any kind. Their eyes are winkless. They always emit a flower-like smell. Their complexions are white. They are cleansed from every sin. They blast the eyes of the sinners that look at them. Their bones and bodies are as hard as a diamond. They regard honor and dishonor in the same light. They all look as if they were of celestial origin. They are all endowed with auspicious marks and great strength. Their heads seem to be like umbrellas. Their voices are deep like that of thunder clouds. The soles of their feet are marked with hundreds

of lines. They have sixty teeth, all of which are white. They have many tongues. With those tongues they seem to lick the very sun whose face is turned towards every direction.[9]

The Avatāras *of Viṣṇu*

The descents of Viṣṇu in visible form (*avatāras*) are narrated in almost all Vaiṣṇava scriptures. There is great variety in both the number and the sequence of *avatāras*. The most widely accepted number is ten (*daśāvatāras*). They are distributed over the four world-ages (*yugas*) of our present aeon.

AVATĀRAS OF THE *KṚTA-YUGA*, THE FIRST WORLD-AGE

Matsya (fish).

Once upon a time, when Manu Vaivasvata was pouring libations under a tree, there arose from the water in the palms of his hands a small fish. When Manu was about to throw it out, it said to him: "Please, do not throw me away, I am afraid of being eaten up by other animals." Manu then put it into a vessel. It increased in size and the fish asked for bigger accommodation. Manu then placed it into a water jar. The fish grew again and asked Manu for bigger accommodation. Thrown into a tank it assumed a huge proportion and asked for more room. Manu then brought him back into the ocean. It assumed enormous size and Manu, terrified, said: "Who are you, but Viṣṇu?" The fish then spoke to Manu: "I have descended for the protection of the universe and the destruction of the wicked. On the seventh day the ocean will submerge the earth. Then a boat will approach you into which you are to take the seeds of all creation. Spend the night of Brahmā on it and tie it with the large serpent to my horn." The fish disappeared and Manu waited at the appointed time for the boat. When the boat appeared he got into it and tied it to the horn of the huge fish under which guise Viṣṇu had appeared.[10]

Kūrma (tortoise).

Hari, in the form of a tortoise served as pivot for the mountain (Maṇḍara, which served as a churning stick when the gods and the demons churned the ocean in order to obtain the nectar of immortality) as it was whirled around.[11]

Nrṣinha (man-lion).

Prahlāda, son of king Hiraṇyakaśipu, who had declared himself the highest ruler, angered his father by worshiping Viṣṇu and extolling Viṣṇu's lordship. Hiraṇyakaśipu unsuccessfully tried to put his son to death by a great many different means. When Prahlāda kept insisting on praising Viṣṇu as Lord, Hiraṇyakaśipu shouted angrily:

"Where is that Lord of the Universe other than me, that you wretch have just mentioned? You insisted that he is everywhere present; why is he not seen in that pillar here? As the universal sovereign I am going to behead you now. Let your Hari, whom you invoke as your refuge, protect you." Thus constantly tormenting his son, the great devotee of Viṣṇu, with angry words, the great and mighty demon Hiraṇyakaśipu jumped from his throne, took his sword and knocked the pillar with his fist. That very moment there arose in the pillar a terrific noise. In order to confirm the assertions of his servant Pralāhda and his presence in all objects, the Lord appeared in the pillar in a strange form, neither animal nor human. Before Hiraṇyakaśipu stood the Lord visibly in the form of a man-lion: it had fierce eyes, shining like molten gold and a face swollen with its mass of hair and mane. It had fearful teeth and a tongue waving like a sword and sharp as a blade of a razor and it looked frightful. Hiraṇyakaśipu rushed against Nṛsinha with a mace. Like a moth that had fallen into a flame, Hiraṇyakaśipu vanished in the splendour of Lord Nṛsinha.[12]

AVATĀRAS OF THE *TRETĀ-YUGA*, THE SECOND WORLD-AGE

Vāmana (dwarf). The story of Vāmana has been told above in the context of Viṣṇu *trivikrama.*

Paraśurāma (Rāma with the battle-ax).

One day when Paraśurāma along with his brothers had gone to the forest, Arjuna's sons came to his father's hermitage, beheaded him while he was meditating, taking his head with them. Paraśurāma, on returning, bewailed his father. He gripped his battle-ax determined to extirpate the whole class of warriors. Going to Mahiṣmatī, Paraśurāma raised in the heart of that city a huge mountain of the Kṣatriyas' heads; with their blood he created a ghastly river that terrified the murderers. Taking the murder of his father as justification, the mighty Paraśurāma rid the world of the Kṣatriyas three times seven times and from their blood created five tanks filled with blood. Having brought back the head of his father he joined it to its trunk.

Descending in the midst of the Bhṛgus, the almighty Lord Śrī Hari, the Soul of the Universe, thus slew several times the kings who had become a great burden on the earth.[13]

Rāma or Rāmacandra. The oldest of the great epics of India, the *Rāmāyaṇa* ascribed to Vālmīki, is entirely devoted to describing the life and the exploits of Rāma. Both the Sanskṛt original and countless re-creations of it in vernacular languages have kept the Rāma story alive in the hearts and minds of the Indian people. The rule of Rāma, the *Rāmarājya*, is invoked even today by political parties as the highest of their goals:

> While Śrī Rāma ruled over the kingdom of Ayodhyā, there were no widows to lament the loss of their husbands, nor was their any danger from beasts of prey or snakes, nor was there any fear of diseases. Old people did not have to perform the last rites for youngsters. Every creature felt comfortable and everyone was devoted to righteousness. Looking only at Śrī Rāma, creatures did not kill each other. As long as Śrī Rāma ruled the kingdom of Ayodhyā people lived to an age of thousand years, were blessed with thousands of sons and remained free from disease and grief. As long as Śrī Rāma ruled people talked only about Śrī Rāma, the whole world appeared to them transformed into Śrī Rāma. Trees in Ayodhyā remained forever firmly rooted and bore fruits and flowers perpetually. Clouds sent down rain when desired and the wind was always delightful. Free from avarice and satisfied with their own occupations the Brāhmaṇas, the Kṣatriyas, the Vaiśyas and the Śūdras remained engaged in their own proper duties. As long as Śrī Rāma ruled, people observed all of their religious duties and never told lies. All were endowed with auspicious marks on their bodies and all were pursuing righteousness. Together with his brothers Śrī Rāma ruled for ten and one thousand years.[14]

While Vālmīki's *Rāmāyaṇa* emphasizes the human qualities of Rāma as son, brother, husband and king, the sixteenth-century *Adhyātma Rāmāyaṇa* sees Rāma's earthly life from beginning to end as a manifestation of the transcendent deity:

> The Lord of Jānakī, who is intelligence itself, although immutable, being requested by the gods to remove the afflictions of the world, took the illusory form of a man and was, as if born in the solar dynasty, and after attaining eternal fame, capable of destroying sins, by killing the foremost of the demons, he again attained his real nature, the Brahmanhood.[15]

AVATĀRAS OF THE *DVĀPARA-YUGA*, THE THIRD WORLD-AGE

Balarāma (Rāma the strong). The elder brother of Kṛṣṇa, the sixth child of Devakī, companion of Kṛṣṇa in many of his exploits, is described as having been fond of wine and hot-tempered. He is considered an *avatāra* of Śeṣa (also called Ananta, the Infinite), the world-snake on which Viṣṇu rests, and is also called Śeṣa and Ananta:

> While the mighty Śeṣa was wandering amidst the forests with the herdsmen in the disguise of a mortal, Varuṇa, in order to provide for his enjoyment, said to his wife Varuṇī (the goddess of wine): "You, Madirā, are always welcome to the mighty Ananta; go therefore and do something for his enjoyment." Varuṇī went and hid in the hollow of a Kadaṃba tree in the woods of Vṛndāvana. Baladeva came there, and smelling the pleasant fragrance of liquor, resumed his ancient passion for strong drink. The holder of the ploughshare was much delighted by the drops of wine oozing from the Kadaṃba tree and gathered and drank them with the herdsmen and women, who celebrated him with voice and lute in songs. Inebriated with wine he called out: "Come hither, River Yamunā, I want to bathe." The river, disregarding the words of a drunken man, did not come. Rāma, in a rage, took his ploughshare, plunged it into the bank and dragged her to him saying: "Will you not come? Now go where you please!" Thus he compelled the river to change its course and follow him wherever he wandered in the woods.[16]

Kṛṣṇa. The most popular among the Viṣṇu *avatāras* is doubtlessly Kṛṣṇa. By many of his worshipers he is regarded not as an *avatāra* in the usual sense – Viṣṇu accepting a fictitious form and appearing in it – but as Viṣṇu manifesting himself fully in his own proper and eternal form, *svayam bhagavān*, the Lord himself.

The best known of all Hindu scriptures, the *Bhagavadgītā*, in the form of a dialogue between Arjuna and Kṛṣṇa, contains a most profound teaching about the essentials of Hinduism. Kṛṣṇa, offering his services to Arjuna as charioteer in the upcoming war between the Pāṇḍavas and the Kauravas, answers Arjuna's questions, reveals to him his divine nature and promises to save him in return for his self-surrender. Kṛṣṇa educates Arjuna to see wisdom as the highest ideal:

> A sage's mind is not troubled in the midst of sorrows, without desire amidst pleasures, free from passion, fear and rage, without affection, not rejoicing at the sight of good nor revolting at the sight of evil.[17]

> Abandoning all desires and acting free from longing, without any sense of mineness or sense of ego one attains to peace.[18]

> Contact with sense objects gives rise to the feeling of cold and hot, pleasure and pain. These come and go and do not last forever. Learn to endure these. One who is not troubled by these, who remains the same in cold and heat, pleasure and pain, is wise.[19]

> When one dwells in one's mind on sense objects, attachment to them arises. From attachment springs desire, from desire rises anger. From

> anger follows bewilderment, from bewilderment comes loss of memory, loss of memory causes the destruction of intelligence; from destruction of intelligence one perishes. A disciplined mind, moving among the sense objects, with senses under control and free from attachment and aversion attains purity of spirit. That purity of spirit brings to an end all sorrow.[20]

About his own mission, Kṛṣna enlightens Arjuna thus:

> Although unborn and imperishable, although the Lord of creatures, established in my own nature I come into existence through my *māyā*. Whenever righteousness declines and unrighteousness arises, I send forth myself: for the protection of the good and the destruction of the wicked, for the establishment of righteousness I come into the world age after age. One who knows the true nature of my divine birth is not born again when leaving this body. Free from passion, fear and anger, absorbed in me, taking refuge in me, purified by austerities and wisdom, many have attained my state of being. As people approach me, so do I accept them: people everywhere follow my path.[21]

In response to Arjuna's fears that engaging in a battle against relations and teachers would earn him punishment in hell, Kṛṣṇa teaches him a new ethic, the ethic of desireless action (*niṣkāma karma*):

> What is action? What is inaction? Even the wise are bewildered in this matter. I will declare to you what action is and knowing this you will be delivered from evil. One has to understand what action is, and likewise one has to understand about inaction. Hard to understand is the way of works. One who sees inaction in action and action in inaction is wise, a yogi, such a one has accomplished all work. One whose undertakings are completely free from desire, whose works have been burned up in the fire of wisdom, such a one is truly learned. Having abandoned all attachment to the fruit of works, ever content, independent, one does nothing, although constantly engaged in work. Having no desires, with the heart and self under control, giving up all possessions, performing actions by the body alone, one commits no wrong. Satisfied by what comes by chance, gone beyond the pairs of opposites, free from jealousy, the same in failure and success, one is not bound even when acting.[22]

> To action alone you have a right, never to its fruit; let not the fruits of action be your motive nor let there be in you attachment to inaction. Do your work, abandoning attachment, with an even mind in success and failure.[23]

Kṛṣṇa also reinforces the belief in reincarnation as a natural and inevitable process only concerning the body, not something to be afraid of:

> Just as a person casts off worn-out garments and puts on others that are new, even so the embodied soul casts off worn-out bodies and takes on others that are new. Weapons do not cleave the Self, fire does not burn the Self, waters do not drench the Self, winds do not parch the Self. The Self is eternal, all-pervading, unchanging and immovable. The Self is the same forever: unmanifest, unthinkable, still.[24]

> One should lift up oneself by oneself; let no one degrade the self; for the Self alone is the friend of the self, and the Self alone is the enemy of the self. To one who has conquered the self by the Self, the Self is a friend, but to one who is not at home in the Self, this very Self will act like an enemy. When one has conquered one's self and has attained to the calm of self-mastery, this Supreme Self abides in oneself ever steady: one is at peace in cold and heat, in pleasure and pain, in honour and dishonor.[25]

Kṛṣṇa's true nature is a deep mystery into which Arjuna is introduced:

> By me all this universe is pervaded through my unmanifest form. All beings abide in me, but I do not abide in them. And yet all beings do not dwell in me. Listen to the divine mystery: My spirit which is the source of all beings, sustains the beings but does not abide in them. As the mighty air is moving everywhere and abides in space, in the same way all beings abide in me. All beings pass into my own nature at the end of a world-age and at the beginning of the next age I send them forth again. Under my guidance nature gives birth to all things, moving and unmoving, and thus the world revolves. The deluded despise me clad in a human body, not knowing my higher nature as Lord of all Beings.[26]

Arjuna, who had been the recipient of Kṛṣṇa's instructions and became convinced of Kṛṣṇa's divinity, expresses the wish to see Kṛṣṇa's true divine form. Kṛṣṇa grants his wish after endowing Arjuna with divine vision. Arjuna describes what he sees:

> In your body, O Lord, I see all the gods and the varied hosts of beings, Brahmā seated on the lotus throne surrounded by sages and heavenly beings. I behold you, of infinite form all-round, with countless arms, bellies, faces, and eyes, but I cannot see your end or middle or beginning, you Lord of the Universe. I see you with your crown, your mace, your discus, glowing like a mass of light, hard to look at, on all sides with the radiance of flaming fire and the sun. You are the imperishable, the Supreme to be realized. You are the ultimate resting place of the universe; you are the undying guardian of the eternal law. You are the Primal Person. I see you as one without beginning, middle or end, of infinite

> power, with numberless arms, with moon and sun as your eyes, your face a flaming fire, whose radiance burns up the universe. This space between heaven and earth is pervaded by you alone, as also the quarters of the sky. O Glorious One, seeing this terrible form of yours the three worlds tremble.[27]

Arjuna also sees the warriors, presently assembled on the battle field, entering the mouth of that Universal Being (*viśvarūpa*) and terrified he asks Kṛṣṇa to assume his human form again and to explain who he is. Kṛṣṇa says:

> Time am I, world-destroying, full and ripe, engaged in subduing the world. Even without you all these warriors standing lined up in the two armies shall perish. Arise and gain glory. Defeating your enemies, enjoy a prosperous kingdom. By me they have been slain already. You be the mere occasion.[28]

The most famous verses of the *Bhagavadgītā*, the so-called *carama-śloka*, contain Kṛṣṇa's final advice to Arjuna and are understood by Hindus generally as a firm promise of salvation:

> Listen again to my supreme word, the most secret of all. I love you greatly and shall tell you what is beneficial for you. Fix your mind on me, be devoted to me, sacrifice to me, prostrate before me: thus you will come to me. This I promise you, because you are dear to me. Abandoning all *dharmas* come to me alone for refuge. Do not grieve, I shall release you from all evil.[29]

The *Bhāgavata Purāṇa* is most explicitly devoted to glorifying Kṛṣṇa. Especially its tenth book is the source of much of Kṛṣṇa devotion. Here is its narration of Kṛṣṇa's birth:

> Now came the most delightful hour, filled with all blessings, when the star Rohinī was at the ascendant and when the rest of the planets were in a most auspicious constellation. The quarters became clear while the firmament was studded with innumerable stars shining brightly. The earth was clearly visible with its towns and villages, its cowherd pens and festive gatherings. The rivers flowed in a limpid stream, ponds blossomed with lotuses, the forest trees, heavy with flowers, rang with the sweet sounds of birds and the buzz of bees. A gentle breeze wafting a fragrant scent blew delightfully, the sacred fires of the brahmins burst into flames. The minds of the good people became cheerful. When that unborn Lord was about to be born, kettledrums sounded in heaven, the heavenly musicians sang, and the celestial damsels danced for joy. Sages and gods

showered flowers, and clouds gently rumbled like ocean waves. When midnight enveloped the earth in darkness and when the time for prayer had come, Lord Viṣṇu, who dwells in all hearts, manifested himself fully through Devakī, who resembled the goddess, even as the full moon appears on the eastern sky. Vāsudeva beheld that extraordinary child with lotus-like eyes, endowed with four arms wielding weapons and emblems such as the conch, a mace, and a discus, bearing on his bosom the Śrīvatsa mark, clad in yellow silk, possessing the charm of a rain cloud, with the Kaustubha gem shining at his neck and his locks bathed in the splendor of a diadem, precious earrings, armlets and bangles. Rapt in joy to behold Śrī Hari as his own son and with eyes wide open, Vasudeva glorified the Lord with a sincere mind.[30]

AVATĀRAS OF THE *KALI-YUGA*, THE FOURTH AND LAST WORLD-AGE

Buddha. When the enemies of the gods had become very powerful, they implored Viṣṇu to help them regain their realm. Viṣṇu promised to do so in the guise of a *māyā-avatāra*, a manifestation of his delusionary power, so as to mislead the Daityas and thus make them perish. He first appeared as the founder of Jainism, discouraging the Daityas from fulfilling the Vedic duties. Then he appeared as Buddha, to complete the work of destruction of the Daityas:

> The same deluder, putting on garments of a red color, assuming a benevolent aspect, and speaking in soft and agreeable tones, addressed the Daityas and said to them: "If you desire either heaven or final release, desist from the slaughter of animals for sacrifice and hear from me what you should do. Know that all is a mind construct. This world subsists without support and is engaged in the pursuit of error which it mistakes for knowledge. It is vitiated by passions and revolves in the confines of *saṃsāra*." Thus these Daityas were induced by the arch-deceiver to deviate from their religious duties by his repeated arguments. When they had abandoned their own faith they persuaded others to do the same and the heresy spread. Many deserted the practices enjoined by Vedas and Dharmaśāstras.[31]

Kalki. The tenth and last *avatāra* will come at the end of the *Kali-yuga* to terminate this present age. He will come riding on a white horse and with a blazing sword re-establish the kṛta-yuga (Golden Age). The entire *Kalki Purāṇa* (an Upa-Purāṇa)is devoted to describing his future exploits. Some Mahā-Purāṇas also contain extensive references to the evils of the *Kali-yuga* and its termination by Kalki.

Lawfulness and righteousness will decrease day by day until the whole world will be wholly depraved. Then wealth alone will confer rank, power will be the only source of right, passion will be the sole bond of union between husband and wife. Falsehood will be the only means of success in litigation, women will be objects merely of sensual gratification. The earth will be valued only for its mineral treasure. The ceremonial thread will be all that makes a brahmin. External signs will be the only distinction between the orders of life. Dishonesty will be the universal means of subsistence, weakness will lead to beggary. Bold and arrogant speech will be the substitute for real learning. Vulgarity will be considered saintliness, any bath will be taken for ritual purification. Mere mutual assent will be considered valid marriage. Fine clothes will be taken as sign of nobility. Any distant water will be esteemed a place of pilgrimage. The one who is strongest will reign over a country thus vitiated by many faults. The people, unable to bear the heavy burdens imposed upon them by their avaricious sovereigns, will take refuge among the valleys of the mountains, glad to feed on wild honey, herbs, roots, fruits, flowers, and leaves. Their only covering will be the bark of trees, and they will be exposed to the cold, to wind and sun and rain. Nobody's life will exceed twenty-three years. Thus in the Kali age decay will constantly proceed until the human race approaches its annihilation.

When the *dharma* based on *śruti* and *smṛti* will be almost defunct, and the end of the Kali age is near, a portion of the Lord Vāsudeva – he who is of the nature of Brahman, the beginning and the end, who comprehends all things – shall descend upon earth. He will be born as Kalki, endowed with the eight superhuman faculties, in the family of Viṣṇuyaśas, an eminent brahmin of Śambala village. By his irrestistible might he will destroy all the *mlecchas* and thieves and all whose minds are bent on unrighteousness. He will re-establish righteousness upon earth; and the minds of those who live at the end of the Kali age shall be awakened and be clear like crystal. Those thus changed by virtue of that special time will become the seeds of human beings and give birth to a race who follows the laws of the Kṛta age. As it has been said: "When the sun and moon and the lunar house of Tiṣya and the planet Jupiter are in one mansion, the Kṛta age shall return.[32]

VAIṢṆAVA PHILOSOPHY AND THEOLOGY

Vaiṣṇavism possesses not only an extensive and colorful mythology but also a great and sophisticated philosophical and theological tradition.

Vaiṣṇava Sāṁkhya

Before Vedānta became the most respected *darśana*, an extensive Sāṁkhya-based Vaiṣṇava theology had been developed. (The meaning of the terms Śaṁkhya and Vedānta, as well as the history of these philosophical systems, are explained in Chapter 6.) The *Bhāgavata Purāṇa* considers Kapila, the founder of Sāṁkhya, an *avatāra* of Viṣṇu and a great teacher of the path of emancipation.

> Kapila, who expounded the true nature of the fundamental principles, was no other than the birthless Lord, descended of his own free will and through his own *māyā* in order to teach humanity the truth of the Self.
>
> The *puruṣa* is no other than the *ātman*, who is beginningless, devoid of attributes, existing beyond *prakṛti*, consisting of the three *guṇas* that thought him in her playful mood. Abiding in *prakṛti*, the *puruṣa* fell a prey to her charms, which obscure knowledge. The *puruṣa* is the all-pervading spirit Viṣṇu, and it is out of his own free will that he accepts *prakṛti*.
>
> In this way the Lord himself, who by His own *māyā* abides unaffected within all living beings as the *puruṣa* and outside them as *kāla* [is the twenty-fifth category].
>
> Therefore through devotion, dispassion, and spiritual wisdom acquired through a concentrated mind, one should contemplate on that Inner Controller as present in this very body, though apart from it.[33]

Another major component of classical Vaiṣṇava theology is the Pāñcarātra doctrine of divine emanations (*vyūha*). Pāñcarātra was formerly an independent branch of Viṣṇu worship and theology before it became merged in Śrīvaiṣṇavism.

> *Vyūha* is the highest Brahman Himself abiding in fourfold form as Vāsudeva, Saṁkarṣaṇa, Pradyumna and Aniruddha for the purpose of meditation and for the creation of the universe. Śrī Vāsudeva is replete with the six qualities. Saṁkarṣaṇa is filled with knowledge and strength. Pradyumna possesses in the highest degree lordship and virility. Aniruddha has consummate potency and splendor. Thus the six qualities are distributed.
>
> Each of the four descends into three sub-*vyūhas* such as Keśava etc. who are the presiding deities of the twelve months and the twelve Ādityas. Their locations are represented in the marks on the bodies of devotees.
>
> Of these, Keśava, shining like gold, bears four discuses. The dark-complexioned Nārāyaṇa bears four conches. Mādhava, bright like sapphire, bears four maces. Govinda, shining like the moon, bears four bows. Viṣṇu, resembling a blue lotus-bloom, bears four ploughs. The red lotus-like Madhusūdana bears four clubs. The fire-colored Trivikrama bears four swords. Vāmana, effulgent like the rising sun, bears four *vajras*. Śrīdhara, who resembles a white lotus, bears four spears. Hṛṣikeśa, bright like lightning, bears four maces. Padmanābha, radiant like the sun, bears

> five weapons. Dāmodara, red-complexioned like an Indragopa insect, bears four cords.[34]

Each of the *vyūhas* has a cosmic and a liberating function. Pradyumna creates the universe and the *śāstra*, which teaches the liberating *dharma*. Aniruddha protects creation and makes known the principles (*tattva*) of liberating teaching and translates them into practice (*tatkriya*). Saṁkarṣaṇa destroys the universe and brings to fruition the actions done (*kriya-phala*) under the aegis of *śāstras*.

Vaiṣṇava Vedānta

After 1000 C.E. the basic philosophy of Vaiṣṇavism was no longer Sāṁkhya but Vedānta. Vaiṣṇava Vedānta is not a straight continuation of Upaniṣadic ideas but an attempt – made at different times by different people in different places – to combine the popular Vaiṣṇava tradition with Vedānta. It begins with the *ācāryas* of Śrīraṅgam, which combined the fervor of the popular religious literature of the Āḷvārs with the *jñāna* of Vedānta. Later other schools of Vaiṣṇava Vedānta developed. In the fourteenth century all existing Vaiṣṇava *saṃpradāyas* were associated with four main traditions.

ŚRĪVAIṢṆAVISM (VIŚIṢṬĀDVAITA)

Śrīvaiṣṇavism as a system originated in Śrīraṅgam, a temple-island in the River Kāverī in Southern India, and Śrīraṅgam has remained the seat of its pontiff. The first of the Śrīraṅgam *ācāryas*, Nātha Muni, was the son of Īśvara Muni, a well-known Pāñcarātra master. He gave the Tamil *Prabandham* of the Āḷvārs the status of a *śruti* (revealed scripture) in Śrīraṅgam and succeeded in establishing himself as the highest authority with regard to doctrine. No writings of his are known to have been preserved.

The successor of Nātha Muni was Yāmunācārya, a scholar who left several works which laid the foundation for Vaiṣṇava Vedānta. As well as the *Stotra-ratna*, a famous hymn in honor of Viṣṇu, he composed a short commentary on the Bhagavadgītā, the *Gītārtha-saṁgraha*, and two systematic treatises: the *Āgama Prāmāṇya*, which attempts to establish the sectarian Vaiṣṇava scriptures as authoritative, and the *Siddhitraya*, a systematic of God, Soul, and Knowledge (which is preserved only incompletely). Over against the monistic Advaita interpretation of the

Upaniṣads, and the assertion that the Supreme is "quality-less" (*nirguṇa*), Śrīvaiṣṇavas maintain the reality of God, souls, and world and insist on God having "qualities" (*saguṇa*). This is the point which Yāmunācārya makes in the following text:

> The real significance of the text: "Reality is one without a second" may now be explained. The person who is considered "without a second" is one who neither has, nor had, nor will have an equal or a superior capable of being counted as a second. How could the world be referred to as a second when it is but a small fraction of the entire collection of entities which constitute His possessions and which are under His sway? The statement: "The paramount ruler of the Cola country now reigning is without a second in the world" is intended to deny the existence of a ruler equal to him. It does not deny the existence of his servants, sons, consort, and so on. Similarly the whole host of *devas*, *asuras* and men, the four-faced Brahmā, and the cosmic egg form but a small part of a drop from the ocean of the greatness of the manifestations of the Lord Viṣṇu who is Lord of all, who is touched neither by sorrows nor by merits, by demerits or anything else and who is the seat of the sixfold qualities of knowledge and the like, and whose greatness cannot be conceived by the mind.[35]

Instead of attributing worldly success or failure to the impersonal operation of karma, Yāmunācārya sees the hand of God in it:

> The Lord then, recognizing one who performs good actions as one who obeys his commands, blesses him with piety, riches, worldly pleasures and final release: while one who transgresses His commands He causes to experience the opposite of all these.[36]

There remains, of course, the crucial problem of the relationship between justice and grace. The "actor" in the principal sense is *īśvara*:

> The inwardly ruling highest Self promotes action insofar as it regards in the case of any action the volitional effect made by the individual soul, and then aids that effort by granting its favor or permission. Action is not possible without permission on the part of the highest Self.[37]

The most important of the *ācāryas* was Rāmānuja (1017–1137), a great organizer and propagator of Śrīvaiṣṇavism as well as a major theologian. His intention was not to build a new system, but to popularize and reformulate Vaiṣṇava Vedānta. Much of his writing consists of polemics against Śaṅkara's Advaita. Rāmānuja's *sādhana* follows closely the

Bhagavadgītā: *prapatti*, self-surrender, is its essence, including *karma*, *jñāna*, and *bhakti*. Thus he explains how one can reach God:

> Now this Supreme Brahman, the highest *puruṣa*, is to be attained. The pathway through which he is to be attained is as follows: By an accumulation of the greatest merit the sins of the past gathered through all past lives are destroyed. A person whose sins are thus destroyed through great merit seeks refuge at the feet of the Supreme Person. Such self-surrender begets an inclination towards him. Then the aspirant acquires knowledge of reality from the scriptures aided by the instruction of holy teachers. Then by a steady effort he develops in an ever-increasing measure the qualities of soul like the control of mind, the control of senses, austerity, purity, forgiveness, straightforwardness, discrimination as to what is to be feared and not feared, mercy and non-violence. He is devoted to the performance of the *nitya* [permanent] and *naimittika* [occasional and optional] duties pertaining to his *varṇa* and *āśrama* and avoids actions prohibited, such a course of conduct being conceived as the worship of the Supreme Person. He offers his all and his very self at the lotus-like feet of the Supreme Person. Actuated by loving devotion to him, he offers perpetual praises and obeisances, engages in perpetual remembrance of him, bows down before him in adoration perpetually, exerts himself always in the godward direction, always sings his glories, always listens to the exalted accounts of his perfections, speaks perpetually of those perfections, meditates upon him continuously, ceaselessly worships him and dedicates himself once and for all to him. The Supreme Person, who is overflowing with compassion, being pleased with such love, showers his grace on the aspirant, which destroys all his inner darkness. *Bhakti* develops in such a devotee towards the highest person, which is valued for its own sake, which is uninterrupted, which is an absolute delight in itself and which is meditation that has taken on the character of the most vivid and immediate vision. Through such *bhakti* is the Supreme attained.[38]

The reason why *bhakti* brings bliss is the blissful nature of *brahman*. Knowing *brahman* means participating in his bliss.

> The Supreme Person is unsurpassed and infinite joy in himself and by himself. He becomes the joy of another also, as his nature as joy is absolute and universal. When *brahman* becomes the object of one's contemplation he (the meditator) becomes blissful. Thus the supreme *brahman* is the ocean of infinite and unsurpassed excellence of attributes. He transcends all evil. The expanse of his glory is boundless. He abounds in surpassing condescension, maternal compassion, and supreme beauty. He is the principal entity. The individual self is subservient to him. If the

> seeker meditates on the Supreme with a full consciousness of this relationship and if the Supreme *Brahman* so meditated upon becomes an object of supreme love to the devotee, then he himself effectuates the devotee's God-realization.[39]

In his last works – three mystical poems – Rāmānuja develops a spiritualistic concept of *mokṣa*: he specifies *bhakti* as *śaraṇāgati* – taking refuge to the Lord – and explains *mokṣa* as *kaiṁkārya prāpti*, eternal service of God.

> When will I see with these eyes my Lord who is my sole treasure, my father, my mother, and my all? When will I touch with these hands those tender, beautiful, lotus-like feet of the Lord, when will I enter into them with all my entire being? When will I enter into that ocean of immortality.[40]

As the name of the system – Śrī Vaiṣṇavism – suggests, Śrī, the consort of Viṣṇu plays an important role. Following the lead of the *Viṣṇu Purāṇa*, Rāmānuja says:

> This Śrī, the Mother of the universe, is eternal and knows no separation from Viṣṇu. Even as Viṣṇu is all-pervading, she is all-pervading. When he becomes a *deva*, she assumes a *devī*-form. When he becomes a man, she too becomes a human being. She makes her form conform to the form of Viṣṇu.[41]

Great importance was attributed by Vaiṣṇavas to the recitation of three specific *mantras* believed to ensure Viṣṇu's grace. The interpretation of these "mysteries" (*rahasya*) occupies much space in the writings of later Vaiṣṇava theologians, as the following text from Vedānta Deśika, second in importance as Śrīvaiṣṇava-teacher only to Rāmānuja, shows:

> Among these three mysteries *Tirumantra* or *Aṣṭākṣara* ["Om, homage to Nārāyaṇa"] has been stated to contain everything within itself and through it the meaning of everything becomes known. The *carama śloka*, [*Bhagavadgītā* XVIII, 66: "Having given up all *dharmas*, surrender yourself to me alone; I will release you from all evil, do not grieve!"] establishes that the adoption of the single means taught in it, self-surrender (*śaraṇāgati*) would secure the benefits of all other means prescribed elsewhere. The *Dvayam* ["I take refuge to the feet of Nārāyaṇa joined with Śrī; Homage to Nārāyaṇa joined with Śrī"], as has been stated in the *Kaṭha Upaniṣad* and elsewhere, is capable of making a person perfect in the discharge of all duties even if it is uttered only once.

Therefore these three mysteries alone are of value to the seeker after salvation. It has been said, "One should ignore what is of no value, what is only of slight value, and even what is valuable and what is more valuable. Only what is most valuable in the *śāstra* one should take, like nectar from the ocean."

The ultimate goal or aim of life (*puruṣārtha*) (namely *mokṣa*) and the means of attaining cannot be ascertained through sense perception (*pratyakṣa*) or inference (*anumāna*). As stated in such passages "It is from the *śāstra* that I know Janārdana," "Therefore in determining what ought to be done and what ought not be done, the only authority that should guide you is *śāstra*" and "One who is well versed in the *Āgamas* or *Vedas* will attain *Brahman*," the only *pramāṇa* [means of ascertaining truth] that exists for our guidance is *śabda* or what is revealed in the *śāstras*. In this context it has been said, "The things that are to be known are many and infinite; the time (at our disposal) is short; the hindrances are numerous; therefore take only what is valuable, like the swan that separates the milk from the water with which it is mixed."

The word "valuable" really means "most valuable," because it refers to what is always and unconditionally valuable. The *śāstras* of those who are outside the pale of the Vedas (like the Buddhists) and likewise of heretics (like the Advaitins) are not valuable at all and are therefore to be ignored. In the first part of the Veda, the portion which treats of rites leading to the attainment of worldly goods is only of very slight value and hence not to be resorted to. That part which treats of the attainment of the good things of *svarga* [heaven] after death, though it may appear valuable to some as leading to fruits higher than worldly goods, is of no use, as, in the final estimate, they are based on sorrow and have other objectionable features. That part, too, which treats of the realization of one's own soul and the means thereof, though a little more valuable, is not of value to those who desire the enjoyment of the Supreme Self. To the man of discerning wisdom, the part of the Veda which treats of the Supreme Brahman, the attainment of Brahman and the means thereof is the most valuable, and is therefore to be preferred.

Even there, the three mysteries which are, as it were, an epitome of the truths that ought to be known and of the means of attaining salvation, which are the distinctive, unique and exclusive doctrines [of our Viśiṣṭādvaita system] are invaluable and therefore to be most preferred. As stated in the *śloka*, "From the many and great *śāstras*, the wise should choose only that which is most valuable as the bee takes in the honey from the flowers," the *jīva* who thirsts for *mokṣa* should prefer as invaluable these three mysteries.[42]

Another important Vaiṣṇava teaching is the assertion that the Lordship of Viṣṇu implies the servitude of all humans:

> In these mysteries Īśvara is disclosed as the *śeṣī*, as one for whom everything else exists. He stands in the relation of a *śeṣī* to both sentient beings and non-sentient things in common. In relation to non-sentient things He is *śeṣī*, because they exist for His purposes. In relation to sentient beings of *jīvas* endowed with intelligence, He is *śeṣī* in the special sense of being *svāmī*, Master whom it is their duty to serve, and this is the manner in which we should understand while uttering the *mantras*. Our being *śeṣa* to the Lord we share in common with non-sentient things but we are *śeṣas* in the special sense also of being His servants (*dāsa*).[43]

Śrīvaiṣṇavism teaches a spiritual practice that leads its followers to union with Viṣṇu. There are many obstacles on the pilgrim's way, as the following text details:

> The hindrances to the attainment are the multitude of obstacles that stand in the way of our attaining *mokṣa*, such as ignorance (*avidyā*), *karma*, and *vāsana* [impressions left in the mind by *karma* in previous births].
>
> The foremost of these hindrances is the punishment inflicted by the Lord for disobedience of His orders from time immemorial. This chastisement causes association with *prakṛti* [matter] with its three qualities and thereby a contraction of knowledge. It brings about a connection between the soul and the body, the senses and the like which are specific modifications of matter. Further it makes the *jīva* subject to the sway of the body and the senses. To quote the words of the Āḷvārs: "With the strong ropes of my sins you have bound me tightly to the body, covered the sores within the body with skin and let me walk away from you ... With the body given by you at the time of creation, I have been wandering about to the satisfaction of the body." This chastisement often consists in placing the *jīva* into the body of animals which can have no knowledge of the *śāstras* and cannot act in accordance with them. Even in births like those of men, it confounds the mind with the views of infidels and heretics and, even in the case of those who escape this, causes, through the concealing agency of the peacock feather of primal matter and its modifications, the bodies and the senses, (1) ignorance of the truth, and (2) erroneous knowledge, and so also (3) subjection to sense-pleasures. As Śrī Rāmānuja says: "This causes obscuration of knowledge of the essential nature of the Lord and also false knowledge. Besides, it makes the *jīva* think that this association is delightful." As a consequence of this, it induces the *jīva* to disobey His orders and do forbidden things for the sake of petty pleasures. To quote again the words of the Āḷvārs: "Is it right for you to confound my soul and excite my five senses by showing me, a sinner, all sorts of petty pleasures?" One act of disobedience leads to further acts of sin. Well has it been said: "Sin committed again and again

> destroys wisdom and the person without wisdom begins further acts of a sinful nature." In consequence the Lord makes the *jīva* wander again and again through the cycle of life in the womb, birth, old age, death, and hell, as stated by Himself, "I throw them always into asuric (demonic) births."[44]

Vaiṣṇavas consider *śaraṇāgati*, "taking refuge [to God]," an unfailing means to win Viṣṇu's grace and to attain liberation from rebirth:

> How can this chief hindrance, divine punishment resulting from disobedience of the Lord's commands, the root cause of this chain of suffering, be removed? The author of *Śrī Bhāṣya* has declared that the only remedy for this hindrance is to obtain the favor of the Lord and that this can be done only by *śaraṇāgati*, self-surrender to the Lord. This declaration is made by him, while commenting on the order in which the senses, the mind and the like have to be controlled as stated in *Kaṭha Upaniṣad.*[45]

Śrīvaiṣṇavas insist on the necessity of a *guru*. Rāmānuja develops this theme in the context of the parable of a young prince who, in the course of a boyish play, leaves his father's court, loses his way, and fails to return:

> The king thinks his son is lost; the boy himself is received by some good Brahmin who brings him up and teaches him without knowing who his father is. When the boy has reached his sixteenth year and is accomplished in every way, some fully trustworthy person tells him, "Your father is the ruler of all these lands, famous for the possession of all noble qualities, wisdom, generosity, kindness, courage, valor and so on, and he stays in his capital, longing to see you, his lost child." Hearing that his father is alive and a man so high and noble, the boy's heart is filled with supreme joy; and the king also, understanding that his son is alive, in good health, handsome, and well instructed, considers himself to have attained all a man can wish for. He then takes steps to recover his son, and finally the two are reunited.[46]

Rāmānuja sees in the "fully trustworthy person" of the parable the true *guru*. The foremost among the *gurus* is Śrī, *mediatrix* between God and man. She is the embodiment of grace and mercy whose endeavors win the forgiveness of God for the *jīva*. The human *guru* should be like her: entirely free from egotism, always desirous of the welfare of others, not swayed by the love of fame or profit. Vedānta Deśika thus describes the qualifications of a spiritual teacher:

> One who desires true (spiritual) wealth and prosperity must secure the help of a preceptor (*ācārya*) with these qualifications: he must be firmly attached to and take his stand on the worthy and proper tradition; he must be possessed of steady and unflinching intellect; he must be free from blemish; he must have mastered the Vedas; he must be deeply attached to the Lord and live, move and have his being in Him; he must be firmly established in *sattva-guṇa*; he must always speak the truth and truth only; he must possess good conduct; he must be free from vanity, jealousy, and other vices; he must keep his senses under control; he must be a lifelong *bandhu* [relation]; he must be full of mercy and compassion; he must never hesitate to point out lapses of conduct; he must always act in a manner conducive to his own and others' welfare.[47]

These are the conditions which the disciple has to fulfill:

> The *ācārya* should be venerated and worshiped as if he were the Lord Himself. For both possess the same qualities: they dispel the darkness of ignorance; they wipe out sins; they bring into existence their own qualities; they confer new life which does away with the old one; they possess the efficacy and power of divine vision; they have unbounded compassion; they are ever sweet and are forever in command. The disciple must be convinced that the teachings of the *ācārya* are beyond remuneration.
>
> A good disciple must have a good intellect, be respectful towards holy people, be of good conduct, desirous to learn about the true nature of things and men, render faithful service to the *ācārya*, must not feel self-important, respect the *ācārya*, await the proper time and opportunity to place his questions and doubts before the *ācārya*, keep his senses under control, control his mind, be not jealous, have faith in the *śāstras*, be tested by the *ācārya*, and be grateful.
>
> The following secret instruction imparted by the *ācārya* should be borne always in mind by the disciple: "Understand that the Lord of Lakṣmī alone is the one who has under His sole control the essential nature, continued existence, activity and fruit of all objects. Never look upon or consider anyone else as the goal of attainment. Do not choose any one else as your help. Realizing that fear and fearlessness both emanate only from Him, do not transgress His commandments."[48]

Rāmānuja's commentary on the last *sūtra* of the *Vedāntasūtras* is a brilliant resumé of Śrīvaiṣṇava theology:

> We know from Scripture that there is a Supreme Person whose nature is absolute bliss and goodness; who is fundamentally antagonistic to all evil; who is the cause of the origination, sustentation, and dissolution of the world; who differs in nature from all other beings, who is all-knowing,

> who by his mere thought and will accomplishes all his purposes; who is an ocean of kindness as it were for all who depend on him; who is all-merciful, who is immeasurably raised above all possibility of anyone being equal or superior to him, whose name is the Highest *Brahman*. And with equal certainty we know from Scripture that this Supreme Lord, when pleased by the faithful worship of his devotees, consisting in daily repeated meditation on Him, assisted by the performance of all practices prescribed for each caste and *āśrama*, frees them from the influence of nescience which is *karma* accumulated in the infinite progress of time and hence hard to overcome, allows them to attain to that supreme bliss which consists in the direct intuition of His own true nature, and after that does not turn them back into the miseries of *saṃsāra*. The text distinctly teaching this is: "He who behaves thus all his life through reaches the world of Brahman and does not return." And the Lord himself declared: "Having obtained me, great-souled men do not come into rebirth, the fleeting abode of misery, for they have reached the highest perfection. Up to the world of *Brahmā* the worlds return again, O Arjuna; but having attained to me, O son of Kuntī, there is no rebirth." As, moreover, the released soul has freed itself from the bondage of *karma*, has its powers of knowledge fully developed, and has all its being in the supremely blissful intuition of the highest *Brahman*, it evidently cannot desire anything else nor enter on any other form of activity and the idea of its returning into *saṃsāra* is therefore altogether excluded. Nor indeed need we fear that the Supreme Lord when once having taken to himself the devotee whom he greatly loves will turn him back into the *saṃsāra*. For he himself has said: "To the wise man I am very dear and dear is he to me. Noble indeed are all these, but the wise man I regard as my very self. For he, with soul devoted, seeks me only as his highest goal. At the end of many births the wise man goes to me, thinking all is Vāsudeva. Such great-souled men are rarely met with." Thus everything is settled to satisfaction.[49]

Shortly after Rāmānuja the unity of Śrīvaiṣṇavism was disrupted: two major schools developed, called Teṅgalais (Southerners, with their centre in Śrīraṅgam) and Vadagalais (Northerners, with their centre in Kāñcīpūram). The split was based on linguistic as well as dogmatic grounds. The Vadagalais maintained that the Sanskṛt scriptures alone were the instruments for salvific knowledge and that one had to cooperate with God in the process of salvation like the young monkey who has to cling to his mother if he is to be carried away from a fire. The Teṅgalais preferred the Tamil holy books and insisted that one had passively to suffer salvation from God like a kitten, which its mother just grabs with her teeth and carries off from the fire.

Pillai Lokācārya is a representative of the "monkey-school:"

> Even the all-loving Father, the Great *Īśvara*, does not force His presence on the soul not yet ripe to receive Him. With infinite patience He waits and watches the struggle of the soul in *saṃsāra* since the struggle is necessary for the full development of the faculties of the soul.[50]

Vedānta Deśika holds the views of the "cat-school:"

> When the Lord, who is omnipotent, who knows all things, and who is by His very nature full of love towards us, has accepted the responsibility (of saving us) there is nothing more remaining to be done by us here for it; let us therefore fix our souls in that boundless sea of supreme bliss and feel the satisfaction (of having attained our object) by becoming rich in rendering service to Him, poor though we may have been before. The person who has adopted surrender (*prapatti*) has from the time of its adoption nothing else to do for attaining its fruit. What had to be done was done by once performing *prapatti*.[51]

Apart from these (and some other) differences, both Vadagalais and Teṅgalais are followers of traditional Śrīvaiṣṇavism. Lokācārya's *Arthapañcaka* is one of the many concise presentations of the essentials of Śrīvaiṣṇavism, which would also be accepted by the other faction. Thus he writes:

> The knowledge of five fundamental truths is essential for an individual soul in this world when intending to lead a spiritual life. It means the correct understanding of (i) the nature of the self, (ii) the nature of the Supreme Self, (iii) the nature of the ultimate end or value of life, (iv) the nature of the means to attain the highest goal of life, and (v) the nature of the impediments obstructing the attainment of the cherished end, God. Each one of these is again fivefold.
>
> The self is of five types, namely, the Eternal, the Free, the Bound, the Lonely, and the Devoted (eager for salvation). The nature of the Supreme Self is fivefold in the form of Absolute (*para*), the Emanations (*vyūha*), the Manifestations (*vibhava*), the Inner Controller (*antaryāmī*), and the Worship-Image (*ārca*). That which is desirable for an individual soul is the object of human life; and that too is fivefold, namely, duty (*dharma*), wealth (*artha*), sensual pleasure (*kāma*), liberation (*mokṣa*), and realization of God (*sākṣātkāra*). The means for attaining the object is also fivefold: action (*karma*), knowledge (*jñāna*), devotion (*bhakti*), surrender to god (*śaraṇāgati*), and regard for the preceptor (*gurūpasati*). The impediments are also fivefold: what is contrary to one's own nature, what is adverse to the nature of the Supreme Self; what obstructs the attainment

of the objects of life; what goes against the means of attainment; and what impedes the realization (of God) ...

(Of the five modes of existence of God) *Ārcāvatāra* is that manifestation of the Lord in which He assumes that form which is agreeable to His devotee, and holds that title which is given to Him by His devotee. He has no form or name for His own sake, but He transforms Himself into the shape desired by His devotee, and bears the name of his choice. Although He is omniscient He behaves as if He were ignorant; though omnipotent He appears as if powerless; though without a desire unfulfilled, He remains as if in need; though the Saviour of all, He requires protection. Thus reversing the relation of the owner and the owned (the order of the object [*sva*] and the subject [*svāmī*]) He makes Himself available to common perception and becomes accessible to all by dwelling in public temples and private sanctuaries to those who adore Him.

Of the five means of attaining salvation the first is activity, which consists first in disciplining the body by the performance of sacrifices, giving gifts, practicing religious austerities, meditation, offering regular morning and evening prayers, performing the five great sacrifices, maintaining the sacred fire, pilgrimages, dwelling in holy places, observing vows, ablutions, leading a religious life during the rainy season, subsisting on fruits and roots, studying scripture, worshiping God, softly repeating the holy *mantras*, offering libations to the forefathers, and performing various prescribed rites. When, as a result of all this, the sins are destroyed, one should make one's own self the subject of one's own attributive consciousness, which, restrained from going out to its natural objects like sound, touch, and others, is in need of an object ...

Devotion consists in continuously contemplating the image of the Lord like an uninterrupted stream of oil and generating a state of affection ... The most effective expedient is absolute surrender (to God). It is easy to practice for those who feel unable to observe the rules of ritual devotion and who cannot tread the path of knowledge, and who have not been able to gain a vision of the Lord. It quickly leads to the desired end and has to be adopted only once; it speedily brings one to the realization of God. This means is readily accessible and quite in keeping with the nature of the aspirant.

Though the Lord is directly accessible, He becomes more accessible through the allegiance to the *guru* as He does through an allegiance to any other deity being the Inner Controller of all; and for that matter the allegiance to the *guru* is an independent measure of equal importance, self-sufficient as well as complementary, to any or all the measures shown above.[52]

The Śrīvaiṣṇava tradition shows vigorous life today in the big pilgrimage centers of Śrīraṅgam, Kāñcīpūram, and Tirupati, visited by millions of people every year. Tirupati is reputed to be the richest temple in the whole of India, and from funds donated by millions of pilgrims the Venkateśvara University has been established. The scholarly, as well as the religious and administrative, succession is in the able hands of the heads of the large Śrīvaiṣṇava establishments.

THE BRAHMA OR MADHVA *SAṂPRADĀYA* (*DVAITA*)

Madhva criticized Rāmānuja for going only halfway in his refutation of Śaṅkara's Advaita. He advocated a radical Dvaita (Dualism) characterized by the "five differences," namely, between God and living beings, between individual living beings, between humans and non-sentient beings, and between individual non-sentient beings. He also exalts the greatness and uniqueness of Viṣṇu and maintains that liberation is only possible through Viṣṇu's grace:

> Brahmā, Śiva, and the greatest of the gods decay with the decay of their bodies; greater than these is Hari, undecaying, because his body is for the sustentation of Lakṣmī ...
>
> Release from bondage is possible only through God's grace. It is bestowed on those who have had a direct vision of God. Such vision is vouchsafed to those who have constantly meditated on him in loving devotion after going through the discipline of sincere study of *śāstras* and cogitation, termed *jijñāsa*, which sets one's doubts at rest and clears the ground for meditation.[53]

> The firm and unshakeable love of God which rises above all other ties of love and affection based upon an adequate knowledge and conviction of his great majesty is called *bhakti*. That alone is the means to *mokṣa*.[54]

> *Mokṣa* would not be worth having if the *ātman* does not survive as a self-luminous entity therein. For the *ātman* is the ultimate goal and target of all desires.[55]

One of his characteristic teachings is the "gradation of bliss:"

> There is a natural gradation among the released souls as well as disparity in their *sādhanas*. The difference in the nature and quality of *sādhanas* must necessarily have a relation to the result. The existence of such a gradation in *mokṣa* is established by reason and revelation. How can anyone oppose it? Just as vessels of different sizes, the rivers, and the Ocean are all "full" of water according to their respective capacities, so also the *jīvas*' "fullness" of bliss is different according to the capacity of their *sādhana*. Those with little capacity are satisfied

> with little bliss. Those with greater capacity require more. Despite the inequalities there is harmony. All causes for jealousy and envy are eradicated.[56]

The released and God are one:

> The released takes everything with the hand of Hari, sees through the eye of Hari only, with the feet of Hari he walks, and this is the state of the released who has attained *sāyuja mukti.*
>
> Those who are fit for this type of *mukti* can enter into the Supreme Lord and at will issue forth, again assume either spirit forms or material bodies, and enjoy all blessings except a few.[57]

The Madhva *saṃpradāya* is a flourishing community, with major centers especially in Karṇāṭaka.

THE RUDRA OR VALLABHA *SAṂPRADĀYA* (PUṢṬIMĀRGA)

Vallabha (1481–1533 C.E.), a Telugu brahmin belonging originally to the Viṣṇuswāmi school, became the founder of a distinct *saṃpradāya* with a specific doctrine of salvation which became known as *puṣṭimārga*, the way of grace. His largest work is the *Subhodinī*, an extensive commentary on that section of the *Bhāgavata Purāṇa* that describes the love games of Kṛṣṇa with the *gopīs*:

> Now that Lord Kṛṣṇa has separated the devotees of Vraja from their experience of the joy of Brahman, that game of His, which is perfectly suited for uniting them with the Joy of Worshiping Him through love, is narrated here.
>
> The Joy of Worship is brought to perfect fulfillment in ordinary women; and it is by means of them that it may come to a man. The suitability of such women to experience Kṛṣṇa's Joy has also been described.
>
> Therefore the Joy of Worshiping Kṛṣṇa through love becomes established perfectly in women. Men will come to experience it through them and in no other way.
>
> For women alone can taste this Joy, and then a man can taste it in women. This is why the blessed Lord Kṛṣṇa delighted in love with women day and night.
>
> Kṛṣṇa's love-games are said to be of five kinds, involving five of his many forms. The first game He plays with the Self, next is the game He plays with the mind. The third game is with speech and breath; the fourth with the senses. The game with the body is called the fifth. With these five games is He Himself fully revealed and established.[58]

> From the famous analysis of the name Kṛṣṇa, which explains *kṛṣ* as "Being" and *na* as "Joy," we know that Kṛṣṇa is the Blessed Lord whose very form is Being and Joy, and who possesses the fullness of perfect qualities. From this it is certain that, because of the defectiveness of anything considered in itself – apart from Kṛṣṇa- there is surely defectiveness in a person who looks upon such a faulty thing as the cause of well-being. Those who do not possess total love for him (by which they would see him in everything) are not fit to experience the game.[59]

The Vallabha *saṃpradāya* is strongly represented in the Mathurā-Vṛṇḍāvana area and in Gujarat.

THE KUMĀRA OR NIMBĀRKA *SAṂPRADĀYA* (*ŚUDDHĀDVAITA*)

Nimbārka (1125–62 C.E.) is a faithful Pāñcarātrin in most respects. A tendency to overemphasize the role of the *guru* is present in his writings, an attitude that led in later times to gross abuses. "*Jīva-Guru-Hari*: this is the eternal secret of all truth."[60]

> *Prapatti* means a complete resignation or self-surrender to the Lord; it consists in depending on the Lord in every respect and at every step, relinquishing one's narrow individuality as a separate self-dependent and self-sufficient being, giving up every other *sādhana* and throwing one's self completely on the mercy of the Lord. One who wants to attain salvation should, after having received instruction from a *guru*, take refuge in the Lord with his whole mind and body, looking upon him as father, mother, friend and master, as knowledge, wealth, and everything, serving him as a son serves his father, a friend his friend, a servant his master. The Lord is ever gracious to one who has thus taken refuge in him. He protects him at all times from all harms and difficulties, regards him as his special ward, as his dear friend, never abandons him in spite of his faults. With his own hands he leads him to salvation, to an attainment of himself.[61]

The attainment of highest fulfillment or *mokṣa* is thus described:

> Having seen there the Lord who is called Mukunda or Kṛṣṇa, from a distance, the *jīva* bows down to Him uttering with happiness the words, "Salutations to your lotus-like Feet," again and again. Then the Lord Kṛṣṇa casts his look of His lotus-like beautiful face, which is tender with kindness and pity, at the *jīva* and welcomes it in an extremely beautiful speech. Then the *jīva* becomes of the nature of the Lord and is liberated from the fetters of *māyā* and never returns to the worldly path again.[62]

The Nimbārka *saṃpradāya* is strongly represented in the Brajmaṇḍala.

The Caitanya Movement and School

Caitanya represents a Vaiṣṇavism in which feelings and emotions are seen as the principal indicators of religiosity. While his learned followers produced under his inspiration a great number of scholarly works, Caitanya himself is credited with only having authored these eight verses:

> The singing of Śrī Kṛṣṇa's name is victorious above all: it cleanses the mirror of the mind, it extinguishes the forest fire of *saṃsāra*, it is the gift of moonshine for the lotus of the heart, it is the power of wisdom, it makes the ocean of joy of divine service surge, it makes us taste holy passion in every syllable, it is a soothing bath for all Selves.
>
> You have revealed your many names in many ways and you have placed into these names your entire being. There is no restriction for singing these names. So great, O Lord is your grace, but my fate in this birth is quite horrible, because there has not arisen in me an overpowering love for your name.
>
> Think of yourself as less significant than a blade of grass, be more forbearing than a tree, do not desire to be honored but render honor to others, always sing the praise of Hari's name.
>
> O Lord of the universe, I do not desire wealth, children, a beautiful wife or a poet's gift: may I have, in life after life, pure love towards you!
>
> O you, son of Nanda! I am really your servant but I have been thrown into the ocean of *saṃsāra*, full of contradictions. Have mercy on me and consider me a particle of dust clinging to your lotus feet.
>
> When will my eyes brim over with a flood of tears at the mention of your name, when will my mouth stammer your name with a breaking voice, and when will the hairs on my body stand up in a shower of ecstasy when chanting your name?
>
> Due to my separation from Govinda a fraction of a moment appears like an aeon to me. My tears are flowing like the rain of the rainy season and the whole world is empty.
>
> Whether He embraces me, devoted to His feet, or whether He crushes me and wounds my innermost being by remaining invisible, whatever He does, the insatiable lover, He is the Lord of my life and no other.[63]

> In the *Kali-yuga* the singing of the name is the great *sādhana*. Through *saṁkīrtana* the sin of the world is destroyed, the heart is purified and practice of all kinds of *bhakti* is initiated.[64]

Sevā, "service," ritual worship of the image that embodies Viṣṇu is one of the foremost, livelong duties of a Vaiṣṇava. The following text gives a fair idea of the inner and outer requirements for such service:

> These are the sixty-four elements of worship: taking refuge at the feet of the spiritual master; Kṛṣṇa initiation and instruction; serving the spiritual master; following the way of the righteous people; enquiry about the right method of worship; renouncing other enjoyments for the sake of Kṛṣṇa; living at holy places and listening to the praises of holy places; accepting food only for the upkeep of the body for the sake of devotion; observing the eleventh day as fastday; regarding as equally holy the holy basil, the holy fig tree, the earth, a cow, a brahmin, and a Vaiṣṇava.
>
> Giving up the company of the wicked; not recruiting many disciples; not enquiring into and discussing various sciences; giving up worry and anger; not speaking ill of other deities; not harassing other living beings; not offending divine service and holy name; not criticizing the spiritual master, Kṛṣṇa, and other devotees; adopting the signs of a Vaiṣṇava; wearing the syllable of Hari's name; wearing flower garlands that had been offered the day before to the deity; dancing before the image; prostrating full-length; rising from one's seat; obsequiousness; frequenting the house of the divine image; circumnambulation of the image; offering *pūjā*; serving food; singing; doing saṅkīrtana; repeating the name of God; reciting hymns; serving *prasāda*; drinking the nectar of the feet of the Lord.[65]

BHAKTI POETS AND MYSTICS

Vaiṣṇavism was always a "people's religion," giving greater emphasis to worship and devotion than to asceticism and philosophical speculation. Its major protagonists were the inspired poets and mystics who lived a life of *bhakti* and who spread it through their songs that people loved to hear and to join in. The *bhakti* poets and mystics used the vernaculars – every major linguistic region of India has its own treasury of spiritual poetry. The translations which follow convey the meaning but they cannot adequately reproduce the puns and the play with words of which Hindu poets are fond.[66]

Sūrdās

The blind poet of Kṛṣṇa *bhakti*, was a follower of the Puṣṭimārga. He flourished in the sixteenth century, and reportedly deeply impressed the Muslim Emperor Akbar who came to listen to him in disguise. His poems express his longing as well as his concern for his fellow-travelers. He belongs to the group of *Aṣṭachāp*, "The Eight Seals," who got their title from using their names as "seals" of identification in the last couplet of their poems.

I have fallen so lowly:
I do not even have one bit of desire for you!
Powerful Māyā has fettered me
in the guise of property, money, and a fair wife.
I see it, I hear it, I know it,
but I still cannot get away from it.
With my own ears I have perceived: it was said
you are the salvation of those who have fallen very low.
I want to get into the boat of deliverance,
but I am unable to pay the fare to the boatman.
I do not ask anything new from you,
you have always been gracious towards the poor.
Incline with favor upon Sūr,
Lord, King of Braja.[67]

Wondrous is this master, wondrous is his servant
wondrous are you, the executor of orders.
Cutting down mango trees and planting thorn shrubs
consigning sandal trees to flames.
Inviting thieves and driving away good people
putting your faith in backbiters.
We are stupid country girls, O Udhava,
we are unable to understand your wisdom!
Sūrdās says: Wondrous is your court
where confusion reigns complete.[68]

When the leaves have separated from the tree
they cannot be fastened back on it again by any device.
In the state of delirium
phlegm will obstruct your throat, your tongue will fail,
Yama will come to snatch away your life-breath.
Mother and father look on in bewilderment
One moment will appear to you like a thousand aeons.
Your love of the world is like the love of a parrot
for the fruit of the silk-cotton tree.
When it touches it with its beak the cotton will fly away.
O madman, do not fall into Yama's trap!
Let your mind rest at the feet of God.
Sūr says that this body is useless
Why do you carry so much conceit in your heart?[69]

Stuck like a fly in the thing-juice, yet far from understanding
he has lost the diamond "God" in the midst of his house.
He is like a deer that sees mirages that do not quench thirst,
even if approached from ten different directions.

Having produced much karma in life after life
in which he fettered himself.
He is like the parrot, who pinned his hope
on the fruit of the silk-cotton tree
Day and night he thought of it.
When he took it into his beak
the shell was empty and the cotton flew up and away.
He is like a monkey, tied on a rope by a juggler
who makes him dance for a few grains at every corner.
Sūrdās says: without devotion to God
You will become just a morsel to eat for the tiger Time.[70]

Tulsīdās

Sūrdās's younger contemporary, Tulsīdās (1532–1623) became most famous as the composer of the *Rāmacaritamānasa*, an Avadhī (Eastern Hindī) re-creation of the *Rāmāyaṇa*, which has become "the Bible of Northern India" and is still known and loved by hundreds of millions today. In addition, he is the author of numerous poems, many of which are sung at the popular *bhajan* sessions throughout India.

Looking at your extremely varied creation
The mind that tries to understand it reels.
A painter without hands has drawn a picture
without colors onto a screen "emptiness."
It cannot be erased through washing
nor does the screen crumble away.
Suffering arises from looking at this body.
In that mirage dwells an extremely ferocious crocodile.
It has no real mouth, but it swallows all
who come to slake their thirst in the imaginary water.
Some call this world real, others unreal,
others assume that it is both real and unreal.
Tulsīdās says: one who has found the true Self
leaves behind all these three errors.[71]

The companions of my birth, my hair, went white.
My concern for people's opinion has gone.
The body is wasted, the hands are trembling,
the light has gone out from the eyes.
The ear can no longer hear any word
and all senses have lost their strength.
The teeth are broken.
I cannot utter any understandable word.

Beauty has disappeared from my face.
Phlegm and bile are covering my throat.
I can call my son only with a movement of my hand.
Brothers, relations and, dearest of all, my wife
are turning me out of my home.
As the moon has got a black mark, of which it cannot get rid
thus I cannot rid myself of the attachment to what is "mine."
Tulsīdās takes refuge to your powerful feet,
which are able to overthrow greed.[72]

Kṛṣṇadās

Kṛṣṇadās, a follower of Vallabha and one of the *Aṣṭachāp* poets, was a contemporary of Sūrdās and in charge of an important temple in the Puṣṭimārga tradition. The themes of his poems are similar to those already mentioned.

You brought much money with you when you entered this city.
Tie it up in your garment to protect it from thieves!
In the business for which you had come, you hardly made any profit.
This is a matter of great concern.
You have fallen into the sleep of falsehood.
Unthinkingly you have lost all your money; you make all sad.
Kṛṣṇadās says: go home!
When Kṛṣṇa comes fall at his feet and find rest![73]

Kabīr

Kabīr (1440–1518) has been claimed by Hindus, Muslims, and Sikhs as their "saint." In his poems he criticizes all denominations and insists on genuine piety and moral integrity as the only true way. Besides the major systematic work, *Bījak*, he composed many poems that enjoy unrivaled popularity with people from all backgrounds.

Those who have gone to the beyond do not come back,
nor do they send messages.
A saint, an ordinary person, a monk, a master,
a guru, a goddess, a god,
Gaṇeśa, Brahmā, Viṣṇu and Śiva,
all are whirling around in ever new births.
A yogi, a mendicant, an ascetic, a heaven-clad, a dervish,
a shaved one, one with matted hair, a pandit,
inhabitants of the world below, the world above,

and all other worlds.
Philosophers, artists, poets,
people skilled in all kinds of things,
kings and beggars – all go round.
Some praise Rām, others Rahim, others call out to Adeś.
Variegated as their costumes may be,
they are all whirled around in the four directions.
Kabīr says: without the word of the *sadguru*
you will not reach your end.[74]

There may be one or two people to whom I can explain it.
All have lost themselves in the business of the belly.
The horse is water, the rider is wind,
like the dew-drop he will fall soon.
In a deep stream, carried away by an unfathomable current,
the boatman's pole is useless.
The "Thing" in the house does not strike the eye.
But the blind, who have lighted a lamp, are making a search.
The fire has caught on, the whole forest of the world is aflame.
Without a Guru one goes astray.
Kabīr says: listen brother monk!
You were born even without the loincloth around your body![75]

You have come into this world to do business and make a profit,
but you have gambled away your stock.
You have not even reached the outskirts of the City of Love.
As you have come, so you shall leave.
Listen my companion! Listen my friend!
What have you done in this life?
You have taken up a load of stones on your head!
Who will lift it from you further down the road?
Your friend is standing on the shore
and you have no mind to meet him.
You are sitting in a shipwrecked boat.
You fool! You will be drowning!
Kabīrdās who observes all this says:
In the end, who is your helper?
Alone did you go forth, and you will eat your own deeds.[76]

Vaiṣṇavism is the numerically strongest of all contemporary Hindu traditions and Kṛṣṇa is no doubt the most popular god in today's India, with Rāma a close second. A very large number of ordained representatives of the above mentioned *saṃpradāyas* continue the heritage of Rāmānuja, Madhva, Vallabha, Nimbārka and Caitanya as well as of many locally worshiped saints, and many other charismatic figures continue praising the greatness of Viṣṇu and his salvific deeds to millions of devotees who throng the great Viṣṇu temples North, South, East, and West.

3 ŚAIVISM

Śaivism, numerically the second strongest branch of Hinduism, is today especially prevalent in Southern India. Its roots go back to the Indus civilization, if not to prehistoric times, but, like Vaiṣṇavas, Śaivas too insist that their religion is "Vedic." Thus we begin by tracing its history from the Vedas.

ŚIVA IN THE *VEDAS*

The adjective *śiva* is used in the *Ṛgveda* as an epithet for several gods in its original meaning "propitious." Rudra, one of the names under which Śiva is invoked, is the addressee of three hymns in the *Ṛgveda*.[1]

> These songs of praise we bring before strong Rudra, to the ruler of heroes, with matted hair, so that humans and animals may prosper in our village and all may be well.
>
> Be gracious to us, O Rudra, and bring us joy; we serve you, the Lord of heroes, with respect.
>
> Whatever well-being and wealth our forefather Manu gained through sacrifices, may we gain under your protection.
>
> May we win your grace, you generous one, by worshiping the gods.
>
> Come to our families and bring them happiness. Our sacrifice is offered to you by faultless heroes.
>
> We invite for help, the wise, the wanderer, the mighty Rudra, perfector of sacrifices.
>
> May he repel from us the anger of the gods: we long for his favor and grace.

> Him with the braided hair we call down with reverence, the reddish wild boar of the sky, of wondrous form.
> May he, his hands holding medicine, grant us protection, shelter, and a firm home.
> To him, the Maruts' father, this hymn is sung a song extremely sweet, to strengthen Rudra's power.
> Grant us, you Immortal, the mortals' food: be gracious to me and my progeny.
> O Rudra do not harm either great or small of us, neither the growing boy nor the full-grown man, do not slay the sire, nor the mother, do not harm our dear bodies,
> Do not harm us in our seed and progeny, harm us not in our living, nor in cows and steeds.
> Do not slay our heroes in the fury of your wrath. We offer you ever more oblations with our songs.
> Like a herdsman I have sung these songs, O Father of the Maruts, give us well-being.
> Your benevolence with which you favor us is blessed: we desire your saving help.
> Far from us may be your shaft that kills humans and beasts, may your bliss be with us you Ruler of Heroes.
> Be gracious to us, O god, and bless us and give us redoubled protection.
> Seeking help we have spoken to him and worshiped him; may Rudra, accompanied by the Maruts, hear our calling.
> This our prayer may be granted by Varuṇa and Mitra, by Aditi and Sindhu, by Earth and Heaven.[2]

> May your bright arrow, shot down by you from heaven, flying upon the earth, pass us uninjured by.
> Inflict no evil on our sons and progeny. Slay us not and do not abandon us, let not your noose, when you are angry, seize us.[3]

Rudra not only inflicts evil but also saves from evil. He can be asked either not to harm his devotees or to provide for them a remedy against the ills sent by him. The Vedic singer implores Rudra to give health, strength, grace, bliss, to protect cattle, to heal all sickness, to help the worshiper in his troubles, to repel all assaults of mischief, to give strengthening balm to the heroes. Rudra is the great physician who possesses a thousand medicines, the remover of woes which other gods have sent, his gracious hand dispenses health and comfort.

One of the most interesting texts in the whole of Vedic literature is the Śatarudriya hymn of the *Yajur-Veda*, connected with the Śatarudriya offering described in the *Śatapatha Brāhmaṇa* introduced by the statement: "Agni has on completion become Rudra and this ceremony is performed to avert his wrath and secure his favor."[4]

> Homage be paid to your wrath, O Rudra, homage to your shaft and homage to your two arms.
>
> Your auspicious form, Rudra, is benevolent and pleasant to look at. With that most auspicious form look upon us.
>
> You mountain hunter, make that shaft, which you hold ready in your hand, auspicious, do not injure man or beast.
>
> You mountain dweller, we greet you with auspicious hymns. May all our people be healthy and well satisfied.
>
> The advocate, the first divine physician has defended us, crushing all serpents, driving away all sorceresses.
>
> That most auspicious one, whose hue is coppery and red and brown, and those Rudras who have their place in various regions, who surround him thousandfold, we implore to hold back their wrath.
>
> Homage to him the blue-necked, the thousand-eyed, the generous.
>
> Loosen your bow-string and cast away, O Lord Divine, the arrows in your hand.
>
> Homage to the golden-armed leader of hosts, Lord of the regions, to the trees with their green tresses, to the Lord of Beasts be homage.
>
> Homage to him whose sheen is like green grass, homage to the radiant Lord of paths, homage to the golden-haired wearer of the sacrificial cord, homage to the Lord of the well-endowed.
>
> Homage to the brown-hued piercer, to the Lords of food be homage. Homage to Bhava's weapon, homage to the Lord of moving things. Homage to Rudra whose bow is bent to slay, to the Lord of fields homage. Homage to the charioteer who injures none: to the Lord of forests homage.
>
> Homage to the red one, the architect, to the Lord of trees homage. Homage to him who stretched the earth, to him who gives relief be homage. Homage to the Lord of plants, homage to the prudent merchant. Homage to the Lord of bushes, to the Lord of foot-soldiers who make their foes weep, be homage.
>
> Homage to the cheat, the arch-deceiver, to the Lord of thieves be homage! Homage to the wearer of sword and quiver, to the Lord of robbers be homage. Homage to the bolt-armed assassins, to the Lord of pilferers be homage. Homage to the sword-bearers, to those who roam at night, to the Lord of plunderers homage.
>
> To the turban-wearing haunter of mountains, Lord of land-grabbers homage. Homage to you who bear arrows and to you who carry bows.
>
> To the strong Rudra bring we these our songs of praise, to him the Lord of heroes with the braided hair, that it be well with all our cattle and our people, that in this village all be healthy and well-fed.[5]

Only a few hymns in the *Atharvaveda* are addressed to Rudra. In *Atharvaveda* VII, 42, Rudra and Soma are mentioned as redeemers from disease and sin. In the hymn reproduced below the two forms of Rudra, Śarva and Bhava, are treated as two distinct persons.

> O Bhava and Śarva, be gracious, do not oppose us, you lords of beings, lords of cattle. Homage to you! Do not let the sharpened arrow fly, do not harm our bipeds or quadrupeds.
>
> Let this Bhava avoid us on every side, as fire the waters, let Bhava avoid us; let him not plot against us; homage be to him.
>
> Yours are the four directions, yours the heaven, yours the earth, yours, O terrible, this wide atmosphere, yours is all this that has *ātman*, that is breathing upon the earth.
>
> Do not harm us, bless us, avoid us, be not angry, let us not come into collision with you.
>
> Be not greedy for our kine, our men; be not greedy for our goats and sheep; elsewhere, formidable One, roll forth, smite the progeny of the mockers.
>
> Bhava is master of the heaven, Bhava of the earth, Bhava has filled the wide atmosphere; to him be homage, in whichever direction.
>
> O King Bhava, be gracious to the sacrificer, for you have become Lord of the Cattle; whoever has faith and says: "There are gods" be you gracious to his bipeds and quadrupeds.[6]

ŚIVA IN THE *BRĀHMAṆAS*

The *Śatapatha Brāhmaṇa* tells us in connection with the Śatarudriya a very interesting story explaining the origin of Rudra-Śiva:

> When Prajāpati had become disjointed the deities departed from him. Only one god did not leave him, *manyu* (wrath). Extended he remained within, he cried and the tears of him that fell down settled on *manyu*. He became the hundred-headed, thousand-eyed, hundred-quivered Rudra. And the other drops that fell down spread over this world in countless numbers, by thousands; and inasmuch as they originated from crying (*rud*) they were called Rudras (roarers). That hundred-headed, thousand-eyed, hundred-quivered Rudra with his strong bow strung and his arrow fitted to his string, was inspiring fear, being in quest of food. The gods were afraid of him.[7]

Another text states that to Rudra is due whatsoever is injured in sacrifice. Several times Paśupati, Śarva, and Bhava are mentioned as names of Rudra. Only in one place is he Rudra-Śiva; here too the kindliness of

Rudra is only the effect of the appeasement made by the sacrificer. His region is the North.

ŚIVA IN THE *UPANIṢADS*

The first and most important Upaniṣad, in which Śiva is identified with Brahman, is the *Śvetāśvatara*. It is to the Śaivas what the *Bhagavadgītā* is to the Vaiṣṇavas.

> There are two unborn beings, the knowing and the unknowing, the one all-powerful, the other powerless. Indeed there is (another) one who is unborn, connected with the enjoyer and the objects of enjoyment. And there is the infinite self, of universal form, non-active. When one finds out this triad, that is *brahman*.
>
> What is perishable is primary matter. What is immortal and imperishable is Hara. Over both the perishable and the soul the one God rules. By meditating on him, by uniting with him, by reflecting on him more and more, there is complete cessation from the illusion of the world.
>
> He who is in the faces, heads, and necks of all, who dwells in the cave of the heart of all beings, who is all-pervading. He is the Lord and the omnipresent Śiva.
>
> That person indeed is the Great Lord, the impeller of highest being, reaching the purest attainment, the ruler, the imperishable light.[8]

Another important text in the same class is the *Atharvaśira Upaniṣad*, younger than the *Śvetāśvatara*. It explains the various names and epithets of Śiva and recommends means to release the Mahāpāśupata *vrata*.

> The *devas* once upon a time went to Mahākailāsa. They asked Rudra, who drives away the disease of delusion relating to the existence of things apart from Brahmā: "Who are you?"
>
> He replied to them thus: "I am the absolute existence, the innermost *Ātman*, the basis of the apprehension of "I" and the like. I existed long before creation, prior to beginningless time. I am present in existence. I shall continue to exist forever in the future. Nothing else exists apart from me, the Parameśvara. Who knows me, knows all the gods as my real form.
>
> This is the Pāśupata *vrata* through which alone can be successfully accomplished the *kaivalya* (final condition) by the *pāśus* ("cattle," designation of unliberated souls), bound by the *pāśa* ("noose," bondage) of the deluded belief in the real existence of things apart from *ātman*, through the attainment of the knowledge of the identity of the *pāśu* with *pati* and the consequent vanishing of the *pāśa*.[9]

ŚIVA IN EPICS AND *PURĀṆAS*

While the *Rāmāyaṇa* and the *Mahābhārata* are predominantly Vaiṣṇava, they also contain many sections relating to Śiva. Most of the Śiva lore, however, is found in the Śaivite *Purāṇas*; some of the more prominent Śiva myths are also mentioned in Vaiṣṇava scriptures. Among these stories the following are most popular:

Dakṣa's Sacrifice

Śiva's interruption of Dakṣa's sacrifice is believed to be the first of Śiva's exploits. It is first mentioned in the *Taittirīya Saṃhitā*. Here is the story as the *Vāyu Purāṇa*, probably the earliest version, tells it:

> Dakṣa has prepared an *aśvamedha* [horse sacrifice] and invites all the gods, except Śiva. His daughter Umā, Śiva's wife, comes to Dakṣa pleading that he should also invite her husband; she feels wronged and dishonored, being the eldest and foremost of Dakṣa's daughters. Sage Dadhīca also remarks that he fears Dakṣa's sacrifice will have a bad end if Śiva is not invited. Dakṣa retorts that this sacrifice was prepared for Viṣṇu:
>
> > Here in this vessel of gold, intended for the Lord of all sacrifices, is the sacrificial offering sanctified by *mantras* and rites according to ordinance. I intend to make this offering to Viṣṇu, who is beyond compare. He is mighty and the master of all and to Him should sacrifices be offered.
>
> Dakṣa does not know of any Rudra other than the eleven Rudras. Umā is sad and asks her husband why he is not going to the sacrifice of his father's, while all the other gods are going there. Śiva himself explains that the gods in ancient times decided that Rudra should not have any part in the sacrifice. Umā is silent reflecting how to obtain for her husband a share – a half or third – of the sacrifice. Śiva then decides to create a "Terrible Being," Vīrabhadra, which will destroy Dakṣa's sacrifice.
>
> There follows a description of this embodiment of Śiva's wrath and of a host of evil and ugly beings that accompany it. They descend upon Dakṣa's sacrifice, scatter everything, drive the gods away, and kill the sacrifice which had assumed the form of a deer. Brahmā, together with the gods and Dakṣa, fold their hands and question the "Terrible Being" about its nature. Vīrabhadra explains his nature and his mission and tells them that they should take refuge with Umā's husband, whose wrath is more

propitious even than the boons of other gods. As soon as he hears it Dakṣa begins praising Śiva.

> I bow to you Lord of all the gods, the destroyer of the forces of the demons. You are thousand eyed, you are fierce-eyed, you are three-eyed. Your hands and feet extend in all directions. Your eyes and head and mouth are turned towards all sides as well. Your ears are everywhere in the universe and you yourself are everywhere.

Śiva is pacified, accepts Dakṣa's homage and grants to him that the sacrifice, though spoilt, be of benefit to him, having spent so much time and pains on it.

The grateful Dakṣa then praises Śiva in a thousand and eight names. At the end he points out that it is always Rudra-Śiva alone who is in all creatures. He did not invite him, because he was creator and all. Or else, he was deluded through the god's subtle *māyā*. But now he takes refuge in Śiva alone. Śiva accepts the praise and devotion and promises Dakṣa his companionship and the fruit of a thousand horse sacrifices and a hundred *vājapeyas*. He then tells him that he had extracted from the Vedas and its six branches the *pāśupata-vrata* – the method of liberating the *paśu* from the *pāśa*. This Pāśupata religion is open to all, regardless of *varṇa* or *āśrama*.

> The recitation of this text itself makes people free from sickness and fear and grants them a journey to Rudraloka from whence there is no return.[10]

The *Bhāgavata Purāṇa*, the only Vaiṣṇava scripture that contains the story, adds some significant details:

> Surrounded by spirits and trolls and ghosts, with his hair scattered about, now laughing and now crying, he roves about uncovered like a madman in frightful crematories. Bathed in the ashes of funeral piles and adorned with a garland of skulls and wearing ornaments of human bones, he is really inauspicious, though bearing the appellation of Śiva. Drunk, he is fond of drunken people and is the lord of goblins and ghosts, who are purely *tāmasik*. At the instance of Brahmā, I gave away my virtuous daughter to such an impure and evil-minded person, the lord of the ghosts.

Dakṣa curses the great Śiva and there and then excludes him from a share of the sacrifices. Nandīśvara, the first servant of Śiva, becomes angry on hearing Dakṣa's curse, and in his turn curses Dakṣa; he should become infatuated and his head should be changed into that of a goat. Bhṛgu utters a counter-curse which clearly shows the Vaiṣṇava background of this version of the story:

> They who observe vows sacred to Bhava and those who follow these latter shall become heretics and act contrary to the true scriptures. Only those who have cast all purity into the wind, are silly-minded and wear matted locks, ashes and bones, shall get themselves initiated into the cult of Śiva worship, where wine and other spirituous liquour will be held in high esteem.

Vīrabhadra comes into existence:

> whose figure touched the skies, who was possessed of a thousand arms, dark like a cloud, with three eyes, bright as the sun, fierce teeth and matted hair, shining like a flaming fire, wearing a garland of skulls and armed with various weapons.[11]

The *Śiva sahasranāma*, which the *Vāyupurāṇa* adds,[12] is not necessarily part of the Dakṣa story; it is very popular with Śaivites even today, who recite it to win Śiva's favor. In it Śiva is identified with the Sun; he is the artificer of the universe; he is in all things; he is Master and Lord of all creatures. He gives boons; he destroys and creates again; he smites and heals. He is worshiped as thousand-eyed, three-eyed, Bhava, Śarva, and Rudra; he is the wielder of the trident; he is red and tawny and has a blue throat; he is white and stainless; he is the embodiment of all kinds of destruction; he is armed with bones and fond of cremation grounds; his bell and his *akṣa-mālā* are mentioned; he is fond of the heart-flesh of all creatures; he is called a tiger and a snake; he is the one who cuts down and pierces and smites; he is time, that is inauspicious. He is the killing, the instrument to kill, and that which is killed.[13]

Śiva Drinks the Poison

For later Śaivism, the myth of Śiva drinking the poison, which appeared after the churning of the ocean, is perhaps the most important one. In this episode Śaivas see the clearest image of Śiva the saviour. Śiva's blue throat is a permanent reminiscence of the deed by which he saved humankind from perishing through poison.

> Engulfing the earth it suddenly blazed up like a fire attended with fumes. And by the scent of that frightful Kālakūta the three worlds were stupefied. And then Śiva, being solicited by Brahman, swallowed that

poison for the safety of the creation. The divine Maheśvara held it in his throat, and it is said that from that time he is called Nīlakaṇṭha. Squeezing into his palm the Halāhala, which was spreading all round, Śiva swallowed it out of compassion. The poison showed its power even on his person: it made him blue at the throat, but this spot became a special ornament to that benevolent soul. Scorpions, snakes and poisonous herbs as well as what other biting creatures there were, took in what little poison leaked from the palm of Lord Śiva while he drank it.[14]

Śiva Destroys Tripura

Another very popular and important Śiva myth connects Śiva with the destruction of Tripura. Three *asuras* practice *tapas* and approach Brahmā for the "boon of immortality from death at the hands of all the creatures of all time." They are told that such a boon is impossible to obtain. Thus they choose another boon:

> We shall reside in three cities over this earth. After a thousand years we will come together and our three cities also will be united into one. That foremost one amongst the gods who will with one shaft pierce these three cities united into one will be the cause of our destruction.

Brahmā, who granted the boon, tells the complaining *devas*:

> Those three cities are to be pierced with one shaft; by no other means can their destruction be effected. None else save Sthāṇu is competent to pierce them with one shaft. You *ādityas*, select Sthāṇu, otherwise called Īśāna and Jiṣṇu, who is never fatigued with work, as your warrior. It is he who will destroy those *asuras*.

The gods pray:

> Slay the Dānavas, wielder of the trident; let the universe, through your grace, obtain happiness! Lord of the world, you are the one whose shelter should be sought. We all seek your shelter.

> Then Śiva, the great lord, seated in the chariot and equipped with everything, got ready to burn the three cities completely, the cities of the enemies of the gods. In an auspicious moment he drew the bow and made a wonderful and terrifying twanging sound. He addressed the great *asuras* and told them his own name. He discharged an arrow that had the splendor of many suns. The arrow, which was constituted by Viṣṇu and whose steel head was Agni, blazed forth and burnt the three *asuras* who

> lived in the three cities. It thereby removed their sins. The three cities reduced to ashes fell on the earth.
>
> Thus was the triple city burnt and thus were the Dānavas exterminated by Maheśvara in wrath, from desire of doing good to the three worlds. After this the gods, the *ṛṣis* and the three worlds became all restored to their natural disposition.[15]

The Burning and Resuscitation of Kāmadeva

A central theme in *Śaiva Purāṇas* is Śiva's burning of Kāmadeva, the god of love and lust, who tries to disturb him in his meditations. In some versions Pārvatī is instigating Kāma to distract Śiva and to marry her. Śiva's first reaction is wrath, and he burns Kāmadeva to ashes. At the wailing of all creatures he restores him to life.

> A great flame of fire sprang up from the third eye of the infuriated Śiva. That fire shot up into the sky, fell on the ground and rolled all over the earth around. Even before the gods had time to say "Let him be forgiven, let him be excused" it reduced Kāma to ashes. When the heroic Kāma was thus slain, the gods became miserable. With pallid face and shaking limbs Pārvatī returned to her palace together with her maids. Overcome with grief at the death of her husband, Ratī fell down unconscious, as if dead. At the request of all the gods, Śiva spoke: "I shall resuscitate Kāma within myself. He will be in my retinue and will always be frolicking around."[16]

The marriage of Śiva and Pārvatī is dealt with at great length in the *Śaiva Purāṇas*: Śaivite philosophers see in the union of Śiva and Śakti the cause of all activity in the universe, the cause also of all salvation. In fact, Śiva is active only after his marriage to Pārvatī, and he performs his great deeds either together with Pārvatī or with her permission.

Śiva the dancer

Śiva Naṭarāja has been immortalized especially in Southern Indian art. The images, however, are not found before the sixth century C.E. Śaiva philosophy, especially in the Śaiva-Siddhānta, has developed a sophisticated philosophy around Śiva Naṭarāja, seeing in it Śiva's fivefold activities symbolized.

The *tāṇḍava* dance is connected with Vīrabhadra, Śiva's terrifying form. It is held on the burning *ghāṭas* and is performed in the company of ghosts and goblins. It is always connected with Devī-Śakti; sometimes

Śāktism and Śaivism become indistinguishable. In some places the *tāṇḍava* dance is even described as Śakti's frenzied dance upon Śiva's corpse.

> The trident-bearing lord of the *devas* performed the *tāṇḍava* at dusk, along with the ghosts and leaders of goblins. After enjoying Śiva's nectar-like dance the Goddess danced in the midst of ghosts happily along with the Yoginīs.[17]

The "beautiful dance," Śiva's *naṭalīlā*, is mentioned always in connection with Śiva's marriage to Umā. The version cited below describes Śiva's dance in connection with his wooing of Pārvatī: appearing as a *sādhu* before Menā, Pārvatī's mother, he begins a beautiful dance which enchants everybody.

> He held a conch in his left and a drum in his right hand. He wore a red cloth and had his knapsack tied on his back. He appeared in the guise of a professional dancer, dancing and singing, blowing the horn and playing on the drum very sweet tunes. Hearing the sweet songs and seeing the delightful dance the people became ecstatic.
>
> Pārvatī, fainting, saw in her heart Śiva's beautiful form, bearing the trident and his other symbols, with ashes all over his body, bedecked with a garland of skulls. He wore a serpent as his sacred thread. Exquisitely white in complexion, the handsome Lord Śiva, the friend of the distressed, the ocean of mercy was repeating the words "*varam vraje*" [which can be translated either as "choose a boon" or "choose a husband"]. Seeing him thus in her heart she worshiped him. In her heart she had chosen the boon when she had said "Be my husband!" He granted that boon with pleasure and vanished.
>
> The mendicant continued his dance. Menā, greatly delighted, brought gems and jewels in gold vessels as a gift. But the dancer did not accept the gifts. He requested the hand of Pārvatī and began to dance and to sing again. Menā, surprised at hearing these words, became furious. She rebuked the mendicant and wished to drive him out. In the meantime Himavat [Pārvatī's father] returned from the Gaṅgā. He saw the mendicant in his courtyard and hearing what had happened became very angry. He ordered his attendants to drive him out. But none of them could push him out; he was hot to the touch like a blazing fire and very brilliant.
>
> He transformed himself into the four-armed Viṣṇu, with crown, earrings and yellow garment. Then Himavat had a vision of four-faced Brahmā, the creator of the worlds, red in color and reciting Vedic hymns. Then he saw him appearing in the form of the the sun, the eye of the universe. After that he appeared to him in the wonderful form of Śiva

> accompanied by Pārvatī. He was smiling and shining beautifully. And again he saw him in the form of a mass of splendor of no specific shape, unsullied, free from attributes and desires, a formless wonder. Thus he saw many forms and figures and was much surprised and delighted.
>
> Then the chief of mendicants begged of Himavat and Menā the hand of Pārvatī as alms. He, the source of great enjoyment, did not accept anything else. Himavat, deluded by Śiva's *māyā*, did not accede to the request. The mendicant vanished from the scene. Then Himavat and Menā realized that Śiva had tricked them and gone to his abode. Thinking about what had happened, they developed deep devotion to Śiva, the cause of salvation, the bestower of divine bliss.[18]

The story of the fully developed Śiva Naṭarāja story is found only in the late *Koyil Purāṇa*, a Southern Indian *sthala-purāṇa*, described in the prose that became classic:

> Śiva went out into a forest in which many Mīmāṃsakas were living. Śiva tried to argue with them, but they only got angry with him and created a fierce tiger to devour him. Śiva seized it and stripped off its skin with the nail of his little finger, wrapping it round like a cloth. Next the Mīmāṃsakas let loose a fierce serpent on Śiva. Śiva took it and put it round his neck like a garland. When Śiva began to dance, the Mīmāṃsakas created a fierce dwarf, Muyālaka, to kill Śiva. Śiva put his foot on the back of Muyālaka and broke his neck. Then he resumed his dance. It is this scene which we see in the Southern Indian bronzes of the Śiva Naṭarāja. The philosophy explaining it has a clear salvific import: the dwarf under Śiva's foot personifies evil, which is subdued by Śiva. The sound produced by his drum is the *anahaṭa* sound, indicative of salvation. The hand which is outstretched shows the *abhaya-mudrā*, the sign of grace. The fire circle in which he dances indicates the consumption of the *māyā*-universe by the appearance of Śiva-reality. The raised foot again is a symbol of freedom. Śiva wears the skull of Brahmā around his neck: all creatures are mortal; Śiva is immortal. The snake around his neck also symbolizes immortality.[19]

ŚAIVITE PHILOSOPHIES

The Pāśupata System

The earliest among the Śaiva schools is the Pāśupata, divided into various subsects, but possessing a common basic philosophy. They believe that Śiva himself originated the Pāśupata system. The following text explains what is meant by it.

By the word *paśu* we are to understand the effect (or created world), the word designating that which is dependent on something ulterior. By the word *pati* we are to understand the cause (or origin); the word designating the Lord, who is the cause of the universe, the ruler.

The cessation of pain is of two kinds, impersonal and personal. Of these, the impersonal consists in the absolute extirpation of all pain; the personal in supremacy, consisting of the visual and active powers.

All that is effected, depending on something ulterior, is threefold: sentiency, the insentient and the sentient. Sentiency is the attribute of the sentients. It is of two degrees according to its nature as cognitive or non-cognitive. The insentient, while unconscious, depends on the conscious. It is of two kinds: effect and cause. As effect it is tenfold: the earth and the other four elements, their qualities, colour, etc. As cause it is of thirteen kinds: the five organs of cognition, the five organs of action and the three internal organs. The sentient souls which are subject to transmigration are also of two kinds: souls associated with organs and souls not associated with organs. The Lord possesses infinite power. Supremacy is essentially connected with him.

Union is the conjunction of the souls with God through the intellect. It is twofold: with action and without action. Action consists of pious mutterings, meditation etc. Inaction consists of pure consciousness.[20]

The Śaiva System or Śaivasiddhānta

The school that Mādhava introduces as Śaiva is better known under the name of Śaivasiddhānta. It is the predominant philosophy of Śaivism in Southern India today. It is based upon the twenty-eight *Śaiva Āgamas* and also incorporated the teaching of the eighty-four *Nāyaṇārs*. The following text explains the basic teachings.

The Supreme has Īśāna as his head, Tatpuruṣa as his mouth, Aghora as his heart, Vāmadeva as his secret parts, Sadyojata as his feet. And this body, created according to his own will, is not like our bodies, but is the cause of the five activities of the supreme which are: grace, obscuration, destruction, preservation and creation.

It must be understood that the word "Śiva" includes in the proper meaning of the term "Lord" all beings who have attained to the state of Śiva, such as Mantreśvara, Maheśvara, the *muktas* who have become Śivas, the teachers and all the means to obtain the state of Śiva.

Paśus are the individual souls. They are of three kinds: the first are those who are under the influence of *mala* only; their *karma* is canceled by maturing or by meditation, contemplation and knowledge, since they have no fetters in the form of enjoyments. The second are those who are under the influence of *mala* and *karma;* in their case the fetters are destroyed at the time of universal *pralaya*. The third are those who are bound by the three fetters of *mala*, *māyā*, and *karma*, they are called *sakala*.

Pāśa is matter. It is fourfold: *mala*, *karma*, *māyā*, and *rodha-śakti*. *Mala* obscures and veils the soul's powers of vision and action. *Karma* is action performed by those who desire a fruit. It is in the form of merit and demerit, like seed and shoot; it is beginningless. In *māyā*, as an energy of the Divine Being, all the world is potentially contained at the time of universal destruction, and at creation everything comes into manifestation again. *Rodha-śakti* is the obscuring power; it is a bond in a metaphorical sense, since this energy of Śiva obscures the soul by superintending matter.[21]

Śrīkaṇṭha's Śaiva-Vedānta, classified within Vedānta under *bhedābheda* ("difference and no difference") may be considered as a special form of Śaiva siddhānta. It is also called "Viśiṣṭa-Śaiva-Vedānta," indicating by its very name its affinity to Rāmānuja's thought:

Through the might of the *vidyā* which consists in the worship of the Supreme Lord, as well as through meditation on the Path which is a subsidiary part of this, He, the favorer of all, becomes pleased and looks upon the knower with favor, which destroys all his sins that so long concealed his real nature from Him. Then he, "with the door revealed" by His grace, comes out through the hundred and first vein that passes through the crown of the head. Others do not so but come out through other veins.

At the time of the soul's departure from the body that very Lord, the Supreme Brahman abiding in the heart of the *jīva*, the Supreme Lord, supremely auspicious in nature, the husband of Umā, the Supreme Soul, being pleased, looks with a favorable glance that removes the stain of mundane blemishes, at the devotee who regularly performs sacrificial acts, like Agni-hotra and the rest, that are enjoined in scriptures, embodying His own commands, and are nothing but a kind of His own worship, who is free from the slightest vestige of prohibited works, who has dedicated all fruits of works to Him alone, who is completely under His control, who is filled with the nectar of knowledge regarding Himself, who is devoid of all desires for selfish fruits, who is endowed with discrimination and the rest, who is devoted to Him alone, who desires for His favor and who possesses knowledge. Through His special grace such a devotee, free from the blemishes of mundane existence comes out through the vein, passing out of the centre crown of the head, which comes to be lighted up, attains the Supreme Place, non-material and Supreme Bliss in nature.[22]

Śrīkaṇṭha insists that Śiva's abode is higher than Viṣṇu's Vaikuṇṭha and Brahmā's Satyaloka, and that the condition of those saved by Śiva is above the *turīya* of the Upaniṣads. *Mukti* means "to realize one's own proper form:"

> Although the real nature, sinless and consisting in attributes similar to those of Brahman, of one who has attained Brahman is existent in him beforehand, yet it is manifested in him through the removal of sins.[23]

When *paśutva*, the "animal nature," disappears, *śivatva*, the "divine nature," becomes the true nature of the soul:

> *Śivatva* means being like Śiva in nature, i.e. having a supremely auspicious form, free from the slightest vestige of sins. "Omniscience" and the rest constitute the nature of Śiva. The freed soul, who is similar to Śiva, is omniscient, eternally knowing, eternally satisfied, independent, omnipotent, and possesses infinite powers. Transmigratory existence consists in a contraction of one's self-knowledge. When the sins, the causes of such a contraction are removed, one becomes omniscient. For this very reason, because of the total extinction of ignorance which causes earthly existence, the wrong identification of the unlimited soul with the limited body ceases. Due to this, it becomes free from old age, death, and grief. Thus, not being subject to *karma*, it becomes independent. As it finds pleasure in its own nature, so it is "eternally satisfied." For this very reason it has no hunger, thirst, and the like.[24]

According to Śrīkaṇṭha the *mukta* is independent, has the "eight qualities" of Śiva, and can assume and discard bodies at will. A particular point in Śrīkaṇṭha's teaching is his assumption that the *mukta* is all-pervasive:

> It is said that the freed souls with their bondage broken by the Great God or the Supreme Brahman – who does good to all like a friend and a father and who has become pleased – become immortal and attain places full of illumination in His World or the Supreme Ether. The freed souls pervade heaven and earth by means of the rays of their own powers. Hence the freed souls, who are one in essence with Śiva, are indeed all-pervasive.[25]

Śrīkaṇṭha describes Śiva's paradise in glowing colors:

> The dwelling place of the husband of Umā is like millions of suns, full of all desirable objects, pure, eternal, indestructible. Having attained that celestial place the souls become free from all miseries, omniscient, capable of going everywhere, pure, full. Further they come to have pure

> sense-organs and become endowed with supreme Lordship. They assume bodies or discard these at will. Those engaged in the pursuit of knowledge and concentration attain this Supreme Place, and they do not return to the frightful earthly existence.[26]

Finally the very name Śiva becomes inclusive of everything:

> The freed souls as well as their world are included in Śiva. Absolutely pure, they all equally possess Śivahood, which consists in being totally different from the state of mundane existence that involves endless cycles of creation and destruction. Omniscient, capable of moving everywhere, tranquil, abodes of eternal and supreme lordship, their veils of sins destroyed completely, perceiving Him everywhere, having Him as their souls, they attain places just as they like and having experienced all objects of desire, they shine forth with Him in all places at all times.[27]

Kāśmīra-Śaivism or Śiva-Advaita

Kāśmīra-Śaivism, the main Śaiva school of Northern India, also called Śaiva-Advaita, Trika, Trika-Śāsana, Rahasya-Saṃpradāya, Trayaṃbaka-Saṃpradāya, is possibly pre-Śaṅkarite. The Pratyabhijñā is the philosophy proper of this system and it is associated mainly with the names of Utpala and Abhinavagupta (950–1020 C.E.) whose disciple Kṣemarāja (975–1050 C.E.) wrote the famous *Pratyabhijñāhṛdaya*, a concise and authoritative exposition of its teachings:

> Absolute consciousness of its own free will is the cause of the manifestation of the universe. It is only when the ultimate consciousness comes into play that the universe opens its eyes and continues as existent, and when it withdraws its movement, the universe shuts its eyes. By the power of her own will, absolute consciousness unfolds the universe upon her screen. This universe is manifold because of the differentiation of mutually related objects and subjects. The individual soul in whom consciousness is contracted, also contains the universe in a contracted form. The magnificent highest Śiva, desiring to manifest the universe which lies in him as identical with Himself, flashes forth in the form of Sadāśiva first as non-differentiated light. Then He unfolds Himself in the totality of manifestations. As the Lord is universe-bodied so the individual has the entire universe in a contracted form as its body. The ensouled being is identical with Śiva, whose body is the universe, because light is his true nature. Knowledge of this truth alone constitutes liberation; want of this knowledge alone constitutes bondage.
>
> When the highest Lord, whose very essence is consciousness, conceals by His will His non-duality and assumes duality all round, then His will

and other powers, though essentially unlimited, assume limitation. Then only does this soul become a transmigratory being, covered with *mala* [impurity]. Thus the willpower of the Absolute whose sovereignty is unrestricted, assuming limitation, becomes *aṇu-mala* [impurity of atomic size], which consists in considering itself imperfect. In the case of knowledge-power, owing to its becoming gradually limited in the world of differentiation, its omniscience becomes reduced to knowledge of a few things only. By assuming extreme limitation beginning with the acquisition of an inner organ and organs of perception, it acquires *māyiya-mala* [impurity in the form of deception] which consists in the apprehension of all objects as different. In the case of the power of action, its omnipotence in this world of differentiation becomes reduced to the ability to do a few things only, and starting with assuming limitation in the form of organs of action, it becomes extremely limited and acquires *karma-mala* [impurity in the form of karma] which consists in doing good or evil.

Thus constituted, this self is called a transmigratory being, poor in Śakti [power]. With the full unfoldment of his *śaktis*, however, he is Śiva himself.[28]

Vīra-Śaivism

The youngest of the major schools of Śaivism is Vīra-Śaivism, connected closely with the name of Basava who reformed an older tradition in the twelfth century. For the Vīra-Śaivas, also called Liṅgāyats, the *liṅga* that they always wear on their bodies – the so-called *iṣṭa-liṅga* – is not only a symbol but the real presence of Śiva. They wear it in order to make their bodies temples of Śiva.

Śrīpati, the author of a Vīra-Śaiva commentary on the Brahmasūtras, holds that

> a *mukta* in the beginning having obtained a status equal to that of Śiva as the result of his meditation and worship, will proceed from one heavenly place to another with a heavenly body and finally become absorbed in Śiva.[29]

Raseśvara-Darśana

Mādhava mentions among the Śaiva-*darśanas* a so-called Raseśvara-*darśana*, the philosophy of a sect which believed in the miraculous powers of mercury to hasten the process of *mukti*.

> Mercury is called *pārada* because it is a means of conveyance beyond the series of transmigratory states. The ascetic who aspires to liberation in

this life should first make to himself a glorified body. As mercury is produced by the creative conjunction of Hara and Gaurī and mica is produced from Gaurī, mercury and mica are identified with Hara and Gaurī as the verse has it: "Mica is your seed, and mercury is my seed; the combination of the two, O goddess, destroys death and poverty."

What higher beatitude is there than a body undecaying, immortal, the repository of sciences, the root of merits, riches, pleasure, and liberation? It is mercury alone that can make the body undecaying and immortal.

Its value is proved even by seeing it, and by touching it: "From seeing it, from touching it, from tasting it, from imparting it, from eating it, from merely remembering it, appear its six virtues." Equal merit accrues from seeing mercury as accrues from seeing all the *liṅgas* on earth.[30]

ŚAIVA POETS AND SAINTS

Among the best-known and most revered singer saints of Śaivism are the sixty-three Nāyanmārs who lived between 700 and 1000 C.E. in Southern India. Their collection of poems (in Tamil) called *Tiru-muṛai* is daily recited in Southern Indian Śiva temples. The Nāyanmārs disregarded caste distinctiona and emphasized moral qualities and devotion. The first part of the *Tiru-muṛai* is called *Devāram*. It is the work of Sambandar, Apparswāmi and Sundaramūrti, whose statues can often be found in Southern Indian temples and who receive worship from the devotees.

Sambandar and Apparswāmi

Sambandar had been fighting vehemently against the Jainas and Bauddhas. According to his teaching, Śiva, the highest god, is formless. Attainment of the state of Śiva is *mokṣa*. The soul should free itself from its *mala* (impurity). For this Śiva's grace is necessary. The most powerful means of reaching it is the *pañcākṣara* (the "five-syllable" invocation *Namaḥ Śivāya*). Thus he says: "The five letters are the final *mantra* through which one must reach Śiva. Worship Śiva with all your heart and you will be saved."[31]

His ears are beringed, He rideth the bull;
His head is adorned with the crescent moon's ray.
White is He with ash from the burning-ground swept;
And He is the thief who my heart steals away.
Great Brahma enthroned on the lotus' full bloom
Erstwhile bowed Him down and His glory extolled,
And singing received the grace of our Lord
Who dwells in famed Brahmāpuram old.

He is our only Lord, conjoined still
To her whose breast no sucking lips have known.
They who in Aṇṇāmalai's hill
where falling waters noisy chatter down
And the hill glistens gem-like, bow before
Our great one who is lord and lady too
Unfailingly for them shall be no more
Dread fruit of good and bad deeds they may do.[32]

Holy Vedas chanting, sacred thread He wears;
All His hosts surround Him, whom the white bull bears.
He comes in His splendor, tiger-skin attired.
"Lord, our naked beggar, above all desired."
Cry ye in your worship, at His feet appeal.
He who dwells in Palani, all your sin will heal.[33]

Three eyes hath His forehead, fair moon crowns His hair;
When Death sought out a victim, Śiva's foot crashed there;
Gory streams of blood flowed, Death it was that died;
Such is He, our father, Umā at his side;
Dwells He aye in Palani, where bees hum around,
Drunk with honeyed sweetness, till its groves resound.[34]

Thou art right and thou art wrong, Lord of holy Ālavāy;
Kinsman, I to Thee belong, never fades Thy light away.
Thou the sense of books divine,
Thou my wealth, my bliss art Thou,
Thou my all, and in Thy shrine with what praises can I bow?[35]

The sacred ash has mystic power, 'tis worn by dwellers in the sky.
The ash bestows true loveliness,
praise of the ash ascends on high.
The ash shows what the Tantras mean,
and true religion's essence tells,
The ash of Him of Ālavāy, in whom red-lipped Umā dwells.[36]

Appar became a martyr for Śiva's sake. He conceived Śiva as beyond the twenty-five *tattvas*. He knows three forms of Śiva: Śiva, the destroyer of the universe; Śiva Pārāpara (*paranjoti*), the unity of Śiva and Śakti; and Stambha, the pillar of light and consciousness, the ultimate goal of spiritual life.

In right I have no power to live,
day after day I am stained with sin.
I read, but do not understand;

I hold Thee not my heart within.
O light, O flame, O first of all.
I wandered far that I might see
Athihai, Vīraṭṭānam's Lord,
Thy flower-like feet of purity.

Daily I'm sunk in worldy sin,
Naught know I as I ought to know,
Absorbed in vice as 'twere my kin,
I see no path on which to go,
O Thou with throat one darkling gem,
Gracious, such grace me grant,
That I may see Thy beauteous feet
You Athihai, Vīraṭṭānam's Lord.

My fickle heart one love forsakes,
And forthwith to some other clings
Swiftly to some one thing it sways
And e'en as swiftly backward swings.
O Thou with crescent in Thy hair
Athihai Vīraṭṭānam's Lord
Fixed at Thy feet henceforth I lie
For Thou hast broken my soul's cord.

The bond of lust I cannot break
Desire's fierce torture will not die;
My soul I cannot stab awake
To scan my flesh with seeing eye.
I bear upon me loads of deed,
Load such as I can ne'er lay down
Athihai Vīraṭṭānam's Lord
Weary of joyless life I have grown.[37]

Evil, all evil, my race, evil my qualities all,
Great am I only in sin, evil is even my good.
Evil is my innermost self, foolish, avoiding the pure,
Beast am I not, yet the ways of the beast I can never forsake.
I can exhort with strong words,
telling men what they should hate,
Yet I can never give gifts, only to beg them I know.
Ah! wretched man that I am, whereunto came I to birth?[38]

He is ever hard to find, but He lives in the thought of the good;
He is the innermost secret of Scripture, inscrutable, unknowable;

He is honey and milk and the shining light.
He is the king of the *devas*,
Immanent in Viṣṇu, in Brahmā, in flame and wind,
Also in the mighty-sounding sea and in the mountains.
He is the great one who chooses Parumpattapuliyūr for His own.
If there be days when my tongue is dumb and speaks not of Him,
Let no such days be counted in the record of my life.[39]

Sundarar

Sundarar (also known as Sundaramūrti) is the author of the hymns that constitute the seventh Tiru-muṛai (eighth century). As a small child he was adopted into the royal household. When he had grown up, a suitable bride was found and everything was prepared for a festive marriage. Just before meeting his bride, Sundara was accosted by an old brahmin who produced a document claiming that Sundarar was the slave of the brahmin's family. Sundarar called the brahmin a madman, protesting that one brahmin could not be the slave of another brahmin. The old man insisted on taking Sundarar to his home. He led him to the temple of Tiru-arutturai and disappeared. Śiva's voice could be heard addressing Sundarar: "You have been saved. Now sing my praises." When Sundarar asked what he was supposed to sing, Śiva told him: "Begin your first hymn with the words 'O madman' since you have given me already this title." Sundaram did as he was told.

O madman with the moon-crowned hair,
Thou lord of men, thou fount of grace,
How to forget Thee could I bear?
My soul has aye for Thee a place.
Venney-nallur, in "Grace's shrine,"
South of the stream of Peṇṇai, there,
My father, I became all thine.
How could I now myself forswear?

I roamed, a cur, for many days,
Without a single thought of Thee,
Roamed and grew weary, then such grace,
As none could win, Thou gavest me.
Venney-nallur, in "Grace's shrine"
Where bamboos fringe the Peṇṇai, there
My shepherd, I became all Thine;
How could I now myself forswear?

From now on for me no birth, no death,
No creeping age, bull-rider mine.
Sinful and full of lying breath
Am I, but do Thou mark me Thine.
Venney-nallur, in "Grace's Shrine"
South of the wooded Peṇṇai, there
My Master, I became all Thine.
How could I now myself forswear?[40]

Our life is all unreal, its end is only dust.
Out of the sea of birth come ruin, pain and lust.
Delay not to do good, but praise Ketāram's king
Whom Viṣṇu as well as great Brahmā vainly sought sorrowing.[41]

Golden art Thou in Thy form,
girt around with the fierce tiger's skin,
Fair shines Thy tangle of hair shines,
crowned with blooms from the kondai's bright tree.
Sov'reign, great jewel art Thou, the red ruby of Maḷapāḍi,
Mother, on Thee, none but Thee, can my heart evermore fixed be.

Clad in the little loin-cloth, my body with holy ash white,
Lo I have come to Thy foot; O my head I beseech Thee, take me.
Portion of sword-eyed Umā, Thou red ruby of Maḷapāḍi
Friend, 'tis on Thee, none but Thee,
can my heart evermore fixed be.[42]

Manikka Vācagar

Tamils hold the *Tiruvācakam*, the "Sacred Words" of Manikka Vācagar (*c.* 650–715 C.E.] in highest esteem. It consists of fifty-one hymns – some containing several hundred stanzas – in honor of Śiva and is recited at worship like a scripture. The translation by G. U. Pope, originally published in 1900, has become a classic in its own right. Its archaisms have been retained in order to reflect the character of the original.[43]

Grass was I, shrub was I, worm, tree,
Full many a kind of beast, bird, snake,
Stone, man, and demon. 'Midst Thy hosts I served.
The form of mighty Asuras, ascetics, gods, I bore.
Within these immobile and mobile forms of life,
In every species born, weary I've grown, great Lord!
Truly, seeing Thy golden feet this day, I've gained release.
O Truth! As the Ongaran dwelling in my soul,

That I may 'scape. O spotless Ohne! O Master of the bull!
Lord of the Vedas! Rising, sinking, spreading, subtile One!
Thou art the heat! and Thou the cold! the Master Thou, O spotless One!
True Wisdom, gleaming bright in splendour true,
To me, void of all wisdom, blissful Lord!
O Wisdom fair, causing unwisdom's self to flee far off!

Thou know'st no increase, measure, end! All worlds
Thou dost create, protect, destroy, enrich with grace,
Release. Thou causest me to enter 'mid Thy servant band.
More subtile Thou than fragrance. Thou'rt afar, art near.
Thou are the Mystic word transcending word and thought.
As when are mingled milk, sweet juice of cane and butter,
Thou dost distil, like honey, in the thought of glorious devotees,
And cuttest off the continuity of births – our mighty One![44]

The sacred foot that danced in Tiḷḷai's city old
Is His, Who in all varied lives has energized;
Revealed in beauty of innumerous, varied qualities;
In earth, in sky, and in celestial worlds.
All ordered lore hath He revealed, and He made void.
My darkness hath He driven for aye far off.
Within His servants' inmost soul that love o'erflows
He dwells, – His glory and His choice.
On great Mahendara's biding hill
In grace He caused the uttered Āgamas appear
He came with the good goddess,
Pleasant and gracious, mingling with men at Kalladam.[45]

He is the Ancient One, Who creates the Creator of all;
He is the God, Who preserves the Preserver of things created;
He is the God, Who destroys the Destroyer;
But, thinking without thought, regards the things destroyed.
To the six sacred sects with their six diverse kinds of men
He is the attainment of deliverance; and Source of being to the heavenly ones.
He is the Possessor of all, Who resembles an insect.
Day by day He to the sun its lustre gave.
In the sacred moon He placed His coolness;
Kindled in the mighty fire its heat;
In the pure ether placed pervasive power;
Endued the ambiant wind with energy;
To the streams that gleam in the shade their savour sweet,
and to the expanded earth its strength He gave;
For ever and aye, me and millions other than me,
All in their several cells has He enclosed.[46]

In this mad world, 'mid stress and strife confused,
  from birth and death that ceaseless spring; –
Where hoarded treasure, women, offspring, tribe
  and learning's store, men prize and seek; –
He calms the storm of mental changing states,
  and clears from error's mists the soul.
To mystic wisdoms's mighty God go thou,
  and breath His praise, O Humming-Bee.[47]

Enter no more the juggling senses' net!
  Bhuyaṅgan's flow'ry feet, the mighty Lord,
Ponder intensely, – other things desire ye not:
  dismiss them, let them go, and pass ye on!
With joyous smile He, entering this world,
  made us – who were like curs impure – His own.
As it befits to draw anigh the Lord,
  let each with no weak faltering step move on.

Each to himself be his own kith and kin!
  each to himself be his own law and way!
For who are "we"? what "ours"? and what are "bonds"?
  illusions all, – let these departing flee.
And, with the ancient servants of the King,
  taking His sign alone for guiding sign,
Shake falsehood off; go on your happy way,
  unto Bhuyaṅgan's golden foot, – our King![48]

In a beautiful stanza he describes the perfection he is hoping for:

I shall raise my hands in prayer to thee;
I shall clasp thy holy feet, and call on thy name.
I shall melt like wax before the flame,
incessantly calling out "my Beloved Father."
I shall cast off this body and enter the celestial city of Śivapura.
I shall behold they effulgent glory.
In joyful bliss shall I join the society of thy true devotees.
Then I shall look up to hear thee say
with thy beauteous lips "fear not" –
the assurance of thy all-embracing love alone
can set my soul at ease and peace.[49]

Śaṅkara

The following Sanskṛt hymn, ascribed to the great philosopher Śaṅkara, summarizes Śiva's great deeds and functions and hails him as saviour from the world of transmigration.

I focus my mind on the Great God alone, the destroyer of Kāma, the Lord of beings, the destroyer of sins, the Supreme Lord, the Adorable One, dressed in the skin of an elephant, the waters of the Gaṅgā cascading from his matted hair.

I adore the Lord, who is ever blissful, who has five faces, the Great God, the Lord of gods, the destroyer of the enemies of the gods, the all-pervading One, the Lord of the Universe, besmeared with ashes, whose three eyes are moon, sun, and fire.

I worship the Five-Faced One, who has Bhāvanī for his wife, the Lord of the Mountains, the Lord of the *Gaṇas*, who has a blue throat, who rides on a bull, whose nature is beyond qualities, the primal cause of everything, the resplendent one, whose body is covered with ashes.

Be propitious, all-pervading Lord, the Consort of Śiva, the Giver of Prosperity, with the crescent on the forehead, holding a spear, with matted hair, the One, the Pervader of the Universe, whose body is the universe.

I adore the Lord, the Supreme Self, the One, the Primordial Cause of the universe, the Actionless, the Formless, who is expressed by the OM, from whom the universe receives its being, by whom it is maintained and into whom it dissolves.

I worship the Lord of Threefold Form, who is beyond all form, who is neither earth, nor water, nor fire, nor air, nor ether; who does not know weariness or sleep, heat, or cold, who has no dwelling place.

I take refuge in Him, the Supreme Purifier, devoid of duality, unborn, eternal, the cause of all causes, the Good, the Absolute, the Illuminator of all luminaries, the Fourth State of Being, beyond darkness, without beginning or end.

Salutations to You, O All-pervading One, You with the many guises. Salutations to You, who are knowledge and bliss. Salutations to You, who can be reached by penance and meditation. Salutations to You, who are known by Vedic knowledge.

O Lord, Wielder of the trident, you All-Pervading One, Lord of the Universe. Great God, the Auspicious One, the Great Ruler, the Three-Eyed One, the Lord of Śiva, the Gentle One, the Destroyer of Kāma and Pura, there is nobody else besides You who is worthy of honor and worship.

O Auspicious One, Great Ruler, O Compassionate One, you Wielder of the Trident, Lord of Gaurī and of all creatures, Destroyer of the bondage of the Jīvas, You, the Lord of Kāśī, out of mercy You project, maintain and destroy the world. You are the Great Ruler.

O Lord Śiva, Destroyer of Kāma, the world is born from You; it exists in You, O Lord of the Universe, O Gracious One, into You, whose sign is the *liṅga*, the world is absorbed again; this world of moveable and immoveable objects is nothing but Yourself.[50]

4 ŚĀKTISM

India has had an unbroken tradition of goddess-worship from prehistoric times to the present. Goddess figurines, resembling those worshiped today in the villages, have been found in the cities of the Indus civilization, and rituals to honor or placate the Goddess are performed everywhere throughout India. While frequently the Goddess is worshiped as the consort of a male god, in Śāktism proper, which has a considerable following in all strata, the Goddess is elevated to the rank of Supreme Being. *Śakti* means power – everything connected with power and empowerment is concentrated in the Goddess. The most generic name of the Goddess is Devī. In most instances the Goddess is characterized by proper names expressing a specific attribute, such as Kālī ("The Black One,") a great feat remembered, such as Mahiṣamardinī ("The Killer of the Demon Mahiṣa,") or a title under which she is worshiped, such as Mahāmātā ("The Great Mother.") There are countless names remembering local apparitions and manifestations of the Goddess, such as Vindhyavāsinī ("The One Who Dwells in the Vindhya Mountains.") The Goddess, as her names reveal, combines the most contradictory features in her person.

DEVĪ IN THE *VEDAS*

The *Ṛgveda* is certainly not the mainspring of Śāktism. There are, however, a few elements in it which merged with the Devī religion of later times and which helped to make Śāktism acceptable to the followers of the Veda. The most important of these elements was the worship of *pṛthivī* (Mother Earth).

> Earth, you the strong one, you carry the heavy weight of the mountains.
> You, the powerful one, quicken the soil with mighty rivers.
> To you, who are so very large, we sing poems of praise.
> You, the bright one, send forth the swift, billowing mists.
> With your great strength you hold the big trees on the ground
> When lightning from the sky sends down torrents from the clouds.[1]

Uṣas (dawn) is praised in several hymns and even called "mother of the gods" in one place, but she does not play any significant role in the further development of Śāktism.

> Dawn, you daughter of heaven, shine upon us with riches;
> You bounteous goddess, give us abundant food.
> Dawn make us abound with horses, cows and all kinds of wealth.
> Speak auspicious words to us, make us partake of great bounty.[2]

A more significant element can be seen in Aditi, the Indian image of the Great Mother. Aditi is the Earth, she is the Infinite, she is the Mother of the gods, she is "filled with splendor."

The *Nirukta* says explicitly:

> Aditi, unimpaired, mother of Gods. Aditi is heaven, Aditi is atmosphere, Aditi is mother, father, and son. Aditi is all the gods, and the five tribes; Aditi is what is born and what shall be born.[3]

The most important goddess text of the *Ṛgveda*, however, is the so-called *Devī-sūkta*, in which Vāk (speech, word) says about herself:

> I travel with the Rudras and the Vasus,
> with the Ādityas and the All-Gods I wander.
> I hold up both Varuṇa and Mitra, Indra and Agni,
> and the Pair of Aśvins.
> I cherish and sustain high-swelling Soma,
> and Tvastar I support, Pūṣan and Bhaga.
> I load with wealth the zealous sacrificer,
> who pours the juice and offers his oblation.
> I am the Queen, the gatherer-up of treasures,
> most thoughtful, first of those who merit worship.
> The Gods have established me in many places
> with many homes to enter and abide in.

> Through me alone all eat the food that feeds them –
> all who see, breathe, hear the word outspoken.
> They know it not, but yet they dwell beside me.
> Hear, one and all, the truth as I declare it.
> I verily, myself announce and utter the word
> that gods and humans alike shall welcome.
> I make the ones I love exceeding mighty,
> make them sages, *Ṛṣis*, Brahmans.
> I bend the bow for Rudra that his arrow may strike
> and slay the hater of devotion.
> I rouse and order battle for the people,
> and I have penetrated Earth and Heaven.
> On the world's summit I bring forth the Father:
> my home is in the waters, in the ocean.
> Thence I extend over all existing creatures,
> and even touch the heaven with my forehead.
> I breathe a strong breath like the wind and tempest,
> the while I hold together all existence.
> Beyond this wide earth and beyond the heavens
> I have become so mighty in my grandeur.[4]

DEVĪ IN THE EPICS

In Vālmīki's *Rāmāyaṇa* we can see the transition and gradual fusion of Vedic and Puranic ideas with regard to the Goddess: the Vedic element is still strong. Aditi plays a comparatively large role as "the mother of the gods," especially as the mother of Viṣṇu, the All-Preserving One.

The *Mahābhārata*, while describing one of the many cruel battle scenes, includes without further introduction a vision of the apparently well-known "Death-Night in her embodied form:"

> A black image, a bloody mouth and bloody eyes, wearing crimson garlands and smeared with crimson unguents, attired in a single piece of red cloth, with a noose in hand, and resembling an elderly lady, employed in chanting a dismal note and standing full before their eyes and about to lead away men and steeds and elephants all tied in a stout cord. She seemed to take away diverse kinds of spirits, with dishevelled hair and tied together in a cord as also many mighty car-warriors divested of their weapons.[5]

An interesting detail is added: the Pāṇḍava soldiers had seen in their dreams this dread figure of the Goddess every night since the battle between them and the Kurus had begun: "The brave warriors of the

Pāṇḍava camp, recollecting the sight they had seen in their dreams, identified it with what they now witnessed."[6]

Her companions the Rakṣasas and Piśācas are described:

> gorging upon human flesh and quaffing the blood. They were fierce, tawny in hue, terrible, of adamantine teeth and dyed with blood. With matted locks on their heads ... endued with five feet and large stomachs. Their fingers were set backwards. Of harsh temper and ugly features, their voice was loud and terrible. They had rows of tinkling bells, tied to their bodies. Possessed of blue throats, they looked very frightful.[7]

The Goddess has now become the deity of war and battleground: Indra, the youthful conqueror God of the Vedas is displaced by Durgā, the nightmarish embodiment of senseless murder. Kṛṣṇa exhorts Arjuna to invoke Durgā on the eve of the mighty battle "for defeat of the foe".

It is not without significance that immediately before the *Bhagavad-gītā* we find a Devī-*stotra*. Durgā is the Goddess of War and Victory. This Durgā-hymn probably was the original introduction to the narrative of the battle, not the lengthy philosophical discussion between Kṛṣṇa and Arjuna.

The *stotra* does not appear as an improvisation for the situation. It looks like an established, well-known hymn for such occasions. Durgā is hymned as "identical with Brahman," "dwelling in the Mandara forest," "free from decrepitude and decay," "black and tawny," "bringer of benefits to her devotees;" Mahākālī, "wife of the universal destroyer," "rescuing from danger," "fierce," "giver of victory," "bearing a banner of peacock plumes," "bearing an awful spear," "holding a sword and shield," "born in the race of the cowherd Nanda," "always fond of buffalo blood," "dressed in yellow robes," "slayer of the *asuras* assuming the face of a wolf," "white in hue," "black in hue," "slayer of the *asura* Kaitabha," "yellow-eyed," "diverse-eyed," "grey-eyed."

> O great Goddess, let victory always attend me through your grace on the field of battle. You always dwell in inaccessible regions where there is fear, in places of hardship, in the abodes of your worshipers and in the nether regions. You always defeat the Dānavas. You are unconsciousness, sleep, illusion, modesty, beauty. You are twilight, day, Savitrī, mother. You are contentment, growth, light. It is you who supports the Sun and the Moon and that makes them shine.[8]

The hymn wins an apparition of Durgā, "who is always graciously inclined towards humankind," and she promises victory to Arjuna and protection to all who invoke her.

> The man that recites that hymn rising at dawn has no fear any time from Yakṣas, Rakṣasas, and Piśācas. He can have no enemies; he has no fear from animals that have fangs and teeth, from snakes as also from kings. He is sure to be victorious in all disputes and if bound he is freed from his bonds. He is sure to get over all difficulties, is freed from thieves, is ever victorious in battle and wins the goddess of prosperity for ever. With health and strength he lives for a hundred years.[9]

A very similar Durga-*stotra* as preparation for battle is recited by Yudhiṣṭhira.[10]

Devī is addressed as

> the Divine Durgā, the Supreme Goddess of the Universe, born of the womb of Yaśodā, the giver of prosperity, the terrifier of Kaṃsa, the destroyer of *asuras*, who ascended the skies when dashed on a stony platform, the sister of Vāsudeva, armed with sword, and shield, always rescuing the worshipers sunk in sin, the eternal giver of blessings.[11]

The purpose of Yudhiṣṭhira's prayer is to obtain a vision of Devī. Whereas in the other Devī appearances her frightfulness and ugliness are emphasized, here her beauty and comeliness stand foremost. She is described both as having four arms and four faces, and as having ten arms, carrying a vessel, a lotus, a bell, a noose, a bow, a discus, and other weapons. She is "the only female in the universe that possesses the attribute of purity." She has "sanctified the celestial regions by adopting the vow of perpetual virginity." She is the slayer of the Mahiṣa-*asura*, the protectress of the three worlds, the foremost of all deities. She is battle-victory. Her eternal abode is on the Vindhya – "that foremost of mountains."

> O Kālī, Kālī, you are the Great Kālī, ever fond of wine and meat and animal sacrifice. Capable of going everywhere at will and bestowing boons on your devotees you are ever followed in your journeys by Brahmā and the other gods. By them that call upon you for the relief of their burdens and by them that bow to you at dawn on Earth there is nothing that cannot be attained in respect of either offspring or wealth. And because you do rescue people from difficulties when they are afflicted in the wilderness or sinking in the great ocean, you are called Durgā by all.

> You are the sole refuge of men when attacked by robbers or while afflicted in crossing streams and seas or in wilderness and forests.[12]

She is called Fame, Prosperity, Success, Steadiness, Wife, Offspring, Knowledge, Intellect, Twilight, Night, Sleep, Light, Beauty, Forgiveness, Mercy, "and every other thing." She saves her devotees from ignorance, loss of children, loss of wealth, disease, death, and fear. Those are the ever-recurring evils from which Devī saves them. Devī appears to Yudhiṣṭhira, promises victory, happiness, long life, beauty, and offspring. The promises of Devī are universal:

> They who will invoke me in exile or in the city, in the midst of battle or of dangers from foes, in forests or in inaccessible deserts, in seas of mountain fastnesses, there is nothing that they will not obtain in this world.[13]

Besides this Great Goddess, the *Mahābhārata* mentions a large number of "mothers" in the company of Kārttikeya (Kumāra) – another war-god. After describing part of the frightful retinue of Kumāra, the names of the "illustrious mothers, the auspicious ones, by whom the mobile and immobile universe is pervaded" are listed.

It is more than probable that they represent a host of local goddesses, village deities with the same functions. Some of them also occur as names of the Great Goddess, some seem to indicate a connection with certain localities. Most of them occur only in this place. After enumerating about two hundred names of mothers, the narrator continues:

> These and many other mothers, thousands of them, of diverse forms, became the followers of Kārttikeya. Their nails were long, their teeth large and their lips protruding. Well built and with pleasant features, youthful, they were decked with ornaments. Rich with ascetic merit they were capable of assuming any form at will.
>
> Some of them shared the nature of Yama, some of Rudra, some of Soma, some of Kubera, some of Varuṇa, some of Indra, and some of Agni, some of Vāyu, some of Kumāra, some of Brahmā, some of Viṣṇu, some of Sūrya, some of Varāha. Charming and delightful to look at, they were beautiful like the *asuras*. They were also inconceivably strong and powerful.
>
> They have their abodes on trees and open spots and road crossings. They live also in caves and burning *ghāṭas*, mountains and springs. Bedecked with ornaments, they wear all kinds of attire and speak a variety of languages. These and many other groups of mothers, inspiring

enemies with dread, followed Kārttikeya at the command of the chief of the celestials.[14]

DEVĪ IN THE *PURĀṆAS*

Devī Mahiṣamardinī

The most prominent myth connected with the Goddess is her killing of the buffalo demon. It is narrated in several *Purāṇas* with significant differences and even in village religion it features prominently.

The *Mārkaṇḍeya-Purāna* reports how for a hundred years *devas* and *asuras* had fought against one another. The *devas* were defeated and Mahiṣa-asura became the lord of heaven. The defeated gods approached Śiva and Viṣṇu for help. Out of the anger of Śiva, Viṣṇu, and all the other gods, Devī was born, "a concentration of light like a mountain blazing excessively, pervading all the quarters with its flames."[15] She received the combination of the essence of all the weapons the gods possess. Several other objects are mentioned that have their importance in Devī-worship: a bell, a noose, a string of beads, a waterpot, a sword, a shield, a necklace, a crest-jewel, earrings, an ax, a lotus, a lion, a drinking cup filled with wine, and so forth. Special mention is made of her "loud roar with a defying laugh." This roaring laughter of Devī terrifies earth and sky. This roar is also the sign of the beginning of the battle between Devī and Mahiṣāsura. With the weapons that she had received she kills thousands of the demons that accompanied Mahiṣāsura. Before Mahiṣāsura falls, all the demon-generals, whose names are mentioned, are killed by Devī.

> Mahiṣāsura terrified the troops of the Devī with his own buffalo-form: some he killed by a blow of his muzzle, some by stamping with his hooves, some by the lashes of his tail, and others by the pokes of his horns, some by his speed, some by his bellowing and wheeling movement, some by the blast of his breath. Having laid low her army Mahiṣāsura rushed to slay the lion of Mahādevī. This enraged Aṃbikā. The powerful Mahiṣāsura pounded the surface of the earth with his hooves in rage, tossed up high mountains with his horns, and bellowed terribly. Crushed by his fast wheeling around, the earth disintegrated, and lashed by his tail the sea overflowed. Pierced by his swaying horns the clouds went into fragments. Cast up by the blast of his breath, mountains fell down from the sky in hundreds.[16]

Finally the demon resumes his buffalo form. In this form the final battle takes place: "Enraged, Caṇḍikā, the Mother of the Worlds, quaffed a divine drink again and again and laughed, her eyes becoming red." Devī receives praise from all the *devas*. In the course of this prayer all the essential qualities of Devī are mentioned, and the basic Devī-philosophy comes to the fore: Devī is "the origin of the universe, the resort of all, the primordial *prakṛti*." She is the "supreme *vidyā* which is the cause of liberation." She is "*durgā*, the boat that carries men across the difficult ocean of worldly existence," she is "Śrī who has taken her abode in the heart of Viṣṇu," and she is "Gaurī, who has established herself with Śiva." Devī offers a boon, and the *devas* choose the following: "Whenever we think of you again, destroy our direst calamities."[17]

Devī Kills Various Other Demons

Devī Mahiṣamardinī sets the pattern for the description of many other battles in which Devī kills demons who have terrorized gods and men. A story very similar to that of Mahiṣāsura is connected with the names of Śumbha and Niśumbha, two demons who had deprived Indra of his sovereignty and his share in sacrifice. They had also usurped the powers of Sun, Moon, Kubera, Yama, Varuṇa, Vāyu, and Agni. This time the *devas*, remembering the boon granted by Devī on the former occasion, go straight to Devī for help. The praises uttered on this occasion are centered around the "Devī who abides in all beings" as consciousness, as intelligence, as sleep, as hunger, as reflection, as power, as thirst, as forgiveness, as peace, as faith, as error, as mother.

The *Mārkaṇḍeya Purāṇa* combines with this story the episode of the demon's wooing of Devī, to become his wife: solicited by his servants Caṇḍa and Muṇḍa, he sends Sugrīva as a go-between. Devī accepts the offer on one condition: she will marry that man who defeats her in battle. Śumbha dispatches Dhūmralocana, the general of the *asura* army to defeat Devī and bring her with him. With the sound *hum* Aṃbikā burns Dhūmralocana to ashes. The lion upon which Devī rides destroys the *asura* army. The *asura* king then dispatches Caṇḍa and Muṇḍa to bind and carry off Aṃbikā. As soon as these come near to seize her,

> Kālī of terrible countenance, armed with sword and noose, bearing a strange skull-topped staff, decorated with a garland of skulls, clad in a

> tiger's skin, very appalling owing to her emaciated flesh, with gaping mouth, fearful with her tongue lolling out, having deep-sunk reddish eyes, and filling the regions of the sky with her roars, and impetuously falling upon slaughtering the great *asuras* ... (issues out of the forehead of Aṃbikā, who herself remains) smiling gently seated upon a lion on a huge golden peak of the great mountain.[18]

Kālī now cruelly kills the men and animals of the *asura* army. It is the same goddess of war we had met in the *Mahābhārata*. Kālī severs the heads of Caṇḍa and Muṇḍa and brings them to Caṇḍikā "as two great animal offerings in this sacrifice of battle." The final victory over Śumbha and Niśumbha is reserved to Caṇḍikā herself. Caṇḍikā promotes Kālī to the position of Cāmuṇḍā. That is the sign for Śumbha to mobilize the entire *asura* army:

> Seeing that most terrible army coming, Caṇḍikā filled the space between the earth and the sky with the twang of her bow-string. Her lion made an exceedingly loud roar and Aṃbikā magnified these roars with the clanging of her bell. Kālī, expanding her mouth wide and filling the quarters with the sound *hum*, overwhelmed the noises of the bow-string, lion and bell by her terrific roars.[19]

This triad of Aṃbikā, lion, and Kālī is joined by the Śaktis from the bodies of Brahmā, Śiva, Guha, Viṣṇu, and Indra – each with the attributes and *vāhana* of the god from which she issued. From the body of Devī also a Śakti issues: "Caṇḍikā, most terrific, exceedingly fierce and yelling like a hundred jackals."

Śiva is sent by Śakti as ambassador to Śumbha and Niśumbha to offer the netherworld to them, provided they return the Trilokas and the oblations to the gods. Each Śakti contributes something specific in overpowering the *asuras*: Kālī pierces the enemies with her spear and crushes their skulls with her staff. Brāhmaṇī robs them of their strength by sprinkling them with water. Maheśvarī slays *asuras* with her trident, Vaiṣṇavī with the discus, Kaumārī with the javelin. Aindrī destroys *asuras* with the thunderbolt, Vārāhī tears their breasts open with her tusks, Nārasiṃhī claws and devours them: "Dazed by the violent laughter of Śivadūtī the *asuras* fell down on earth: she then devoured those who had fallen down." The *asura* army flees. One Raktabīja, however, advances: whenever a drop of Raktabīja's blood falls to earth, another *asura* of his stature arises. These battle the Mātṛs, "and those *asuras* that were born from the blood of Raktabīja pervaded the whole world; the *devas* became intensely alarmed at this."

Devī orders Cāmuṇḍā to drink the blood of the *asura* before it falls to earth and to devour the *asuras* that have come already into existence. Finally Devī kills him. Then Śumbha and Niśumbha advance in rage to kill Devī and the lion. Devī intercepts the weapons hurled against her with her own weapons. Śumbha is knocked down by the ax of Devī. Before Niśumbha falls under Devī's trident, Devī blows her conch, twangs her bowstring, and fills the four quarters with the sound of her bell. Her lion fills earth and sky with his roar, Kālī produces an enormous noise by striking the earth with both hands, Śivadūtī gives vent to a terrible peal of laughter. After Niśumbha is struck by Devī's trident he regains consciousness, resumes fighting, is pierced by Devī's arrow, and another demon issues out from him.

> Then the Devī, laughing aloud, severed the head of him who issued forth with her sword. Thereupon he fell to the ground. The lion then devoured those *asuras* whose necks he had crushed with his fierce teeth and Kālī and Śivadūtī devoured others. Some great *asuras* perished being pierced through by the spear of Kaumārī. Others were repulsed by the water purified by incantation of Brāhmaṇī. Others fell, pierced by a trident wielded by Maheśvarī, some were powdered on the ground by the blows from the snout of Vārāha. Some Dānavas were cut to pieces by the discus of Vaiṣṇavī, and others again by the thunderbolt discharged from the palm of Aindrī.[20]

Another interesting feature is interwoven with the final killing of Śumbha: the demon challenges Devī by declaring that she is not fighting by her own strength but is relying on the strength of others. In order to show that she is alone in the world, she re-absorbs all those Śaktis who previously had been fighting separately. A fierce battle follows in which the Devī destroys the weapons of the *asura* by shouting the *mantra hum*. The fight is carried on not only on earth, but also in the sky. Finally Devī pierces Śumbha with a dart through the chest and throws him to the earth, which shakes at the fall. The result of this victory wrought by Devī becomes apparent in universal relief:

> When that evil-natured was slain, the universe became happy and regained perfect peace and the sky grew clear. Flaming portent-clouds that were in evidence before became tranquil, and the rivers kept within their courses when he was stricken down. When he had been slain, the minds of

> all the bands of devas became overjoyed, and the Gandharvas sang sweetly. Others sounded their instruments, and the band of Apsarās danced; likewise favorable winds blew; the sun became very brilliant; the sacred fires blazed peacefully and tranquil became the strange sounds that had risen in different quarters.[21]

The reinstated *devas* praise Devī as their saviour:

> O Devī you who remove the sufferings of your supplicants, be gracious. Be propitious, O Mother of the whole world. Be gracious, O Mother of the universe. Protect the universe. You are, O Devī, the ruler of all that is moving and unmoving.[22]

She is addressed as the "cause of final emancipation," as "the bestower of enjoyment and liberation," as "intent on saving the dejected and distressed that take refuge with her," as the one "who removes all sufferings," as the one "who possesses the benevolence of saving the three worlds," as "the one who took away the life of Vṛtra," as "the one who frees from all fear and from all evils."

Devī promises to those, who worship her, protection and the destruction of future demons: in the twenty-eighth Manvantara under Vaivasvata Manu, Śumbha and Niśumbha will be born again – the Devī promises to destroy them as Vindhyavāsinī, born of Yaśodā. The *dānavas*, descendants of Vipracitti, will be slain by her in an Atirudrā form. She will then be called Raktadantā, because her teeth will become red from their blood. At the time of a drought of a hundred years Devī will be born of the *munis* "but not womb-begotten" as the Śatākṣī; maintaining the world with life-sustaining vegetables born of her own body she will be known as Śakhāmbhārī. She will slay the *asura* Durgama and will therefore be known as Durgādevī. She will slay the *rakṣasas* in the Himālayas for the protection of the *munis* and will be known as Bhīmadevī. As Bhrāmaradevī she will kill the *asura* Aruṇa "for the good of the three worlds."

Devī utters promises of salvation to those who pray to her with the above-mentioned hymns, and who remember her salvific deeds. Those who observe the Devī-*vrata* on the eighth, ninth, and fourteenth *tithi* "shall not experience anything wrong, robbers or kings, of weapons, fire and flood." Devī promises never to forsake a place where her praises are sung. The blessings which are connected with Devī's presence are that: enemies perish, welfare accrues, evil portents subside, the unfavorable influence of planets vanishes, a bad dream is turned into a good dream; it frees children from seizures, promotes friendship, and destroys demons, goblins, and ogres.

> The chanting and hearing of the story of my manifestations remove sins, and grant perfect health and protect one from evil spirits ... He who is on a lonely spot in a forest, or is surrounded by forest fire, or who is surrounded by robbers in a desolate spot, or who is captured by enemies, or who is pursued by a lion, or tiger, or by wild elephants in a forest, or who under the orders of a wrathful king is sentenced to death, or has been imprisoned, or who is tossed about in his boat by a tempest in the vast sea, or who is in the most terrible battle under a shower of weapons, or who is amidst all kinds of dreadful troubles, or who is afflicted wih pain – such a man on remembering this story of mine will be saved from his straits.[23]

Various Forms and Manifestations of Devī

The *Devī Purāṇas* are also known as Devī-*avatāras*. They have the same function which Vaiṣṇavas ascribe to Viṣṇu-*avatāras*, namely to protect the world in successive ages from demons and other evil. The numerous goddesses are but manifestations of One Supreme Goddess:

> Bhavanī is worshiped by the gods in all her incarnations. She always kills demons by incarnating herself on earth and she protects all creation in heaven, earth, and the nether world. This Mahādevī was again born from the womb of Yaśodā and killed the demon Kaṃsa by placing her foot on his head. From that time on people on earth have installed this "giver-of-joy-to-Yaśodā" on the Vindhya mountain and reintroduced her worship.[24]

DEVĪ IN THE *TANTRAS*

In the *Tantras* the Goddess comes to occupy the supreme position: according to these texts, Brahman, being neuter and incapable of creation, produced Śiva and Śakti. Śiva without Śakti is powerless. Śakti is the cause of liberation, Śiva the cause of bondage.

> The Goddess is the great *Śakti*. She is *Māyā*, for of her the *māyā* which produces the *saṃsāra* is. As Lord of *Māyā* she is *Mahāmāyā*. Devī is *avidyā* because she binds, and *vidyā* because she liberates and destroys the *saṃsāra*. She is *prakṛti* and as existing before creation is the *Ādya Śakti*. Devī is the *vācaka Śakti*, the manifestation of *Cit* in *Prakṛti*, and the *vācya*

> *Śakti* or *Cit* itself. The *Ātma* should be contemplated as Devī. Śakti or Devī is thus the Brahman revealed in its mother aspect (*Śrīmātā*) as creatrix and nourisher of the worlds. Kālī says of herself in Yoginī Tantra: "I am the visible form of Being-Consciousness-Bliss, I am *brahman*, the throbbing, pulsating *brahman*."[25]

The earliest Devī-Durgā texts are hymns to the goddess and the bulk of later Devī religious literature again consists of hymns, *mantras*, descriptions of rituals, feasts, and ceremonies. Whereas Devī-mythology is comparatively uniform, Devī-worship takes innumerable forms. The worship of Devī is usually connected with some material object that represents Devī; she is *prakṛti*, matter-nature, never "pure spirit."

The great Advaitin Śaṅkara composed some of the most popular hymns to Devī:

> O mother, may all my speech, howsoever idle, be the recitation of *mantra*; may all my actions with my hand be the making of *mudrā*; may all my walking be *pradakṣinā*; may all my eating and other functions be *homa* rites; may my act of lying down be a prostration before you; may all my pleasures be an offering to the *ātman*. Whatsoever I do, may it be counted as worship to you.[26]

Śaṅkara also composed a hymn to the goddess under her form as Annapūrṇā, the provider of nourishment:

> Annapūrṇā, Mother Divine, you create happiness, grant gifts and dispel fear. You ocean of beauty, who bestows purity, wash away all sins. You are truly the Great Goddess, who purifies the family dwelling in the Himālaya.
> Presiding Goddess of Kāśī, you vessel of mercy, please give me alms.
>
> Annapūrṇā, Mother Divine, you are dressed in golden cloth bedecked with jewels, garlanded with a necklace of pearls, surrounded by the scent of perfume.
> Presiding Goddess of Kāśī, you vessel of mercy, please give me alms.
>
> Annapūrṇā, Mother Divine, giver of the bliss of yoga, destroyer of foes, inspirer of devotion to righteousness and prosperity, resplendent like the light of moon, sun, and fire, protectress of the three worlds, granter of all desires and prosperity.
> Presiding Goddess of Kāśī, you vessel of mercy, please give me alms.
>
> Annapūrṇā, Mother Divine, you made your dwelling on Mount Kailāsa, you are Gaurī, Umā, Śaṅkarī, you give insight into the meaning

of the Vedas; you are the components of the syllable OM, you open widely the door to emancipation.
Presiding Goddess of Kāśī, you vessel of mercy, please give me alms.

Annapūrṇā, Mother Divine, you support all beings, visible and invisible. In your body is contained the whole universe. You destroy your own playful creation and make the lamp of wisdom shine. You delight the mind of the Lord of the Universe.
Presiding Goddess of Kāśī, you vessel of mercy, please give me alms.

Annapūrṇā, Mother Divine, Bhagavatī, you are the mistress of all humans on earth. Your blue-black locks are arranged in beautiful braids. You are the goddess who forever provides food. You give happiness to all and make their life propitious.
Presiding Goddess of Kāśī, you vessel of mercy, please give me alms.[27]

ŚĀKTA PHILOSOPHY

In contrast to other Hindu philosophies that diminish or deny the reality of matter over spirit, Śakta texts emphasize the non-difference between matter and spirit and the reality of *māyā* as creative power, not as illusion. Śakti is "Ādya-Prakṛti," original matter, "Mūla-Prakṛti," the root of nature.

The omnipotent Goddess, who is consciousness, who is truly the "I-consciousness," creates appearances of the world upon it like reflections in a mirror by her willpower, or the power of *māyā* known as liberation.

All this world is reflected, like in a mirror, in consciousness. Seeing the reflections, one actually sees the mirror; likewise, experiencing the world appearance, one sees pure consciousness, God, the Self. Just as a mirror without reflecting a pot remains a mirror, so the highest consciousness remains itself, pure and undifferentiated, as soon as the world appearance created by thought activity is gone.

And since there is not the least touch of sorrow and pain in it, it is pure joy in essence. As it is the goal of all desires, it is bliss and joy in itself. The nature of the self is bliss, since this is what one desires.

Do not conclude that there is no such thing as the world. Such thinking is imperfect and defective. Such a belief is impossible. One who tries to negate the whole world by the mere act of thought brings it to existence by that very act of negation. Just as a city reflected in a mirror is not a reality but exists as a reflection, so also this world is not a reality in itself but is consciousness all the same. This is self-evident. This is perfect knowledge.

> There is no such thing as bondage or liberation. There is no such thing as the seeker and the means for seeking anything. Partless, Non-Dual, Conscious Energy, Tripurā alone pervades everything. She is both knowledge and ignorance, bondage and liberation too. She is also the means for liberation. This is all one has to know.[28]

Śāktism also accepts the possibility of *jīvanmukti*. According to the *Devī Bhāgavata Purāṇa* one thought of Devī in her revealed form can transform one instantly into a *mukta*.

> There is one supreme *brahman* diffused throughout the universe. It is worshiped by the worship of the universe, because everything exists in it. Even those who look to the fruit of action and are governed by their desires and by the worship of different gods and are addicted to various rituals go to and enter That. One who sees everything in Brahman and who sees Brahman everywhere is undoubtedly known as a true Kaula, one who has attained liberation while yet living.[29]

DEVĪ IN OTHER HINDU SYSTEMS

Śaṅkara's Advaita

Śaṅkara recognizes *śakti* as the root of all phenomenal existence, as the root of bondage and creation:

> This world, when being dissolved is dissolved to that extent only that the *śakti* of the world remains and is produced from the root of that *śakti*. Belonging to the Self, as it were, of the Omniscient Lord, there are name and form, the figments of nescience not to be defined either as being or as different from it, the germs of the entire expanse of the phenomenal world, called in *śruti* and *smṛti*, *māyā*, *śakti* or *prakṛti* of the Omniscient Lord. Different from them is the Omniscient Lord himself.[30]

Rāmānuja's Śrīvaiṣṇavism

Rāmānuja, the master exponent of Śrīvaiṣṇavism, commenting on a quote from the *Viṣṇu Purāṇa* writes about *śakti*:

> "The *śakti* of Viṣṇu is the highest, that which is called the embodied soul is inferior, and there is another third energy called *karma* or nescience, actuated by which the omnipresent *śakti* of the embodied soul perpetually undergoes the afflictions of wordly existence.[31] These and other texts teach that the highest Brahman is essentially free from all imperfection

> whatsoever, comprises within itself all auspicious qualities, and finds its pastime in originating, preserving, re-absorbing, pervading, and ruling the universe; that the entire complex of intelligent and non-intelligent beings in all their different estates is real and constitutes the *rūpa* or *śakti* of the highest Brahman.[32]

The lesson which he draws from the *Purāṇa* text is the following:

> It declares that the highest Brahman, that is Viṣṇu, possesses two *rūpas*, called *śaktis*, a *mūrta* and an *amūrta* one, and then teaches that the portion of the *mūrta* namely the *kṣetrajñā* (embodied soul) which is distinguished by its connection with matter and involved in nescience – that is termed *karma*, and constitutes a third *śakti* – is not perfect.[33]

Caitanya's Gauḍīya Vaiṣṇavism

In Gauḍīya Vaiṣṇavism the *śaktis* of Viṣṇu play a major role:

> There is an infinite *śakti* in the Lord ... That mother of the world, Śrī, is the eternal *śakti* of Viṣṇu and is indissolubly united with the Lord. As Viṣṇu is all-pervading, so is she also.
>
> Viṣṇu has three *śaktis*, the highest among them is Śrī and she is not different from the Lord. Thus taught the great teacher Mahāprabhu to his disciples.
>
> The power of the transcendent Viṣṇu is revealed as manifold and innate: namely intelligence-power (*Jñāna-śakti*), strength-power (*Bala-śakti*), and action-power (*Kriyā-śakti*).
>
> The Viṣṇu *śakti* is called Parā, the Aparā *śakti* is called Kṣetrajñā, and the third *śakti* is that which is called Avidyā and Karma, the energy found in matter.
>
> His highest energy, called Parā-Śakti, is not within the scope of minutes and hours or any other division of time.
>
> In him exists this one *śakti* which is threefold, namely Hlādinī (bliss-giving), Sandhinī (existence-giving) and Samvit (consciousness-giving).
>
> Viṣṇu is one indeed and so is Laskṣmī, his eternal consort. They become many assuming various forms due to their *śaktis*.[34]
>
> *Hlādinī* [*śakti*] is so named because of giving delight to Kṛṣṇa who tastes delight through that power. Kṛṣṇa himself is delight. *Hlādinī* is the cause of the *bhakta*'s delight; the essence of *hlādinī* is called *prema*. Rādhā is the modification of Kṛṣṇa's love. Her name is the very essence of the delight-giving power. *Hlādinī* makes Kṛṣṇa taste delight. Through *hlādinī* the *bhaktas* are nursed.[35]

Kāśmira Śaivism

In the Śaiva system of Pratyabhijñā a number of Śaktis of Śiva play a great role. In the Śaiva system as described by Mādhava the grace of Śiva is personified as *rodhaśakti*.

DEVĪ IN MODERN HINDUISM

Rāmakrishna Paramahamsa

One of the foremost devotees of the goddess of the modern age and one of the best-known and most widely acknowledged saints of modern India was Rāmakrishna Paramahamsa. He spent many days in a trance before the image of the Goddess, in whose temple he served as priest and on many occasions spoke about her in his conversations. He insisted on the exclusivity of religious dedication:

> Do you aspire after Divine grace? Then propitiate the Mother, the Primal Energy (*śakti*). Yes, she is Mahāmāyā Herself. She is it Who has deluded the whole world, and is conjuring up the triple device of creation, maintenance, and dissolution. She has spread a veil of ignorance over all, and unless She unbars the gate, none can enter the "Inner Court." Left outside, we see only the external things, but the Eternal One, Saccidānanda, remains ever beyond our ken.
>
> The Divine Śakti has two aspects: Vidyā and Avidyā: Avidyā deludes and is the mother of Kāminī-Kañchana, "woman and gold"; and it binds. But Vidyā is the source of devotion, kindness, knowledge and love, and it takes us towards God.
>
> This Avidyā has to be propitiated, and hence the institution of Śakti worship. Various are the ways of worship for gratifying Her: as Her "handmaid," or "hero," or "child." Śakti sādhana is no joke. There are very strenuous and dangerous practices in it. I passed two years as Mother's "handmaid" and "friend." Mine, however, is the mood of the "child," and to me the breasts of any woman are like unto my mother's.
>
> Women are so many images of Śakti. In the western parts of this country the bridegroom holds a knife in his hand during marriage, and in Bengal a nutcracker. The idea is that he will cut the bonds of Māyā with the help of the bride who is Śakti herself. This is Vīrabhava, "the way of the hero." But I never practiced it. Mine is the attitude of the child.[36]

Aurobindo Ghose

Aurobindo Ghose, whose Westernized father sent him as a young boy of seven to England in order to receive a thoroughly Western education, rediscovered his native spiritual heritage as a young revolutionary in a British prison in Calcutta. Withdrawing into solitude in the then French colony of Pondicherry, he spent the rest of his long life preparing for *śakti-nipāta*, the descent of the Śakti which was to transform him into the avatāra of the twentieth century. He entrusted the management of his ashram and the communication with the world at large to "the Mother," about whom he had this to say:

> Nothing can be done except through the force of the Mother. When I speak of the Mother's force I do not speak of the force of Prakṛti which carries in it things of the Ignorance but of the higher Force of the Divine that descends from above to transform, the nature.
>
> There is a force which accompanies the growth of the new consciousness and at once grows with it and helps it to come about and to perfect itself. This force is the Yoga-Shakti. It is here coiled up and asleep in all the centers of our inner being (Chakras) and is at the base of what is called in the *Tantras* the Kuṇḍalinī Shakti. But it is also above us, above our head as the Divine Force – not there coiled up, involved, asleep, but awake, scient, potent, extended and wide; it is there waiting for manifestation and to this Force we have to open ourselves – to the power of the Mother. In the mind it manifests itself as a divine mind-force or a universal mind-force and it can do everything that the personal mind cannot do; it is then the Yogic mind-force. When it manifests and acts in the vital or physical in the same way, it is there apparent as a Yogic life-force or a Yogic body-force. It can awake in all these forms, bursting outward and upwards, extending itself into wideness from below; or it can descend and become there a definite power for things; it can pour downwards into our body, working, establishing its reign, extending into wideness from above, link the lowest in us with the highest above us, release the individual into a cosmic universality or into absoluteness and transcendence.
>
> Certainly, in a sense the descent of the higher powers is the Divine Mother's own descent – for it is she who comes down in them.[37]

The Revival of Śāktism

There is a definite revival of the Goddess religion in India today and virtually all of contemporary Hinduism includes worship of *śakti*.

However, this new Goddess religion is not a mere resurrection of medieval Tantrism. It blends with the post-independence assertion of India's nationhood and a worldwide rediscovery of nature as a vehicle of transcendence. As V. S. Agrawala writes:

> Mother Earth is the deity of the new age ... the *kalpa* of Indra-Agni and the *yuga* of Śiva-Viṣṇu are no more. The modern age offers its salutations to Mother Earth whom it adores as the super-goddess ... The physical boundaries of the Motherland stretch before our eyes but her real self is her cultural being which has taken shape in the course of centuries through the efforts of her people ... Mother Earth is born of contemplation ... Let the people devote themselves truthfully to the Mother Land whose legacy they have received from the ancients. Each one of us has to seek refuge with her. Mother Earth is the presiding deity of the age, let us worship her. Mother Earth lives by the achievements of her distinguished sons.[38]

5 SMĀRTAS

Smṛti, "tradition" was mentioned as a source of Hinduism (almost) equal in importance to *śruti*, "revelation." In daily life it carried even greater weight. *Śruti* was often couched in language accessible only to the brahmin specialists and was referred to only in particular contexts. *Smṛti* applied to everybody and had universal significance in all life situations. Since orthodox Hinduism consisted mainly of a minute ordering of life (some speak of "orthopraxy" instead of "orthodoxy," to underscore the great importance of "ritual correctness" over articulations of belief) those texts that related to this ordering were of the utmost importance. It is not without deeper significance that the authorship of the most respected of such works, the *Manu-smṛti*, is ascribed to the father of humankind and its first lawgiver. The *Manu-smṛti* begins with the creation story, linking the division of castes and their rights and duties to the creator himself.

> In order to protect the universe the most replendent one assigned separate duties and occupations to those who sprang from his mouth, arms, thighs and feet. To Bṛāhmaṇas he assigned teaching and studying the Veda, sacrificing for their own benefit and for others, giving and accepting of alms. The Kṣatriya he commanded to protect the people, to bestow gifts, to offer sacrifices, to study the Veda, and to abstain from attaching himself to sensual pleasures. The Vaiśya he told to tend cattle, to bestow gifts, to offer sacrifices, to study the Veda, to trade, to lend money, and to cultivate land. One occupation only the Lord prescribed to the Śudra, to serve meekly these other three castes. Man is stated to be purer above the navel than below; hence the Self-existent has declared the purest part of

> him to be his mouth. As the Brāhmaṇa sprang from Brahman's mouth, as he was first-born, and as he possesses the Veda, he is by right the Lord of this whole creation. For the Self-existent produced him first from his own mouth, in order that offerings might be conveyed to the gods and forefathers and that this universe might be preserved ...
>
> The very birth of a Brāhmaṇa is an eternal incarnation of the sacred law; for he is born to fulfill the sacred law, and becomes one with Brahman. A Brāhmaṇa coming into existence, is born as the highest on earth, the lord of all created beings, for the protection of the treasury of the law. Whatever exists in the world is the property of the Brāhmaṇa; on account of the excellence of his origin the Brahmana is indeed entitled to it all. The Brāhmaṇa eats but his own food, wears but his own apparel, bestows but his own in alms, other mortals subsist through the benevolence of the Brāhmaṇa.[1]

The *Manu-smṛti* explains its own importance as a summary of *dharma*:

> In this work the sacred law has been fully stated as well as the good and bad qualities of human actions and the immemorial rule of conduct for all the four castes. The rule of conduct is highest law (*ācāraḥ paramo dharma*) whether it be taught in the revealed texts (*śruti*) or in the sacred tradition (*smṛti*); hence a twice-born man who possesses regard for himself should always be careful to follow it. A Brāhmaṇa who departs from the rule of conduct does not reap the fruit of the Veda, but he who duly follows it will obtain the full reward. The sages who saw that the sacred law is thus grounded on the rule of conduct, have taken good conduct to be the most excellent root of all austerity.[2]

The text then briefly itemizes the content of the work, covering all aspects of traditional religious and secular law as well as a great deal of traditional belief with regard to rebirth and final destination.

Besides the *Manu-smṛti* there existed dozens of similar texts of a more regional importance, that were the recognized law books for many centuries. Since the observation of the rules contained in these *Smṛtis* was deemed to be "highest *dharma*," many brahmins did not find it necessary to join one of the numerous *saṃpradāyas* associated with Viṣṇu, Śiva, or Devī to find salvation. They distanced themselves from what they believed to be sectarianism and called themselves Smārtas. They are fairly numerous, especially in Southern India, and are defenders of traditional *dharma*. Śaṅkara, the great Advaitin, is held to have been a Smārta: he introduced *pañcāyatana pūjā*, the collective worship of five deities instead of the exclusive worship of one.

6 HINDU PHILOSOPHIES

THE ANTECEDENTS

Reflection and speculation, the characteristics of what we call "philosophy," have been the hallmark of Hinduism from its earliest days to the present. Many Hindu scriptures are highly philosophical; in India there was never a hard and fast distinction made between philosophy and theology, as in the West.

The *Ṛgveda* contains hymns that could be called philosophical, such as the famous "Hymn of Creation:"

> Then there was neither being nor non-being, neither air nor sky. What was moving about, where, and under whose protection? What was the impenetrably deep water?
>
> Then there was neither death nor immortality, there was no sign of day or night. According to its own nature the One was breathing without a wind. Besides this there was no other.
>
> In the beginning there was darkness enveloped by darkness; all this was an indistinguishable dark mass of water. The lifeforce was enclosed by the void, the one was born through the power of its inner urge.
>
> In the beginning desire entered it, the first seed of thought. Searching in their hearts, by deep pondering the sages found that being was tied to non-being.
>
> They stretched their measuring thread across. Was there an above, a below? There were creative powers and forces of expansion; beneath was desire, above fulfillment.
>
> Who knows for certain, and who can tell for sure whence it originated and where this world came from? The gods were born after this world's creation: who can know from whence it has arisen?

> Whence this world has come, and whether He, the Overseer, made it or not – he alone knows and does not know.[1]

The *Upaniṣads*, the basis for later Vedānta philosophy, are a string of profound sayings and insights into the nature of reality. They suggest that our ultimate destiny depends on finding out the truth about the world and ourselves.

> In the beginning this world was just being, one only, without a second. Some people say: "In the beginning this world was just non-being, one only, without a second; from that non-being being was produced." But how could that be? How could being be produced from non-being? On the contrary: in the beginning this world was just being, one only, without a second. It thought to itself: I wish I were many. Let me bring forth myself. It sent forth fire. That fire thought: May I be many, may I grow forth. It sent forth water. Therefore, when a person grieves or works, water is produced from the heat. That water thought: May I be many, may I grow forth. It sent forth food. Therefore whenever it rains there is abundance of food. So food for eating is produced from water.[2]

> Verily this self is Brahman, made of knowledge, of mind, of breath, of seeing, of hearing, of earth, of water, of wind, of space, of energy and non-energy, of desire and non-desire, of anger and non-anger, of virtuousness and non-virtuousness. It is made of everything. According as one acts, according as one conducts onself, so does one become. The doer of good becomes good. The doer of evil becomes evil. One becomes virtuous by virtuous action, bad by bad action. As is one's desire so is one's resolve, such an action one performs; what action one performs, that one procures for oneself. One who is without desire, who is freed from desire, whose desire is satisfied does not pass on to another birth. Being *brahman* he enters into *brahman*. One who has found and has awakened the Self that has entered this composite body, that one is the maker of everything, the creator of all; the world is that one's; that one is the world itself. In the cave of the heart lies the ruler of all, the lord of all, the king of all. That one does not become greater by good action nor less by bad action. That is the Lord of all, the overlord of beings, the protector of beings.[3]

> This body, truly, is mortal. It has been appropriated by death. But it is the standing-ground of that bodiless, deathless Self. One who is in a body has been appropriated by pleasure and pain. There is no freedom from pleasure and pain for one who is in a body. One who is bodiless, is untouched by pleasure and pain.[4]

> The Self, hidden in all beings, does not reveal itself to everyone. It is seen by those of subtle and concentrated mind. Having realized that which is

without sound, without touch, formless, imperishable, and also without taste and smell, eternal, without beginning or end, beyond all manifestation – one is liberated from death. When all desires that dwell in the heart are destroyed, when all the knots of the heart are rent asunder, then a mortal becomes immortal and here in this very body attains the inifinite.[5]

The Self is below, the Self is above, the Self is to the west, the Self is to the east, the Self is to the south, the Self is to the north. The Self, indeed is this whole universe.[6]

The Self which is free from evil, from aging, from death, from sorrow, from hunger, from thirst, whose desire is the Real, whose conception is the Real – that should be searched out, and one should strive to understand it. One obtains all worlds and all desires if one has found out and understands that Self.[7]

The one who dwells in all things, yet is other than all things, whom all things do not know, whose body all things are, who controls all things from within – That is your Self, the Inner Controller, the Immortal. That is the unseen Seer, the unheard Hearer, the unthought Thinker, the un-understood Understander. Other than That there is no seer. Other than That there is no hearer. Other than That there is no thinker. Other than That there is no understander. That is Your Self, the Inner Controller, the Immortal.[8]

Verily, this self is Brahman, made of knowledge, of mind, of breath, of seeing, of hearing, of earth, of water, of wind, of space, of energy and non-energy, of desire and non-desire, of anger and non-anger, of virtuousness and non-virtuousness. It is made of everything.[9]

By discerning that which is soundless, touchless, formless, imperishable, tasteless, constant, odorless, without beginning, without end, higher than the great, stable – one is liberated from the mouth of death.[10]

This *ātman* is not to be obtained by instruction, nor by intellect, nor by much learning. It is to be obtained only by the one whom it chooses, to such a one the *ātman* reveals its own being. This *ātman* is not to be obtained by one devoid of fortitude, nor through heedlessness, nor through a false notion of austerity. But one who strives by these means, provided one knows, into this *brahman*-abode this *ātman* enters.[11]

THE SIX ACCEPTED SYSTEMS (*ṢAḌDARŚANA*)

Not satisfied with the aphoristic wisdom of these sources, and keen to construct an all-embracing world-view, Hindu thinkers developed a number of philosophical systems, called *darśanas*, "theories." In the early (Indian) middle-ages Hindus began to differentiate between *āstika*, "orthodox," and *nāstika*, "heterodox," schools: among the latter were listed Buddhism, Jainism and Cārvāka (an early Indian form of materialistic philosophy). The orthodox systems were classified in a stereotypical six, paired into three groups: Nyāya-Vaiśeṣika, Sāṁkhya-Yoga, Pūrva and Uttara Mīmāṃṣā.

Nyāya-Vaiśeṣika

VAIŚEṢIKA

Vaiśeṣika is an early kind of atomistic physics, with a religio-metaphysical orientation. Nyāya, which later developed into a sophisticated study of epistemology and logic, was also practiced with a view to find emancipation.

> The means to prosperity and salvation is *dharma*. The attainment of salvation is the result of the cognition of the six categories of substance, quality, action, class concept, particularity and inherence. The substances are: earth, water, fire, air, ether, time, space, *ātman*, and mind. The qualities are: taste, color, odor, touch, number, measure, separation, contact, disjoining, prior and posterior, understanding, pleasure and pain, desire and aversion, and volitions. Action (*karma*) is as upward movement, downward movement, contraction, expansion, horizontal movement. The feature common to substance, quality and action is that they are existent, non-eternal, and substantive; they effect, cause and possess generality and particularity.[12]

A major part of the *sūtra* consists in a further elucidation of the various terms mentioned, in much the same way as the early Greek philosophers of nature analyzed and described the elements, their qualities, and the interrelations. The teaching which distinguishes Vaiśeṣika most from other philosophies is its theory of *viśeṣa*, as explained in the following text:

> *Viśeṣas* are the ultimate specificatives or differentiatives of their substrates. They reside in such beginningless and indestructible eternal substances as the atoms, *ākāśa*, time, space, *ātman* and *manas* – inhering in their entirety in each of these, and serving as the basis of absolute differentiation of specification. Just as we have with regard to the bull, as distinguished from the horse, certain distinct cognitions – such, for

> instance as (a) that is a "bull," which is a cognition based upon its having the shape of other bulls, (b) that it is "white," which is based upon a quality, (c) that it is "running swiftly," which is based upon action, (d) that it has a "fat hump," which is based upon "constituent parts," and (e) that it carries a "large bell," which is based upon conjunction; so have the Yogis, who are possessed of powers that we do not possess, distinct cognitions based upon similar shapes, similar qualities, and similar actions – with regard to the eternal atoms, the liberated selves and minds; and as in this case no other cause is possible, those causes by reason whereof they have such distinct cognitions – as that "this is a peculiar substance," "that is a peculiar self" and so forth – and which also lead to the recognition of one atom as being the same that was perceived at a different time and place – are what we call the *viśeṣas*.[13]

According to the teaching of the Vaiśeṣikas, there are many different *ātmans* distinguished by their relative and specific *viśeṣas*. An ordinary person, however, is able to recognize their diversity only on account of externally perceptible actions, qualities, and so on. Only a Yogi has the "insight into the essence of the soul itself and thus into the real cause of their diversity."

> For the sake of complete emancipation one ought to devote oneself to *śīla* [morality], *dāna* [charity], *tapas* [austerities], and *yoga*. From these comes supreme merit which leads to the attainment of emancipation and *tattva-jñāna* [metaphysical knowledge]. "Prosperity" is enjoyment of pleasure in *svarga* [heaven]. Knowledge of ultimate truth brings *mokṣa* [liberation], when merit and demerit have been completely destroyed and *ātman* [Self] and *manas* [body-dependent mind] no longer come in contact with each other, that is when the nine things are no longer produced.[14]

These "nine things" are: *buddhi* (understanding), *sukha* (happiness), *duḥkha* (suffering), *icchā* (desire), *dveṣa* (hatred), *prayatna* (effort), *dharma* (righteousness), *adharma* (unrighteousness), *saṃskāra* (innate propensity).

NYĀYA AND NAVYA-NYĀYA

The *Nyāya* system is composed of two parts: *adhyātma-vidyā*, or metaphysics, and *tarka-śāstra*, or rules of debate, often simply called logic. Thus the *Nyāya Sūtra*, famous for its acute analysis of discursive thought, as such also has substantial sections on suffering, soul, and salvation. It begins with the following aphorism:

> It is the knowledge of the true character of the following sixteen categories that leads to the attainment of the highest good: (1) The Means of Right Cognition; (2) The Objects of Right Cognition; (3) Doubt; (4) Motive; (5) Example; (6) Theory; (7) Factors of Inference; (8) Cogitation; (9) Demonstrated Truth; (10) Discussion; (11) Disputation; (12) Wrangling; (13) Fallacious Reason; (14) Casuistry; (15) Futile Rejoinder; and (16) Clinchers.
>
> Suffering, birth, activity, mistaken notions, folly – if these factors are cancelled out in reverse order, there will be *mokṣa*.[15]

In the twelfth century *Navya-Nyāya*, or the "New Logic," arose. The *Tattva-cintāmaṇi* by Gaṅgeśa, the major work of the new school, emphasized the *pramāṇas*, the means of valid cognition, devoting one chapter each to perception (*pratyakṣa*), inference (*anumāna*), analogy (*upamāna*), and verbal testimony (*śabda*). Quite unique in Indian philosophy are the Nyāya arguments for the existence of *Īśvara*.

> From effects, combination, support, etc. and traditional arts, authority, *śruti*, and so on, an everlasting omniscient being must be assumed.

The commentary on this text explains:

> The earth etc. must have had a maker, because they have the nature of effects like a jar; by a thing's having a maker we mean that it is produced by some agent who possesses the wish to make, and has also a perceptive knowledge of the material cause out of which it is to be made. "Combination" is an action, and therefore the action which produced the conjunction of two atoms, initiating the *dvyaṇuka* at the beginning of a creation, must have been accompanied by the volition of an intelligent being, because it has the nature of an action like the actions of bodies such as ours. "Support" etc.: the world depends upon some being who possesses a volition which hinders it from falling, because it has the nature of being supported ... By traditional arts etc.: the traditional arts now current, such as that of making cloth, must have been originated by an independent being, from the very fact that they are traditional usages like the tradition of modern modes of writing. "From authority": the knowledge produced by the Vedas is produced by a virtue residing in its cause, because it is right knowledge, just as in the case in the right knowledge produced by perception. "From *śruti*": the Veda must have been produced by a person, from its having the nature of a Veda like the *Āyur Veda* ... At the beginning of creation there must be the number of duality abiding in the atoms, which is the cause of the measure of the *dvyaṇuka* but this number cannot be produced at that time by the distinguishing perception of beings like

> ourselves. Therefore we can only assume this distinguishing faculty as then existing in *Īśvara.*[16]

> *Īśvara* indeed supports the efforts of people, i.e. if a person tries to attain something special, it is *Īśvara* who attains it; if *Īśvara* does not act, the activity of people is fruitless.[17]

Sāṁkhya-Yoga

SĀṀKHYA

Sāṁkhya, literally "number," because of the enumeration of twenty-five *tattvas* (principles) out of which the whole universe is formed, comes closest to the ancient Greek philosophy of nature. It is, however, designed to lead to transcendental liberation, as the opening verse of the *Sāṁkhyakārikā* makes clear: "From torment by threefold misery the inquiry into the means of terminating it. The discriminative knowledge of the evolved, the unevolved and the knower is the means of surpassing all sorrow."[18]

Sāṁkhya presupposes distinct individualities, in contrast to the monistic philosophy of Advaita Vedānta:

> The plurality of *puruṣas* follows from the fact of individual death and individual birth, and from the fact that the organs of cognition and action are individual; moreover not all people are active at the same time and the relationship of the three *guṇas* varies from person to person.[19]

Against the objection that the postulated omnipresent *prakṛti* (*materia prima*) cannot be perceived they respond: "The non-perception is due to its subtlety, not to its non-existence, since it is cognized from its effects."

Human suffering is attributed to the misperception that the *puruṣa* (the spirit-self) is subject to bondage and change:

> Certainly no *puruṣa* is in bondage and none is liberated nor has he to undergo any changes; it is *prakṛti*, dwelling in many forms, which is bound, freed and subject to change. *Prakṛti* binds herself sevenfold and through one form she causes liberation for the benefit of *puruṣa.*[20]

YOGA

Yoga, literally "joining," is the reversal of the evolution described in Sāṁkhya. Some of the later *Upaniṣads* are brief compendia of Yoga. The *Tejobindu Upaniṣad* gives a fairly detailed description of *Rāja-yoga.*

The *Yoga-sūtra* itself – a short work of but 194 aphorisms ascribed to Patañjali – consists of four *pādas* (parts), with the subject-titles *samādhi* (trance), *sādhana* (means of realization), *vibhūti* (preternatural accomplishments), and *kaivalya* (ultimate aim):

> Yoga is the cessation of all changes of the mind ... The *yoga* of action is constituted by *tapas* (austerities), *svādhyāya* (scriptural study), and *īśvara praṇi-dhāna* (meditation with the Lord as object) ... *Dhāraṇā* is the fixation of the intellect on one topic. *Dhyāṇa* is the one-pointedness in this effort. *Samādhi* is the same (concentration) when the object itself alone appears devoid of form, as it were ... *Kaivalya* is realized when the *guṇas*, annihilated in the objectives of a person, cease to exert influence, or when *citta-śakti*, the power of consciousness, is established in her own proper nature.[21]

Pūrva- and Uttara-Mīmāṃsā

Mīmāṃsā, "enquiry," is the name of two very different systems of Hindu theology which have one thing in common: they claim to be but an exposition of the true meaning of the Veda. *Pūrva-Mīmāṃsā* (often simply called *Mīmāṃsā*), the "earlier enquiry," has *dharma* as its proper subject and the *karma-kāṇḍa* of the Vedas as its scriptural source. *Uttara-Mīmāṃsā*, the "latter enquiry," better known as Vedānta, has *brahman* knowledge as its subject and the *jñana-kāṇḍa* of the Veda as its scriptural basis. Vedānta literally means "end of the Veda." It is used both to describe the *Upaniṣads* (the end-portion of the Veda as well as the assumed aim or end of its teaching) and the systematic philosophy built on Upaniṣadic teachings as contained in the *Vedānta-sūtras*. Though historically there was a considerable amount of friction between the two systems, they are also in many ways complementary and are considered the two most orthodox of the six Hindu systems.

PŪRVA-MĪMĀṂSĀ

The basic text of Pūrva-Mīmāṃsā are the *Mīmāṃsā-sūtras* attributed to Jaimini (third century B.C.E.). Most of its literature consists of commentaries and subcommentaries to these aphorisms from which we select a few:

> Now, then, an enquiry into *dharma*.
> *Dharma* is that which is indicated by Vedic injunctions for the attainment of the highest good ...

> Sense-perception is not a means of knowing *dharma*, as it apprehends only things existing at the present time.
>
> The relation of the word with its denotation is inborn – instruction is the means of knowing *dharma* – infallible regarding all that is imperceptible; it is a valid means of knowledge, as it is independent ...
>
> The purpose of the Veda lying in the enjoining of actions, those parts of the Veda which do not serve that purpose are useless; in these therefore the Veda is declared to be non-eternal ...
>
> The one result [of ritual actions] is heaven, as that is equally desirable for all.[22]

The *Śābarabhāṣya* (*c.* 200 C.E.) provides extensive comment on the *sūtras* and answers objections that had meanwhile been formulated by opponents. While Jaimini's *sūtras* cover less than a hundred pages in print, Śābara's commentary fills over two thousand pages. The following is a translation of part of Śābaras's exposition of the very first of Jaimini's *sūtras*:

> The words of the *sūtras* are, so far as possible, to be understood in that same sense which they are known to convey in common speech; it is not right to assume meanings for them on the basis of elliptical and other devices, or to attribute to them any special technical signification. It is only in this way that all that would have to be done would be to explain the Vedic texts directly (with the help of the *sūtras*); otherwise (if we did not take the words of the *sūtras* in their ordinary sense) it would be necessary for us to explain the extraordinary (technical) meanings of the words of the *sūtras* themselves, and then the texts of the Veda. This would involve a great exertion.
>
> Objection: "In common parlance the term *atha* (next) is found to be expressive of sequence to an event; in the case of the present *sūtra*, however, we do not find any event; and yet there must be an event in sequence, whereto the enquiry into *Dharma* would come in. It is only thus that the word *atha* could be taken in an ordinary sense."
>
> Answer: "Reading of the Veda would be the required event; as it is only after reading the Veda has been accomplished that enquiry into *dharma* follows."
>
> Objection: "It cannot be so; as it is possible to have an enquiry into *dharma* after some other event also – even before the reading of the Veda."
>
> Answer: "The Teacher has used the term 'next' in reference to that particular enquiry into *dharma* which is not possible without reading of the Veda. Why so? Because in the course of the enquiry there will be various kinds of discussion over Vedic texts (and until we have studied the texts there can be no discussion of them). Further, we are not asserting

> that there is to be no enquiry into *dharma* prior to the reading of the Veda, and that the enquiry is to follow immediately after (Vedic study). In fact, the single sentence (contained in the *sūtra*) could not deny the possibility of the enquiry into *dharma* before the reading of the Veda, and at the same time affirm the immediate sequence of the enquiry to the reading . . ."[23]

The eighth-century Mīmāṃsaka Kumārila Bhaṭṭa offers in his *Śloka-vārttika*, *Tantra-vārttika*, and *Tup-ṭīka* lengthy subcommentaries to Śābara's *Bhāṣya* as well as extensive anti-Buddhist polemics. The following is part of his commentary on Śābara's *Bhāṣya* to the second *sūtra*. In it he rejects together with the (Buddhist) notion of an "omniscient Buddha," the very idea of an omniscient person whose words could have the same authority as the Veda.

> An omniscient person is not seen by us at the present moment; nor is it possible to prove (by inference) that such a one ever existed before. Nor can the existence of the Omniscient One be proven by Scriptures; for in that case there would be mutual interdependence. And how can one ever believe the authenticity of a Scripture composed by another human? Nor can we get at any other Scripture (save the Veda) which is eternal. If the eulogies (occurring in the Veda in praise of such an Omniscient Person) were eternal, then non-eternality would belong to the Scripture itself. The eternality of the Scripture (Veda) having been established, all other assumptions (of an Omniscient Author and the like) become needless. For men could prove the existence of *dharma* by means of the same (scripture) whereby you seek to prove the existence of an Omniscient Person. One who, convinced of the truthfulness of Scripture writers with regard to their assertions in connection with the relation of the senses or their objects, would base their authority even in the case of matters of faith on the fact of these latter assertions proceeding from one whose assertion has been found true in the former case – such a one would thereby prove the authenticity (of Buddha's) assertions to depend on something else.[24]

Parthasārathi Miśra (*c.* 1050–1120 C.E.) wrote a very influential Pūrva-Mīmāṃsā manual entitled *Śāstradīpikā* ("The Lamp of Doctrine") in which he not only comments on the *sūtras* of Jaimini's text but also critically examines Buddhist and Advaita views as well as the explanations given by the great Mīmāṃsakas of the past, such as Kumārila Bhaṭṭa and Prabhākara, ending each section with a *siddhānta*, i.e. a statement containing the true and final position arrived at. Here is the *siddhānta* to the long discussion of the second *sūtra*:

> Is there no *pramāṇa* [proof] by which to establish *dharma*? Do perception etc. alone serve as *pramāṇa*? Or the Veda only? Or either? Or conjointly? Because *śabda* [verbal testimony] derives its validity from some other *pramāṇa* which bestows validity on it and by itself cannot serve as *pramāṇa* (*śabda* brings to mind what has been cognized by other *pramāṇas*) and since perception etc. are incapable of bringing within their purview (*dharma* which is supersensuous) *dharma* is bereft of any *pramāṇa* – this is one view. That it is cognizable by perception etc. is the second view. That Yogins can have direct perception while moderns have to fall back upon the Veda is the third view. Because of the amazing variety observed in the world we are driven to conclude by implication something unseen (*adṛṣṭa*) and so we arrive at *dharma* of a general nature. Then on the authority of the Veda we learn what its specific nature is, viz. *agnihotra* etc. Hence a different view is that conjointly they (*arthāpatti* and *codanā*) establish *dharma*. The final view or *siddhānta* is that *codanā* (Veda) alone is the *pramāṇa* and that it alone is the valid means of the apprehension (of *dharma*, i.e. its validity cannot be questioned). Therefore these two statements thus emphasized – Veda alone is the right means of knowing *dharma*, and Veda is *pramāṇa* – indubitably constitute the thesis.[25]

Pūrva-Mīmāṃsā, while theologically largely superseded by Vedānta, remained of great importance for the praxis of Hinduism: the interpretation of traditional law that governs the daily life of Hindus is done even today on the basis of Mīmāṃsā principles and the renewed interest in Vedic studies has also given new impetus to the study of the Mīmāṃsakas and their sophisticated analysis of Vedic texts.

UTTARA-MĪMĀṂSĀ OR VEDĀNTA:

The *Vedānta Sūtra*, also called *Brahma Sūtra*, ascribed to Bādarāyaṇa (fifth century B.C.E.), is the basic text of the Vedānta *darśana*. The *Vedānta Sūtra* is divided into four *adhyāyas*, chapters, each subdivided into four *pādas*, literally "feet" or parts, which again are made up of a varying number of *sūtras* or aphorisms. The 550 brief *sūtras*, often only fragments of sentences, require extensive commentary to become meaningful. They can be interpreted in a variety of ways, and thus a number of mutually incompatible schools of Vedānta developed in the course of time. Several of these have been mentioned in the context of Vaiṣṇava and Śaiva philosophies. We briefly introduce here the school of Advaita, founded by Śaṅkara (788–820 C.E.) which propounds a non-sectarian interpretation of the *Vedānta Sūtras*.

The special question with regard to the enquiry into Brahman is whether it presupposes the understanding of *dharma*. To this question we reply: No! Because for a person who has read the Vedānta it is possible to begin the inquiry into the nature of *brahman* before having studied the *dharma*. The study of *dharma* results in transitory heaven and this depends on the performance of rituals. The inquiry into the nature of *brahman*, however, results in *mokṣa*, lasting liberation. It does not depend upon the performance of ceremonies. A few presuppositions preceding the inquiry into the nature of *brahman* will have to be mentioned. These are:

1. Discrimination between the eternal and the non-eternal.
2. Renunciation of the desire to enjoy the fruit of one's actions either here or hereafter.
3. Practice of the basic virtues like peacefulness, self-restraint and so on.
4. Strong desire for liberation.

If these conditions are fulfilled, then a person may inquire into *brahman* whether before or after the *dharma*-inquiry; but not if these conditions are not fulfilled. The object of desire is the knowledge of *brahman* and complete understanding of it. Knowledge is therefore the means to perfect *brahman*-cognition. The complete knowledge of *brahman* is the supreme human goal, because it destroys the root of all evil, namely *avidyā*, which is the seed of *saṃsāra*. One may now ask: is *brahman* known or unknown? If *brahman* is known then there is no need for further inquiry; if *brahman* is unknown we cannot begin an inquiry. We answer: *brahman* is known. *Brahman*, omniscient and omnipotent, whose essential nature is eternal purity, consciousness and freedom, exists. For if we contemplate the derivation of the word *brahman* from the root *bṛh-*, to be great, we understand at once that it is eternal purity, etc. More than that: the existence of *brahman* is known because it is the *ātman*, the self of everyone. For everyone is conscious of the "self" and no one thinks: I am not. *Ātman* is *brahman*. If the existence of the self was not known each one would think: I am not. But if *ātman* is generally known as *brahman*, one does not have to start an inquiry. Our answer is: No. Because there is a diversity of opinions regarding its nature. Uneducated people and the Lokāyatās are of the opinion that the body itself, having *caitanya*, consciousness, as an attribute, is the *ātman*. Others believe that the sense-organs, endowed with the potency to experience, are the *ātman*. Others again believe that *cetana*, reasoning, or *manas*, mind, is the *ātman*. Others again believe the self to be simply a momentary idea, or that it is *śūnya*, emptiness. Some others explain that there is besides the body some supernatural being, responsible for the transmigrations, acting and enjoying; others teach that this being enjoys only but does not act. Some believe that besides these there exists an omniscient, omnipotent *Īśvara*, and others finally declare that the *ātman* is that enjoyer ... The *sūtra*,

> therefore presents a discussion of the Vedānta texts with the motto: "Inquiry into *brahman*," which proceeds with appropriate arguments and aims at supreme bliss.[26]

In a short treatise entitled *Sarva-vedānta-siddhānta-saṅgraha* ("summary of all the final conclusions of Vedānta") he further explains:

> According to *śruti* all that is manifest has proceeded from *brahman*. Apart from *brahman* they cease to be, therefore they are not eternal. Whatever consists of parts and whole cannot be eternal. This truth holds good even if it is Vaikuṇṭha. Therefore to consider any particular object to be eternal would be an error of imagination. To distinguish, in the light of what the *śruti* says, and with the help of one's power of reasoning, between that which is eternal and that which is not eternal is known as *viveka*.[27]

One of Śaṅkara's original ideas, vigorously rejected by other interpreters of the *Brahma Sūtras*, is his notion of *adhyāsa* ("super-imposition") which he defines as follows:

> It is an awareness, similar in nature to memory, that arises on a different (foreign) basis as a result of some past experience ... Superimposition has neither beginning nor end but flows on eternally, appears as the manifested universe and its apprehension, conjured up agentship and enjoyership, and is perceived by all persons. In order to eradicate this source of evil and in order to acquire the knowledge of the unity of the Self a discussion of Vedānta is begun.
>
> To attribute to that which is real the nature of the properties of unreal objects is known as superimposition ... The supreme *brahman* is characterized by truth, knowledge and bliss, and that is the only reality. The universe is perceived to be real, because it is superimposed upon *brahman*, just as the blue color is superimposed upon the sky... Whatever is negated by means of proof must needs be unreal. But that which is not so disproved ... must be real, if it is true at all times ... ignorance is the cause ... it is *anirvācanīya* (one cannot say it is and cannot say it is not).
>
> It is unreal in itself but has *brahman* as its basis and abides in *brahman*, but *brahman* is not tainted by it ... the animate and the inanimate ... prove the existence of *brahman* ... Thus when one says "I do not know *brahman*" even that should be taken as proof of the existence of *brahman*.[28]

A further notion peculiar to Śaṅkara is his understanding of *māyā* as neither reality nor pure illusion, but the basis of superimposition and therefore of bondage:

> Pure consciousness has *māyā* for its adjunct and is reflected in and through it. It is then endowed with the quality of all-knowingness and with an abundance of *sattva*. It is that which is the cause of creation, preservation, and dissolution of the universe. It is then known as the unmanifested [*avyākṛta*], the primordial element [*avyakta*] and as Lord [*Īśvara*]. The Lord is then endowed with the quality of all-knowingness, and is regarded as the illuminator of knowledge ... Īśvara the first cause of all ... the world is known as the sheath of Īśvara ... everything merges in Iśvara at the time of final dissolution.[29]

A split developed among the immediate disciples of Śaṅkara. The two factions became later known as the "Vivaraṇa" and the "Bhāmatī" schools, named after two celebrated subcommentaries on Śaṅkara's *bhāṣya*, written by Prakāśātman (*c.* 1000 C.E.) and Vācaspati Miśra (*c.* 850 C.E.). They differed on the role which ritual played in the process of emancipation and also on the question as to whether the locus of *avidyā* (ignorance) was in the individual *jīvātman* or in the universal *brahman*.

In course of time many systematic treatises were written that popularized the ideas of Śaṅkara. The *Aṣṭāvakra Saṃhitā*, from whom some extracts follow, purports to be the work of the ancient Ṛṣi Aṣṭāvakra ("broken in eight places") teaching Advaita Vedānta in stately Sanskṛt verses.

> If you aspire after liberation, shun the objects of the senses like poison, and seek forgiveness, sincerity, kindness, contentment, and truth as nectar. You are neither earth, nor water, nor fire, nor air, nor ether. In order to gain liberation, know the Self as witness of all these and pure consciousness. Virtue and vice, pleasure and pain are properties of the mind, not of you. You are neither doer nor enjoyer, you are ever free.[30]

> One who considers oneself free is free indeed and one who considers onself bound remains bound. "As one thinks, so one becomes," is a popular saying in this world which is very true.[31]

> In me, the unlimited ocean, the vessel of the universe moves about, impelled by the wind of its own nature. I am not moved by it.
>
> In me, the unlimited ocean, the wave of the universe rises or vanishes according to its own nature. I am neither increasing nor decreasing by it.
>
> In me, the unlimited ocean, the universe of imagination develops. I am tranquil and formless. In this alone I dwell.
>
> The Self is not in the object and the object is not in That which is infinite and stainless. It is free from attachment and desire and is still. In this alone do I dwell.

> I am pure Consciousness. The world is like a magic show. How should there be in me any notion of attractiveness or repulsiveness?[32]

> It is bondage, when the mind desires anything or grieves about anything, rejects or welcomes anything, feels angry or happy about anything. Liberation is attained when the mind does not desire or grieve or reject or accept or feel happy or angry. It is bondage when the mind is attached to any particular sense organ. It is liberation when the mind is not attached to any sense-organ. When there is no "I" there is liberation; where there is "I" there is bondage. Considering this, refrain from accepting or rejecting anything.[33]

Advaita Vedānta was kept alive through the centuries by a galaxy of famous scholars, who were often heads of the *maṭhas* founded by Śaṅkara. They are also called Śaṅkarācāryas and *Jagad-gurus* ["world-teachers"] and continue to spread the message of Advaita. Advaita Vedānta became also the preferred philosophy of modern Hindu intellectuals.

The most prominent and most widely known of these is Sarvepalli Radhakrishnan (1889–1975). He not only lectured beautifully and wrote widely on philosophical matters, but also was a major public figure in early post-independence India. After serving as India's ambassador in several countries, he became Vice-president (1952–62) and President (1962–67) of India. He considered himself "the conscience of the nation" and showed how the principles of Advaita Vedānta could be applied to contemporary social and economic problems. He also felt a need to defend Hinduism against its critics both inside and outside India and created a lofty reinterpretation:

> The mystic religion of India, which affirms that things spiritual are things personal and that we have to reflect them in our lives, which requires us to withdraw from the world's concerns to find the real and return with renewed energy and certitude to the world, which is at once spiritual and social, is likely to be the religion of the new world.[34]

At the same time he recognized the great importance of the spiritual traditions of all of humankind for the formation of a viable new civilization:

> We cannot base the new civilization on science and technology alone. They do not furnish a reliable foundation. We must learn to live from a new basis, if we wish to avoid the catastrophe that threatens us. We must

> discover the reserves of spirituality, the sense of the sacred found in all religious traditions and use them to fashion a new type of man who uses the instruments he has invented with a renewed awareness that he is capable of greater things than mastery of nature. The service to which man must return is man himself, the spirit in him.[35]

> The new world order must have a deep spiritual impulse to give it unity and drive. It alone can give a rational basis to the social programme ... There is no other source from which salvation can come to a world wandering ever more deeply into tragedy ... If we are centred in the spiritual reality we shall be freed from the greed and the fear which are the basis of our society which is anarchic and competitive. To change it into a human community in which everyone's physical and psychical advance is provided for, we have to enlarge our consciousness, recognize life's purpose and accept it in our own work.[36]

Over against a purely otherwordly spirituality as proclaimed by some Hindu sages of the past, he affirmed the need to engage in work in and for the world:

> The life eternal is to be realized on this earth itself. Love of man is as fundamental to religion as worship of God. We must seek our evolution through the medium of this life, by transforming it, by changing it over.[37]

He blended new, Western evolutionary ideas with ancient Vedāntic notions of the immanence of *brahman* in everything:

> The God who is responsible for this world, who is the consciousness of the universe, is working through brute matter from which he has to liberate himself, and liberate us. He himself is suffering in each and all of us. This suffering will be at an end, when the potential world spirit of the whole becomes the actual consciousness of each part, when God becomes "all in all" – when the solitary limited God becomes the Pantheistic Absolute.[38]

7 MODERN HINDUISM

The vast majority of Hindus today keep following the teachings and practices of the various traditions of Vaiṣṇavism, Śaivism and Śāktism as outlined above. What is called "modern Hinduism" consists of a large number of Hindu reform movements of the nineteenth and early twentieth centuries. They had and have a relatively small number of followers and by no means replaced or superseded the major traditional forms of Hinduism.

RĀJĀ RĀM MOHAN ROY AND THE BRAHMO-SAMĀJ

Rām Mohan Roy, educated in both traditional Hindu and Muslim learning, was one of the first Indians to learn English and to seek employment with the East India Company in Calcutta. Later in life he devoted himself to developing an all-embracing new religiosity. He protested against image worship and superstition and attempted to base the new universal religion on the *Upaniṣads*. In his introduction to the translation of the *Kaṭha-Upaniṣad* he explained its purpose:

> To assist the European Community in forming their opinion respecting Hindoo-Theology rather from the matter found in their doctrinal scriptures than from the Purāṇas, moral tales or any other modern works or from the superstitious rites and habits daily encouraged and fostered by their self-interested leaders. Idolatry destroys to the utmost degree the natural texture of society, and prescribes crimes of the most heinous nature, which even the most

> savage nations would blush to commit, unless compelled by the most urgent necessity.[1]

After coming into contact with the English missionaries in Serampore [Srirampura], a Danish enclave not far from Calcutta, he wrote in 1820 *The Precepts of Jesus: The Guide to Peace and Happiness*, a small book that to Rām Mohan Roy's surprise led to a major controversy.

> I feel persuaded that by separating from the other matters contained in the New Testament the moral principles found in that book will be more likely to produce the desirable effects of improving the hearts and minds of men of different persuasions and degrees of understanding … This simple code of religion and morality is so admirably calculated to elevate men's ideas to high and liberal notions of God who has equally submitted all living creatures, without distinction of caste, rank or wealth, to change, disappointment, pain and death and has equally all admitted to be partakers of the bountiful mercies which he has lavished over nature and is also so well fitted to regulate the conduct of the human race in the discharge of their various duties to themselves, and to society, that I cannot but hope the best effects from its promulgation in its present form.[2]

He came to the conclusion that Christ's message had been misinterpreted by later Christians and that Western Christianity rested on a gross misunderstanding of Jesus' words. In his introduction to the *Kena-Upaniṣad* he talked about the difficulty of founding religion either on a tradition or on subjective reason:

> The best method perhaps is neither to give ourselves up exclusively to the guidance of the one or the other, but to endeavour to improve our intellectual and moral faculties relying on the Goodness of the Almighty Power, which alone enables us to attain that which we earnestly and diligently seek.[3]

The Brahmo-Samāj sent some young people to Benares to study the *Upaniṣads*. They returned with the notion that one could neither accept divine inspiration nor inerrancy for these texts. They also rejected the idealistic Advaita interpretation of the *Upaniṣads* and thus Debendranath Tagore, one of its leaders, finally abandoned Śaṅkara as his guide in understanding them.

> But when in the Upaniṣads I came across "I am He," "Thou art That," then I became disappointed with them also. These Upaniṣads could not

> meet all our needs, could not fill our hearts. I came to see that the pure heart was filled with the light of intuitive knowledge – this was the basis. Brahman reigned in the pure heart alone. The pure unsophisticated heart was the seat of Brahmoism. We could accept only those texts of the Upaniṣads which accorded with that heart. Those sayings which disagreed with the heart we could not accept.[4]

He compiled an anthology *Brahmo-dharma-grantha* which became the official book of rituals of the new Brahmo-Samāj liturgy. From 1857 onwards every member of the *Tattvabodhinī-Pātrikā* carried the "creed" of the Brahmo-Samāj:

> In the beginning there was only the supreme spirit, there was nothing else. He created all this, that is. He is infinite in wisdom and goodness; He is everlasting, all-knowing, all-pervading, all-sustaining, formless, changeless, one only without a second, almighty, self-dependent and perfect; there is none like unto Him. Our welfare here and hereafter consists only in worshipping Him. To love Him and to do His bidding is to worship Him.[5]

In his testament he summarized his ethical principles thus:

> Let only that be done which promotes well-being. Do not evil to an evildoer... Evil should be overcome by good. Contend with no one. Restrain anger, and imbued with love and charity, behave justly to all. Let love be thy rule of conduct with regard to others. He who desires the good of mankind must look on others as he looks on himself.
>
> He who adores and loves man is a saint.[6]

Keshub Chandra Sen (1838–1884) joined the Brahmo-Samāj in 1857. He rejected all Hindu *saṃskāras* and designed "purified" sacramental rituals in his *Anusthāna Paddhati*. He opposed caste and wanted to give women more prominence in public life. Increasingly coming under Christian influence, he called himself "Jesudās" (Servant of Jesus). In a lecture on "Jesus Christ, Europe and Asia" he said:

> I cherish great respect for the Europeans, not for any secular considerations but for the sake of Jesus Christ, whom they profess to follow and whom, I believe, is their mission to make known to us in words as well as deeds. It is the bounden duty of all Europeans in India so to prove their fidelity to him in all the avocations of their private and public life, that through the influences of their example the spirit of true Christian righteousness may leaven Native Society ... I am proud that I am an Asiatic; and was not Jesus Christ an Asiatic? Yes and his disciples were

> Asiatics ... In Christ we see not only the exaltedness of humanity but also the grandeur of which Asiatic nature is susceptible ... And thus in Christ Europe and Asia, the East and the West may learn to find harmony and unity.[7]

Sen conceived his *Nava Vidhāna* ("New Dispensation") as "Religion of Comparative Theology," as "the realized science of religion." It was to be the "Church of the Holy Spirit." His speculations about the Divine Trinity give a good picture of his understanding of Christianity. The Trinity is

> the treasury in which lies the accumulated wealth of the world's sacred literature ... the loftiest expression of the world's religious consciousness ... an Oriental conception ... *Sat-Chit-Ānanda* was, is and shall be for ever India's God.[8]

The acceptance formula for members of the Brahmo-Samāj resembles the traditional baptismal formula of the Christian churches. Thus the minister asks the applicant:

> Dost thou believe in the Church Universal which is the depository of all ancient wisdom and the receptacle of modern science, which recognizes in all prophets and saints a harmony, in all scriptures a unity, and through all dispensations a continuity, which abjures all that separates and divides and always magnifies unity and peace, which harmonizes reason and faith, yoga and *bhakti*, ascetism and social duty in their highest forms, and which shall make of all nations and sects one kingdom and one family in the fullness of time?[9]

Today the Brahmo Samāj has only a few thousand members and does not exercise any visible influence on the Hindu community at large. It did not fulfill the hopes of those who saw in it the future religion of India, a blend of Hindu metaphysics and Christian ethics.

DĀYĀNANDA SARASVATĪ AND THE ĀRYA-SAMĀJ

The Ārya-Samāj, founded by Swāmi Dāyānanda Sarasvatī in 1875 as a radical Hindu reform movement, has been called "The Church Militant of Hinduism." Dāyānanda not only wanted to stem the Christian missionary onslaught but also to purify Hinduism from all post-Vedic accretions and to return to the pristine Vedic tradition. On the other hand he also endeavoured to modernize Hinduism and to make it again a socially and politically engaged religion.

These are the "Ten Principles of the Ārya-Samāj" as promulgated by him:[10]

1. God is the primary cause of all true knowledge and of everything known by its means.
2. God is All-truth, All-knowledge, All-beatitude, Incorporal, Almighty, Just, Merciful, Unbegotten, Infinite, Unchangeable, Without a beginning, Incomparable, the Support, and the Lord of All, All-pervading, Omniscient, Imperishable, Immortal, Exempt from fear, Eternal, Holy, and the Cause of the Universe. To Him alone worship is due.
3. The Vedas are the books of true knowledge and it is the paramount duty of every Ārya to read or hear them read, to teach and read them to others.
4. An Ārya should always be ready to accept truth and to renounce untruth.
5. All actions must conform to virtue, i.e. should be performed after a thorough consideration of right and wrong.
6. The primary object of the Samāj is to benefit the whole world, viz. by improving the physical, spiritual, and social condition of mankind.
7. All ought to be treated with love and justice and with due regard to their merits.
8. Ignorance must be dispelled and knowledge diffused.
9. No one should be contented with his own good alone, but everyone should regard his or her prosperity as included in that of others.
10. In matters which affect the general social well-being of our race none should allow his or her individuality to interfere with the general good, but in strictly personal affairs, everyone may act with freedom.

The Ārya-Samāj became the nursery of many movements and political parties that strove both to modernize and to reform Hinduism, with the ambition to re-establish Hindu rule in India.

THE RĀMAKRISHNA MOVEMENT

In Chapter 4 (*Śāktism*) mention was made of Rāmakrishna Paramahamsa the great devotee of Kālī. He and the movement that carries his name must also to be highlighted in the context of Hindu reform and renovation.

Rāmakrishna Paramahamsa

Rāmakrishna Paramahamsa was born Gadadhar Chatterji on February 17, 1836 in Kamarpukur/Bengal into a poor but strictly orthodox brahmin family. Invited to become priest in a newly built temple near Calcutta, he spent the rest of his life in worship and ecstasy before the Goddess. A small circle of pious men formed around him. One of them noted down the conversations and the utterances of Rāmakrishna. They were later published (in Bengalī) and appeared in English under the title *The Gospel of Rāmakrishna*.

Answering the classical Hindu question whether one should do "work" or withdraw into pure contemplation, he says:

> Perform your duties in an unselfish spirit. Always try to perform your duties without desiring any result. All without exception perform work. Even to chant the name and glories of God is work as is the meditation of the non-dualist on "I am He": Breathing is also an activity. There is no way of renouncing work altogether. So do your work, but surrender the results to God ... You may try to increase your income, but in an honest way. The goal of life is not the earning of money but the service of God. Money is not harmful if it is devoted to the service of God ... One doesn't have to do one's duty after the attainment of God, nor does one feel like doing it then ... As you advance nearer and nearer to God, He will reduce your activities little by little.[11]

He warned, however, that "work" must not be an aim in itself. It is a means to God-realization:

> Sambhu Mallick once talked about establishing hospitals, dispensaries and schools, making roads, digging public reservoirs, and so forth. I said to him: "Don't go out of your way to look for such works. Undertake only those works that present themselves to you and are of pressing necessity – and those also in a spirit of detachment." It is not good to become involved in many activities. That makes one forget God ... Work is only a means to the realization of God. Therefore I said to Sambhu: "Suppose, God appears before you, then will you ask Him to build hospitals and dispensaries for you? A lover of God never says that. He will rather say: 'O Lord, give me a place at thy Lotus Feet. Keep me always in Thy company. Give me sincere and pure love for Thee.'[12]

When confronted by the question, which of the many religions was the best he countered with his famous simile of the many bathing *ghāṭs* all leading to the same holy water:

> There are several bathing *ghāṭs* in a large tank. Whoever goes choosing whichever *ghāṭ* he pleases to take a bath or to fill his vessel reaches the water and it is useless to quarrel with one another by calling one's *ghāṭ* better than another. Similarly there are many *ghāṭs* that lead to the water of the fountain of Eternal Bliss. Every religion of the world is one such *ghāṭ*. Go direct with a sincere and earnest heart through any of these *ghāṭs* and you shall reach the water of Eternal Bliss. But say not that your religion is better than that of another.[13]

> Many are the names of God and infinite the forms through which He may be approached. In whatever name and form you worship Him, through that He will be realised by you.[14]

> Men may partition their lands by measuring rods and boundary lines, but no one can so partition the all-embracing sky overhead. The sky surrounds all and includes all. So the unenlightened man in his ignorance says that his religion is the only true religion and that it is the best. But when his heart is illumined by the light of true knowledge, he comes to know that above all these wars of sects and creeds is the one Existence-Knowledge-Bliss.[15]

> Coming to the Kālīghāṭ temple, some, perhaps, spend their whole time giving alms to the poor. They have no time to see the Mother in the inner shrine. First of all manage somehow to see the image of the divine Mother, even by pushing through the crowd. Thus you may or may not give alms, as you wish. You may give alms to the poor to your heart's content, if you feel that way ... *Karmayoga* is very hard indeed. In the Kaliyuga it is extremely difficult to perform the rites enjoined in the scriptures. Nowadays man's life is centred in food alone ... In the *Kali-yuga* the best way is *bhaktiyoga*, the path of devotion – singing the praises of the Lord and prayer. The path of devotion alone is the religion of this age.[16]

The core of religion is faith in God, not attachment to religious objects, as he explains:

> A man wanted to cross a river. A sage gave him an amulet and said, "This will carry you across." The man, taking it in his hand, began to walk over the water. Before he had gone half the way, he was seized with curiosity, and opened the amulet to see what was in it. Therein he found, written on a piece of paper, the sacred name of Rāma, the Lord. At this the man said depreciatingly, "Is this the whole secret?" No sooner did this scepticism

enter his mind than he sank down. It is faith in the Name of the Lord that works wonders; for faith is life and want of faith is death.[17]

He tells the famous writer Bankim Chandra Chatterje, who argued that "doing good" was the most important aspect of religion:

Charity, doing good! How dare you say you can do good to other? ... Kindness belongs to God alone. How can a man lay claim to it? Charity depends on the Will of Rāma ... If a householder gives in charity in a spirit of detachment, he is really doing good to himself and not to others. It is God alone that he serves – God who dwells in all beings, and when he serves God through all beings, he is really doing good to himself and not to others ... This is called *karmayoga*. This too is a way to realize God.[18]

Similarly in a conversation with another visitor:

Trailokya: If a man lives in the world, he must accumulate some money. He has to practice charity.

Rāmakrishna: What! First accumulation of money and then God! And how great is their charity and kindness! They spend thousands of rupees in the marriage of their daughters but the next-door neighbour with his family may be starving, and they feel constrain in giving him a handful of rice. They have to think long before doing so. While people are starving they think "Never mind, whether neighbours live or die, it is of little consequence to me; let me and my family live well!' And they talk of kindness to all beings.

Trailokya: Among householders also there are good men. Pundarika Vidyanidhi, the follower of Sri Chaitanya was a householder.

Rāmakrishna: He had drunk of the bliss of God up to his neck, had he drunk a little more he could not have lived a householder's life.[19]

He rejects the opinion of the Brahmo-Samājis, that one can serve and love God and the world at the same time:

They talk of leading a religous life while living as householders. But that is like a man sitting in a closed room with just a ray of light peeping through an aperture of the roof. Can one see the sun if the roof be overhead? What good is one ray of light? Lust and wealth are the roof. Can one see the sun without removing the roof? Worldly people are imprisoned, so to say, in the room.[20]

Swami Vivekānanda

Narendra Nath Dutt, universally known under his Samnyāsi name "Vivekānanda" carried the name of Rāmakrishna into the world and made it synonymous with a wholly new type of Hindu religious order. Born 1863 into a well-to do middle-class family, he received a modern education and expected to enter a prosperous career. When his father suddenly died he found himself in the position of sole provider for the family. Despairing and frustrated he became an "atheist." But on encountering Rāmakrishna at Dakshineswar he experienced a "conversion" and became Rāmakrishna's favorite disciple. After Rāmakrishna's death he founded, with some other fellow-devotees, the Rāmakrishna Mission. Appearing as Hindu delegate to the World Parliament of Religions in Chicago in 1993, he became world famous through his brilliant speeches, in which he presented a new kind of Hinduism that was open to the world. He became a hero for the Indians who continue to emulate his zeal and patriotism. While staunchly Hindu, he nevertheless criticized many popular Hindu beliefs and customs and admonished his fellow Hindus to change:

> The first of all worships is the worship of the Virāt – of all those around us. The first gods that we have to worship, are our own countrymen.[21]

> We must revive the old laws of the Rishis, we must initiate the whole people in the code of our old Manu and Yājñavalkya with a few modifications here and there to adjust them to the changed circumstances of the times.[22]

> I do not propose any levelling of caste. Caste is a very good thing. Caste is the plan we want to follow. What caste really means, not one in a million understands. There is no country in the world without caste. In India we reach from caste to a point where there is no caste. Caste is based throughout on that principle. The plan in India is to make everybody Brāhmaṇa, the Brāhmaṇa being the ideal of humanity. If you read the history of India you will find that attempts have always been made to raise the lower castes. Many are the classes that have been raised. Many more will follow till the whole will become Brāhmaṇa ... Indian caste is better than the caste which prevails in Europe or America. I do not say it is absolutely good. Where will you be if there were no castes? Where would be your learning and other things if there were no caste. There would be nothing left for Europeans to study if caste had never existed. The Mohammedans would have smashed everything to pieces. Where do you

find the Indian society standing still? It is always on the move. Sometimes, as in times of foreign invasions the movement has been slow, at other times quicker. Caste should not go but should be only adjusted occasionally. Within the old structure is to be found life enough for the building of two hundred thousand. It is sheer nonsense to desire the abolition of caste. The new method is – the evolution of the old.[23]

To the reformers I would point out that I am a greater reformer than any one of them. They want to reform little bits, I want root and branch reform. Where we differ is the method: theirs is the method of destruction, and mine is that of construction. I do not believe in reform, I believe in growth. I do not dare to put myself in the position of God and dictate to our society, this way thou shouldst move and not that ... This wonderful national machine has worked through ages.[24]

This is my objection against the reformers. The orthodox have more faith and more strength in themselves, in spite of their crudeness. But the reformers simply play into the hands of the Europeans and pander to their vanity. Our masses are gods as compared with those of other countries. This is the only country where poverty is not a crime. They are mentally and physically handsome.[25]

To what a ludicrous state are we brought! If a *bhaṅgi* (sweeper; an outcaste) comes to anybody as a *bhaṅgi*, he would be shunned as a plague; but no sooner does he get a cupful of water poured upon his head with some mutterings of prayers by a padri and gets a coat to his back, no matter how threadbare, and comes into the room of the most orthodox Hindu, I don't see the man who then dares refuse him a chair and a hearty shake of hands. Irony can go no further. And come and see what they, the padris are doing here in the Deccan. They are converting the lower classes by lakhs, and in Travancore, the most priest-ridden country in India, where every bit of land is owned by the Brahmins, and the females, even of the royal family, hold it as high honour to live in concubinage with the Brāhmaṇas – nearly one fourth has become Christian.[26]

Our best work is done, our greatest influence is exerted, when we are without the thought of self. All great geniuses know this. Let us open ourselves to the one Divine Actor and let Him act, and do nothing ourselves. Be perfectly resigned, perfectly unconcerned; then alone can you do any true work ...

... Those who give themselves up to the Lord do more for the world than the so-called workers. One man who has purified himself thoroughly accomplishes more than a regiment of preachers. Out of purity and silence comes the word of power. Be like a lily, stay in one place and expand your petals and the bees will come of themselves.[27]

After every happiness comes misery; they may be far apart or near. The more advanced the soul, the more quickly does one follow the other. What we want is neither happiness nor misery. Both make us forget our true nature; both are chains, one iron, another gold; behind both is the Ātman, who knows neither happiness nor misery. These are states and states must ever change; but the nature of the soul is bliss, peace, unchanging. We have not to get it, we have it; only wash away the dross and see it ...

... There is no possibility of ever having pleasure without pain, good without evil, for living itself is just the lost equilibrium. What we want is freedom, not life, nor pleasure, nor good. Creation is infinite, without beginning and without end, the ever moving ripple in an infinite lake. There are yet unreached depths and others where the equilibrium has been regained but the ripple is always progressing, the struggle to regain the balance is eternal. Life and death are only different names for the same fact, the two sides of one coin.[28]

8 HINDU NATIONALISM
HINDU JĀGARAN

Political Hinduism can claim ancient roots: In "classical India," i.e. before the coming of the Muslims, it was a matter of course that public as well as private life in the Hindu kingdoms was governed by Hindu principles, as laid down in the *Manu-smṛti* and other law books. All that changed with the coming of the Muslims and then with the British Rāj. The "Hindu Awakening" advocated by today's Hindu political parties is about a century old. It was born out of the struggle for independence from colonial rule and the fear that the end of the European domination of India could bring a return of Muslim rule.

BALGANGADHAR TILAK

The first major proponent of Hindu nationalism was Balgangadhar Tilak (1856–1920) called by the British "The Father of Indian Unrest." Like Dāyānanda Saraswatī he wanted Hinduism to be strong but also cleansed from its social evils. In a speech in Bombay 1918 he lashed out against untouchability, defended by the orthodox as part of the Hindu tradition:

> If God were to tolerate untouchability, I would not recognize Him as God at all. I do not deny that it was the Brahman rule that introduced the practice of untouchability. This is a cancer in the body of Hindu society and we must eradicate it at all costs.[1]

Tilak was also the originator of the formula which became the *mantra* of the independence movement: *Swarāj is my birthright and I will have it.*

CASTE CONFERENCES

From 1887 onwards the higher castes held so-called "Caste-Conferences" for self-protection. They wanted to save orthodox Hinduism and with it their caste privileges. The *Indian Social Reformer* commented:

> The idea of caste conferences has always been repugnant to us, even when they have for their object the prosecution of social reforms. The caste sentiment is so ingrained in the Hindu mind, it so deeply permeates every fibre of our being and it so thoroughly colours our outlook, that it seems to us the only effective course for those who wish to see this state of mind altered is resolutely to cut themselves off from anything savouring of the idea.[2]

THE SERVANTS OF INDIA SOCIETY

One of the most important and most influential organizations of a moderate political religious Hinduism around the turn of the twentieth century was the Servants of India Society, founded in 1905 in Poona by M. Gopal Krishna Gokhale. Its programme stated:

> For some time past the conviction has been forcing itself on many earnest and thoughtful minds that a stage has been reached in the work of nation-building in India, when for further progress, the devoted labours of a specially trained agency applying itself to the task in a true missionary spirit are required . . . The Servants of India Society has been established to meet in some measure those requirements of the situation. Its members frankly accept the British connection as ordained in the inscrutable dispensation of Providence, for India's good. Self-government within The Empire for their country and a higher life generally for their countrymen is their goal. This goal, they recognize, cannot be attained without years of earnest and patient effort and sacrifices worthy of the cause. Much of the work must be directed towards building up in the country a higher type of character and capacity than is generally available at present, and the advance can only be slow . . . one essential condition of success in this work is that a sufficient number of our countrymen must now come forward to devote themselves to the cause in the spirit in which religious work is undertaken. Public life must be spiritualized. Love of country must so fill the heart that all else shall appear as of little moment by its side. A fervent patriotism which rejoices at every opportunity of sacrifice for the motherland, a dauntless heart which refuses to be turned back from its object by difficulty or danger, a deep faith in the purpose of

> Providence which nothing can shake – equipped with these, the worker must start on his mission and reverently seek the joy which comes of spending oneself in the service of one's country. The Servants of India Society will train men prepared to devote their lives to the cause of the country in a religious spirit, and will seek to promote by all constitutional means, the national interests of the Indian people. Its members will direct their efforts, principally (1) towards creating among the people by example and by precept, a deep and passionate love of the motherland, seeking its highest fulfilment in service and sacrifice; (2) organizing the work of political education and agitation, basing it on a careful study, of public questions and strengthening generally the public life of the country; (3) promoting relations of cordial goodwill and co-operation among the different communities; (4) assisting educational movements, especially those for the education of women, the education of backward classes and industrial and scientific education; (5) helping forward the industrial development of the country; and (6) the elevation of the depressed classes.[3]

RABINDRANATH TAGORE (THAKUR)

Rabindranath Tagore (1861–1941) is often called "the Leonardo da Vinci of the Hindu Renaissance." In 1913 he was the first Indian to receive the Nobel prize for Literature for his collection of poems *Gītāñjalī* (English 1912). Besides writing, Tagore was active in developing Śāntiniketan, an experimental school founded by his father, into an educational institution of international rank. He painted, he composed music, and he became engaged in many social and political issues of his time. His vision of a free and independent India became an inspiration to many of his compatriots:

> Where the mind is without fear – and the head is held high, where knowledge is free; where the world has not been broken up into fragments by narrow domestic walls, where words come out from the depth of Truth, where tireless striving stretches its arms towards perfection, where the clear stream of reason has not lost its way into the dreary desert sand of dead habit, where the mind is led forward by thee into ever-widening thought and action – into that heaven of freedom my Father, let my country wake.[4]

While clearly an Indian patriot, Tagore was also a citizen of the world, encouraging his fellow citizens not to lose sight of the larger context of their lives:

> The idea of the humanity as our God, or the divinity of Man the Eternal, is the main subject of this book. This thought of God has not grown in my mind through any process of philosophical reasoning. On the contrary, it has followed the current of my temperament from early days until it suddenly flashed into my consciousness with a direct vision ... On the surface of our being we have the ever changing phases of the individual self, but in the depth there dwells the Eternal Spirit of human unity beyond our direct knowledge ... The first stage of my realization was through my feeling of intimacy with nature.
>
> I have mentioned in connection with my personal experience some songs which I had often heard from wandering village singers, belonging to a popular sect of Bengal, called Baüls, who have no images, temples, scriptures, or ceremonials, who declare in their songs the divinity of Man, and express for him an intense feeling of Love. Coming from men who are unsophisticated, living a simple life in obscurity, it gives us a clue to the inner meanings of all religions, for it suggests that these religions are never about a God of cosmic force, but rather about the God of human personality.[5]

> And I say of the Supreme Man, that he is infinite in his essence, he is finite in his manifestation in us the individuals. As the *Isopanisad* declares, a man must live his full term of life and work without greed, and thus realize himself in the Being who is in all beings. This means that he must reveal in his own personality the Supreme Person by his disinterested activities.[6]

The "forest university" Śāntiniketan was founded in 1901 as an experimental school by Maharsi Debendranath Tagore with the aim to provide an education that was close to nature and not Christian. Out of it grew in 1921 the Viśva-Bhāratī-University under the direction of Rabindranath Tagore. In its prospectus its aim and mission was described like this:

> To study the mind of man in its realization of different aspects of truth from diverse points of view. – To bring into more intimate relation with one another through patient study and research, the different cultures of the East on the basis of their underlying unity. – To approach the West from the standpoint of such a unity of the life and thought of Asia. – To seek to realize in common fellowship of study the meeting of the East and the West, and thus ultimately to strengthen the fundamental conditions of worldpeace through the establishment of free communication of ideas between the two hemispheres. – And, with such ideals in view to provide at Śāntiniketan a Centre of Culture where research into and study of the religion, literature, history, science, and art of Hindu, Buddhist, Jain,

> Islamic, Sikh, Christian, and other civilizations may be pursued along with the culture of the West, with that simplicity in externals which is necessary for true spiritual realization, in amity, and good fellowship, and co-operation between the thinkers and scholars of both Eastern and Western countries, free from all antagonisms of race, nationality, creed or caste.[7]

Rabindranath Tagore had expressed his aims like this:

> I have given an opportunity to the children to find their freedom in Nature by being able to love it. For love is freedom ... I tried to create an atmosphere in my institution, giving it the principal place in our programme of teaching.[8]

AUROBINDO GHOSE

Aurobindo Ghose (1872–1950) too, was mentioned before as a modern Śākta. He was also a prominent exponent of Hindu nationalism, as well as of a humanistic spiritual universalism.

> The true and full spiritual aim in society will regard man not as a mind, a life and a body, but as a soul incarnated for a divine fulfilment upon earth, not only in heavens beyond, which after all it need not have left if it had no divine business here in the world of physical, vital and mental nature.[9]

> A large liberty will be the law of a spiritual society and the increase of freedom a sign of the growth of human society towards the possibility of true spiritualisation.[10]

> To make all life religion and to govern all activities by the religious idea would seem to be the right way to the development of the ideal individual and ideal society and the lifting of the whole life of man into the Divine.[11]

> A spiritual religion of humanity is the hope of the future. By this is not meant what is ordinarily called a universal religion, a system, a thing of creed and intellectual belief and dogma and outward rite. Mankind has tried unity by that means; it has failed and deserved to fail, because there can be no universal religious system, one in the mental creed and in the vital form. The inner spirit is indeed one, but more than any other the spiritual life insists on freedom and variation in its self-expression and means of development. A religion of humanity means the growing realisation that there is a secret spirit, a Divine Reality, in which we are all one, that humanity is its highest present vehicle on earth, that the human race and the human being are the means by which it will progressively reveal itself here. It implies a growing attempt to live out this knowledge and bring about a kingdom of this Divine Spirit upon earth.

By its growth within us, oneness with our fellow-men will become the leading principle of all our life, not merely a principle of co-operation, but a deeper brotherhood, a real and an inner sense of unity and equality and a common life. There must be the realization by the individual that only in the life of his fellow-men is his own life complete. There must be the realization by the race that only on the free and full life of the individual can its own perfection and permanent happiness be founded. There must be too a discipline and a way of salvation in accordance with this religion, that is to say, a means by which it can be developed by each man within himself so that it may be developed in the life of the race.[12]

The greatness of the ancient Indian civilization consists in the power with which it did this work and the high and profound wisdom and skill with which, while basing society, ordering the individual life, encouraging and guiding human nature and prosperity, it turned them all towards the realization of its master idea and never allowed the mind it was training to lose sight of the use of life as a passage to the infinite and a discipline for spiritual perfection.[13]

Freedom and harmony express the two necessary principles of variation and oneness – freedom of the individual, the group, the race, coordinated harmony of the individual's forces and of the efforts of all the individuals in the group, of all groups in the race, of all races in the kind – and these are the two conditions of healthy progression and successful arrival.[14]

MAHĀTMĀ GANDHI

Mohandas Karamchand Gandhi (1869–1947), probably the best known Indian of the twentieth century, understood his engagement for Indian Independence always as an act of worship and saw himself first and foremost a religious educator, a reformer of Hinduism. His ultimate aim was to establish Rāmarājya in India, the Kingdom of God on earth. The means to do so was *satyāgraha*, "truth-grasping," based on *ahiṃsā*, "non-violence" and unshakable faith in God.

Let me state my faith: As a Congressman, wishing to keep the Congress intact, I advise suspension of non-cooperation, for I see that the nation is not ready for it. But as an individual I cannot, will not do so, as long as the Government remains what it is. It is not merely a policy with us, it is an article of faith. Non-Cooperation and Civil Disobedience are but different branches of the same tree, called *satyāgraha*. It is my *kalpadruma*, my *Jam-i-Jam*, the Universal Provider. *Satyāgraha* is search for truth, and God is Truth. *Ahiṃsā* or non-violence is the light that reveals that Truth to me. Therefore, I cannot and will not hate the

> Englishmen. Nor will I bear their yoke. I must fight unto death the unholy attempt to impose British methods and British institutions on India. But I combat the attempt with non-violence . . . I have repeatedly stated that *satyāgraha* never fails and that one perfect *satyāgrahi* is enough to vindicate Truth . . . *Satyāgraha* is an attribute of the spirit within. It is latent in every one of us. Like *Swarāj* it is our birthright. Let us know it.[15]

A crucial ingredient of Gandhi's freedom struggle was his call for *svadeśi*, the exclusive use of articles produced in India, thereby eliminating India's economic dependence from outside.

> *Svadeśi* is that spirit in us which restricts us to the use and service of our immediate surroundings to the exclusion of the more remote. Thus as for religion, in order to satisfy the requirements of the definition, I must restrict myself to my ancestral religion, that is, the use of my immediate religious surrounding. If I find it defective I should serve it by purging it of all defects.[16]

Contrary to other Hindu reformers, Gandhi was not against caste:

> *Varṇāśrama dharma* defines man's mission on this earth. He is not born day after day to explore avenues for amassing riches and to explore different means of livelihood, on the contrary man is born in order that he may utilize every atom of his energy for the purpose of holding body and soul together, to the occupation of his forefathers. That and nothing more or nothing less is *varṇāśrama dharma*.[17]

> I believe that if Hindu society has been able to stand, it is because it is founded on the caste system. The seeds of *Swarāj* are to be found in the caste system . . . I believe that inter-dining and inter-marriage are not necessary for promoting national unity . . . Caste is another name for control . . . The caste system is a natural order of society. In India it has been given a religious coating . . . I oppose all those who are out to destroy the caste system.[18]

His notion of *ahiṃsā* implied not only the abstention from harming others but active engagement on behalf of all.

> Non-violence is an active force of the highest order. It is soul force or the power of Godhead within us. Imperfect man cannot grasp the whole of that Essence – he would not be able to bear its full blaze, but even an infinitesimal fraction of it, when it becomes active within us, can work wonders.[19]

Gandhi did not want any "Gandhianism" to survive him:

> I lay claim to nothing exclusively divine in me. I do not claim prophetship. I am but a humble seeker after Truth and bent upon finding it. I count no sacrifice too great for the sake of seeing God face to face. The whole of my activity whether it may be called social, political, humanitarian or ethical is directed to that end. And as I know that God is found more often on the lowliest of His creatures than in the high and mighty, I am struggling to reach the status of these. I cannot do so without their service. Hence my passion for the service of the suppressed classes.[20]

> There is no such thing as "Gandhism," and I do not want to leave any sect after me. I do not claim to have originated any new principle or doctrine. I have simply tried in my own way to apply the eternal truths to our daily life and problems ... The opinions I have formed and the conclusions I have arrived at are not final. I may change them tomorrow. I have nothing new to teach the world. Truth and non-violence are as old as the hills. All I have done is to try experiments in both on as vast a scale as I could do. In doing so I have sometimes erred and learned by my errors. Life and its problems have thus become to me so many experiments in the practice of truth and non-violence. By instinct I have been truthful, but not non-violent ... In fact it was in the course of my pursuit of truth that I discovered non-violence.[21]

> There is the danger of your Sangh [i.e. the Gandhi-Seva-Sangh] deteriorating in a sect. Whenever there is any difficulty you will turn to my writings in *Young India* and *Harijan* and swear by them. As a matter of fact my writings should be cremated with my body. What I have done will endure, not what I have said or written ... I want you to face the problems that will come before you this week in the spirit of what I have said ... Forget me therefore, my name is an unnecessary adjunct to the name of the Sangh.[22]

> Let Gandhism be destroyed if it stands for error. Truth and *ahiṃsā* will never be destroyed, but if Gandhism is another name for sectarianism it deserves to be destroyed. If I were to know, after my death, that what I stood for had degenerated into sectarianism, I should be deeply pained. We have to work away silently. Let no one say that he is a follower of Gandhi. It is enough that I should be my own follower. I know what an inadequate follower I am of myself, for I cannot live up to the convictions I stand for. You are not followers but fellow students, fellow pilgrims, fellow seekers, fellow workers. We have to make truth and non-violence not matters for mere individual practice but for practice by groups and communities and nations.[23]

When questioned how he knew that what he was doing was the right thing, Gandhi always referred to the "still small voice within," a *daimonion* that guided him when all other means failed:

> What then is Truth? A difficult question, but I have solved it for myself by saying that it is what the voice within tells you.[24]

> I have no special revelation of God's will. My firm belief is, that He reveals Himself daily to every human being, but we shut our ears to the still small voice. We shut our eyes to the Pillar of Fire in front of us. I realize His omnipresence.[25]

> I will give you a talisman. Whenever you are in doubt, or when the self becomes too much with you, apply the following test: recall the face of the poorest and the weakest man whom you may have seen and ask yourself if the step that you contemplate is going to be of any use to *him*. Will he gain anything by it? Will it restore him to a control over his own life and destiny? In other words, will it lead to Swarāj (self-rule) for the hungry and spiritually starving millions? Then you will find your doubts and your self melting away.[26]

> There come to us moments in life when about some things we need no proof from without. A little voice within tells us, "You are on the right track, move neither to your left nor right, but keep to the straight and narrow way."[27]

> There are moments in your life when you must act even though you cannot carry your best friends with you. The "still small voice" within you must always be the final arbiter when there is a conflict of duty.[28]

VINOBA BHAVE

When Gandhi began, on October 17, 1940, his Individual Satyāgraha he made Vinoba Bhave, one of his most loyal followers, head of this movement. Later Vinoba Bhave initiated an ambitious social reform program on a voluntary basis and after Gandhi's death was considered his legitimate heir. He propagated *Sarvodaya*, "uplift of all" as the solution of India's and the world's social and economic ills:

> Those who believe in Mahātmā Gandhi's ideology decide to form themselves into a Brotherhood.
> Name: *Sarvodaya Samāj* (*Sarvodaya* means the "welfare of all," *Samāj* is "brotherhood.")

Aim: to strive towards a society based on Truth and Non-violence in which there will be no distinctions of class and creed, no opportunity for exploitation, and full scope for the development of both individuals as well as groups.

Basic Principle: insistence on the purity of the means as well as that of the end.

Programme: for the achievement of the aim, the following programme is to be worked:

1. Communal harmony (friendship between followers of different faith and sects).
2. Abolition of class distinctions.
3. Prohibition.
4. Promotion of cottage industries.
5. Village Sanitation.
6. Basic Education.
7. Equality of status and rights for both men and women.
8. Health and cleanliness.
9. Economic equality.
10. Development of agriculture.
11. Organization of labour.
12. Welfare of aboriginals.
13. Organization of students.
14. Service of lepers.
15. Relief work.
16. Naturopathy.
17. Other similar activities.

These items are mainly for India. Programmes for different countries can be drawn up in accordance with local conditions.

Membership: whoever accepts the above aim and the basic principle and tries to work them out is eligible for the membership of the Samāj. On sending his name and address to the Secretary, he will be registered as a member of the *Sarvodaya Samāj*.

Sarvodaya Day: in order to propagate the ideal of *Sarvodaya*, the 30th January (the day of Gandhijis passing away) shall be observed at all places as the *Sarvodaya* day.

Sarvodaya Conference: in order to facilitate mutual contacts and exchange of views among the members, there shall be an Annual Conference in April, during the National Week.

Function: the functions of the *Samāj* will be advisory and not mandatory.

Committee: to carry on and promote the work of the *Sarvodaya Samāj*, a Sub-Committee has been nominated by the *Sarva Seva Saṅgha*. The function of the Committee is to maintain a register of members of the *Samāj* and generally act as a liaison between the *Samāj* and its members

> and otherwise to implement the resolution of the Conference relating to the formation of the *Sarvodaya Samāj*.[29]

> I submit therefore, in all humility, that Marx is today out of date and Manu's Code has, of course, no value; even Gandhi's thought, as developed by him within his lifetime, cannot solve our contemporary problems. The whole of our social fabric has undergone vast changes during this decade; particularly our political patterns are completely outmoded and retrograde in relation to the needs of the hour.[30]

> In a capitalist society even personal virtue becomes a monopoly of the few, like any other natural resource; stoicism is associated with the *sādhu* or ascetic, truth with the *rishi* or sage and non-violence with the *yogi* or philosopher. Now this monopolistic ownership has also to be divested; and human qualities have to become the common attribute of the community as a whole.[31]

He is contrasting his ideal of *Loka-śakti* (people/civil power) with the present rule of *Hiṃsā-sakti* (violence/military power) and *Daṇḍa-śakti* (punitive/legal power of the state):

> In this society, call it *Sarvodaya* society for want of a better name, everybody who eats would be enjoined to do productive physical labour. All who eat would work and all who work would eat. Each would work according to his or her capacity and get according to his or her need.[32]

> At least, I for one, see the salvation of India through only this double-edged weapon, namely freedom from the lure of money and performance of body-labour. In it I see the acme of Gandhiji's philosophy, a synthesis with Communism and an antidote to both Communism and Capitalism.[33]

He articulates the philosophy of *Bhūdān* as follows:

1. Property or means of production to be owned by society.
2. Distinction between manual and intellectual work must go.
3. Productive physical labour must be regularly performed by everybody be he an intellectual or an administrator.
4. No arms to be used in self-defence.

Vinoba always believed in the good in humankind:

> A man's heart is always good at the core. It may get rusted on the outside on account of various internal factors but its goodness remains always the same, whatever the outward appearance. It is like the head of a cabbage whose outer layer may be bad but the inside layers retain their freshness.

> The workers should have firm faith in this internal goodness and strive to reach for it, undismayed by outer appearances.
>
> Man is born through love, he grows through love, he thirsts for it in his last moments and feels supremely comforted when he gets it. If, therefore, his entire life, in its beginning, the middle and the end, depends upon love, if that is for him the source of his greatest delight, why would he not feel prompted to participate in *Bhoodān* and *Sampatti-Dān*, which are but an aspect of this all-embracing law of love, and give to his poorer brethren a due share of what he has in land and wealth?[34]

When he was refused entry to the main temple at Jagannath Puri because he was accompanied by a European woman, he stated:

> I believe that if Hinduism were to confine itself to its own people and cling to its narrow groove it would give a mortal blow to its own self and would be simply destroyed.[35]

Vinoba Bhave's volunteers went out to the villages to prepare for his coming. Those *Loka-Sevaks* (people-servants) had to sign the following pledge:

1. I believe in truth, non-violence and non-possession and I will endeavour to the best of my ability to live up to them.
2. I believe that real freedom can be realized by the awakening of the *Loka-nīti* (the universal law of humanity). Therefore I will not associate myself with any king of politics in any form.
3. I will ever serve with a spirit of devotion and self-sacrifice without expecting anything in return.
4. I pledge myself to work for the abolition of all differences of caste, class and creed.
5. I will devote most of my time and thought to the realization of the *Sarvodaya*-ideal through non-violent revolution based on *Bhoodān* (which has now developed into *Grāmdan*) and supported by village industries.[36]

THE HINDŪ MAHĀSABHĀ

The Hindū Mahāsabhā, founded in 1909 by Pandit Mohan Malaviya, was the first political party in India that campaigned on a Hindu platform. Its *Election Manifesto* of 1966, repeating much of its early program, proclaimed:

Hindustan is the land of the Hindus from times immemorial. The Hindū Mahāsabhā believes that Hindus have a right to live in peace as Hindus, to legislate, to rule, to govern themselves in accordance with Hindu genius and ideals and establish by all lawful and legal means a Hindu State, based on Hindu Culture and tradition, so that Hindu Ideology and way of life should have a Homeland of its own.

The Hindū Mahāsabhā comprises in its fold all those who call themselves Hindus, irrespective of their religion of Bhāratīya origin, caste and creed and language, united for the purpose of building up a true Democracy with a dynamic force and progressive conception capable of assimilating all modern scientific inventions and modern social economic thoughts.

"One who regards this land of Bhārat from Indus to the Seas as his fatherland as well as holy land is a Hindu."

The cardinal creed of Hindū Mahāsabhā is:

1. Loyalty to the unity and integrity of Hindustan.
2. Hindū Mahāsabhā reiterates once again that it is pledged to the re-establishment of Akhand Bhārat by all legitimate means and it shall try its level best to undo the mischief and betrayal of the Congress in partitioning the country on the basis of religion.

The re-unification of Hindustan is an article of faith for Hindū Mahāsabhā and it stands by it. Passage of time neither changes its creed nor shakes its confidence in its ultimate realisation of its ideals.

The Hindū Mahāsabhā reiterates its clarion call, as given by Vir Savarkar as far back as 1939, "Hinduise Politics and Militarise Hinduism."

In the past the people of the country ignored the warnings and suggestions of Hindū Mahāsabhā with fatal consequences for the nation. There would have been no Pakistan today if the people had paid heed to the policy and programme of the Hindū Mahāsabhā.

Hindū Mahāsabhā is of the considered opinion that the present Constitution is altogether unsuited to the genius of the people of Hindustan, as it is a mere collection of disjointed fragments from various heterogenous constitutions of different countries of the Western World, like the U.S.A., Britain, France, etc., and there is hardly anything "Indian" about it.

The present Constitution of India suffers from a serious lacuna in as much as it fails to define its moral and ethical inspiration, thereby leading to a serious decline in the moral values of respect for the nation as a whole.

Hindū Mahāsabhā therefore stands for recasting the Constitution of the country with a view to bring it in consonance with the tradition and culture of the Hindus to make it a truly democratic Hindu State.

> The Hindū Mahāsabhā considers it absolutely essential to amend the present Constitution in such a way as to make it binding on the Central and/or State Government to ban the slaughter of cows, calves, bulls and bullocks of every age and condition, under all circumstances, by law.
>
> The Hindū Mahāsabhā stands for social and economic justice with its moorings in the moral and spiritual past of this sacred land. Hindū Mahāsabhā believes that all sections of the society of this country should get equality of opportunity in life and are assured of a decent standard of living. The Hindū Mahāsabhā aspires to create a social order based on "Hindutva" which advocates class-coordination and social-consciousness, as against class-conflict and individual consciousness advocated by the other political parties who constantly harp on only material and selfish gain.
>
> The industrial, agricultural, labour and other economic programmes of the Mahāsabhā are based on the aforesaid principles, which suit the genius of the people and on which the Hindu nation and civilisation have survived for thousands of years.
>
> The Hindū Mahāsabhā stands for the restoration of all Hindu temples like those of Śrī Viśvanāthji in Vārāṇasī, Śrī Rāma Janmabhūmī in Ayodhyā, and Śrī Krishna Janmabhūmī in Mathurā etc. which are now in illegal possession of Moslems and the Mahāsabhā aspires to repair and renovate all Hindu temples as far as possible.
>
> Hindū Mahāsabhā stands for Hindu, Hindī and Hindustan – where a Hindu way of life is to be re-established. Our emphasis is not on materialism but on spiritualism. A social and economic order, based on Hindu view of life, can only stabilise the present imbalanced structure of Bharat, – nay of the world.[37]

THE RĀṢṬRĪYA SVAYAMSEVAK SAṄGH (R.S.S.)

Hindu nationalists always had a sense of divine mission. They believed that Hindus were a chosen people and that Hindu *dharma* was there to save the whole world. M. S. Golwalkar, the second Sarsaṅghachalak of the R.S.S., wrote:

> The mission of reorganising the Hindu people on the lines of their unique national genius which the Saṅgh has taken up is not only a great process of true national regeneration of Bharat but also the inevitable precondition to realise the dream of world unity and human welfare ... It is the grand world-unifying thought of Hindus alone that can supply the abiding basis for human brotherhood ... This knowledge is in the safe custody of the Hindus alone. It is a divine trust given to the charge of the Hindus by destiny.[38]

The same ideas have recently been echoed by A. Chatterjee: "We Hindus are not just a religious community like the Mohammedan and the Christian but a nation unto ourselves. The term 'Hindu' is the name of our nationality." He goes on expanding this notion: "The traditional homeland of Hindus is Bhāratavarsha. It is a quite distinct geographical entity ... It appears as if Nature, or the Supreme Being if you like, has specially created this country as the motherland of a particular nation." The foreign bodies on Hindu soil are Islam and Christianity. The author compares Muslims and Christians to "drug-addicts" because of the "foreign culture" they subscribe to. He complains about "those baneful ideologies – Islam and Christianity – which have created in the minds of some of our own people, a hostility against their original culture."[39]

> The basic notes of Christian theology are not very different from that of Islam, but considerable liberalism now sweeps across the Christian societies of the world so that by and large it has ceased to be important for the Christians now to really believe in their theology. We can, therefore, find a large number of persons among Christians in India ... who may be following the mode of worship of alien religions, but who have retained a reverence for *sanātana dharma*, a sentiment for the culture of their ancestors, a cognition in their minds of the nationality of Hindus, and an emotional bond with its distinctive features. Such persons continue to be part of the Hindu nation.[40]

THE BHĀRATĪYA JANATĀ PARTY (B.J.P.)

Often Hindu politicians use the term *Rāmarājya* instead of *Hindu rāṣṭra*. Thus L. K. Advani, the charismatic leader of the B.J.P. wrote:

> Śrī Rāma is the unique symbol, the unequalled symbol of our integration, as well as of our aspiration to live the higher values. As Maryāda Purushottama Śrī Rāma has represented for thousands of years the ideal of conduct, just as Rāma Rājya has always represented the ideal of governance.[41]

Also the figure of Kṛṣṇa as statesman is emphasized. Not only is his historicity affirmed, also his rule is praised as

> not based on force but on renouncing, truth, compassion, justice, and humanity. His only aim is universal wellbeing (*abhyudaya kalyāṇ*). Kṛṣṇa's political science would be a cure from the universal selfishness of today and the frightful wars of our time.[42]

V. A. Pai Panandiker, Director of the Centre for Policy research in New Delhi, holds that *dharma* was also "a central concern" of his Centre: "*Dharma* in that sense goes even beyond human rights and democracy."[43] C. Badrinath, a researcher at the Centre, declares: "The true identity of Indian civilization has been dharmic and not 'Hindu' nor was there ever any such thing as 'Hinduism'" (which he calls an invention of Christian missionaries).[44]

> The one concern from which everything in Indian thought flowed, and on which every movement of life ultimately depended, is *dharma*, order. Not any positivistic order, but the order that is inherent in all. *Dharma* means that, whereby whatever lives, is sustained, upheld and supported. It is a secular view of life, not a "religious" one, but it is not secularism either. It cuts across the religious-secular polarity of Western thought.[45]

Clearly distancing himself from modern Western notions and trying to meet Hindu nationalists halfway he goes on:

> The *dharmic* culture ... attached utmost importance to the proper use of words, which, if used carelessly, must invoke wrong things, create wrong perceptions and bring about false consciousness. The use of the word "religion" in relation to Indian civilisation has had that effect in modern India, leading to much conflict and disorder. *Dharma* is not religion. Indian civilisation is not "religious." Religion is by nature divisive, *dharma* unites.[46]

9 OPPOSITION TO HINDU NATIONALISM

THE DALITS ("OPPRESSED")

The major opposition against Hindu nationalism today seems to come from the Dalits who have organized themselves and are representing the former untouchables, outcastes, "scheduled castes" (or whatever names were given to the lowest strata of Hindu society). They number over 200 million. Not all of them are organized and those who are organized belong to various, often mutually competing groups. Anti-Hindu sentiments have a history among these people: Dr Ambedkar, a Mahar (sweeper-caste), publicly rejected Hinduism in the 1930's and with thousands of fellow-Mahars embraced Buddhism. While Ambedkar had demanded a total abolition of caste (and on these grounds became a bitter enemy of Mahātmā Gandhi who wanted to induct the "Harijans" into the Śūdra caste) the new leaders are now promoting a new "caste identity theory."

V. T. Rajashekhar, the editor of *Dalit Voice* (a Bangalore fortnightly newspaper) recently proclaimed:

> Each caste is a nationality and unless each nationality is assured its share in all spheres, India's democratic structure, unity and integrity cannot be ensured. That means the entire bullshit built by our "Hindu nation" heroes, their drummer boys in the "national" toilet papers and academic circles falls to the ground. India is not a "nation" but a conglomeration of "nations" in which the basic building brick is caste (*jāti*). It is caste that is emerging as the "nation" in India. There is no "Hindu nation." There is

> no other nation. Each caste is a nation. Caste cannot be destroyed and hence we have to live with it ... Even Muslim and Christian delegates admitted the pull of caste in their religions and the fact that religion does not bind the followers of that religion. Strengthen every *jāti*, brahmins will be dead soon.[1]

HINDU SECULARISM

Under the leadership of Jawaharlal Nehru the Indian Congress adopted at its meeting in Karachi 1931 the resolution that in free India "(t)he State shall observe neutrality in regard to all religions." Nehru, the "secular Hindu," was very critical both of the popular Hinduism of his day and its religious leaders whom he accused of obscurantism. He believed that the role of religion would diminish in proportion to India's economic growth. This was not to be the case.

Secularism was enshrined in the preamble to the Indian Constitution in a 1977 amendment, that declared India a "Sovereign Socialist Secular Democratic Republic." Indian secularism is quite different from European secularism, as the following statement by Dr Shankar Dayal Sharma, at that time Vice-President of India, explains:

> Secularism in the Indian ethos is a matter of basic relevance to our polity and to the contribution that our country can make towards a better future for the world as a whole. Our understanding of this word, however, is vastly different from that in the West ... We in India understand secularism to denote *Sarva Dharma Sambhava* (the co-existence of all religions), an approach of tolerance and understanding of the equality of all religions.
>
> The *Ṛgveda* propounds: "Truth is one, the learned may describe it differently." Thus a core idea of secular thought is expressed, recognising the many paths of logical and intuitive access to absolute truth, acknowledging and providing a conceptual basis to a philosophy of the co-existence of all religions whereby apparently different bodies of religious thoughts are seen as converging to the same and only truth.
>
> The *Bhagavadgītā* clearly states: "Behave with others as you would with yourself. Look upon all the living beings as your friends, for in all of them there resides one soul. All are but part of that universal soul. A person who believes that all are his soul-mates and loves them all alike, never feels lonely. Divine qualities of such a person such as forgiveness, compassion and service will make him lovable in the eyes of his associates. He will experience intense joy throughout his life."

> Thus a philosophical and ethnological composite is provided by ancient Indian thought for developing secular thought and outlook. This enlightenment is the true nucleus of what is now known as Hinduism. An enormously powerful and humanistic body of secular thought formed the true substance of Hinduism – and should be recognised as such.[2]

After appreciative comments about the contributions of each of the major religious communities towards a "secular ethos" he concluded:

> In recent years there has been a Wrealisation of the need to separate religion from politics. The issue has received attention by intellectuals and activists. It is important to be clear about what is intended when sensible and patriotic people talk of keeping religion and politics separate. The objective, in my view, should be to prevent communalism from entering politics. Communal opportunism has to be kept away from our political affairs. That is very necessary. But communalism should not be confused with religion. The history of our secular ethos tells us so ...
>
> Secularism in the Indian ethos is a matter that requires to be nurtured by every citizen every day in all his actions. This feature of our national polity has an importance which is not confined to our nation alone. There is a message in it to all the peoples and the nations of the world, indicating the path for a better future for humankind.[3]

10 THE NEW UNIVERSAL HINDU GURUS

While the traditional Hindu *saṃpradāyas* continue to flourish and to attract millions to their regular temple-worship routines and festivities, a new independent type of *guru* has recently arisen in India whose authority is not based on the ordination within a traditional *saṃpradāya* or the headship of an important temple complex, but on charisma and personal achievement. Their number is fairly large; some have reached national, or even international prominence. Their teaching is eclectic, idiosyncratic, ecumenical, addressing contemporary social and political issues. Their influence is considerable and in many ways they represent "contemporary Hinduism" better than academic philosophers or heads of major traditional religious institutions. The few names mentioned here stand for a very large number of contemporary *gurus* who are reaching out to many millions in India and abroad.

SWĀMI RĀMA TĪRTHA

Swāmi Rāma Tīrtha (1873–1906) relinquished his position in the mathematics department at Forman College, Lahore in 1901 in order to teach Vedānta in Japan and the U.S.A. where he gained a large following. His teaching is practical and to the point:

> The bullock of the oil machine goes round and round its limited circle for the whole day, and in spite of his hard labour, he remains where he was, and does not advance even an inch. Similarly the worldly man remains engrossed in his family affairs, day and night, like the bullock of an oil

machine, but does not know where he is going to and what he is aiming at. Yes, but at the time of his death, when he realizes that he has wasted his whole life for nothing, it is then too late. He then weeps and repents for his failure, but in vain. Ultimately he dies in pain and anguish with repentance. O man, engrossed in family snares, remember that this world is not the place of rest. Here you have to work and to be progressive. Spread your hands to embrace others. Increase your fellow-feeling and love for all, so that your limited circle of selfish life may expand unlimitedly to become a straight line, and so that your life may follow the straight path of righteousness. Advance, advance and be progressive, till you leave this transitory world and its affairs far behind.[1]

There is, no doubt, something in human existence which is specially connected with religion and its goal. It is "Reality." But "Reality" is no part of human existence, rather human existence can be (so to say) called a part of that "Reality." The "Reality" is an endless ocean in which human beings are like waves. That "Reality" is named *ātma* [self] in Hindu scriptures. It is All-pervading and Omnipresent.

As regards the connection between the *ātma*, the Real Self, and the individual limited self, it is stated in the Hindu scriptures that "to rise above names and forms and to give up the limitations of body, mind and intellect, is to become All Knowledge, All Bliss and All Energy." For example, the bubbles and the waves of the river, on giving up their names and forms, are in reality pure water which is sweet, crystal clear, all-pervading and interpenetrating.[2]

RAMAṆA MAHARṢI

Ramaṇa Maharṣi (1879–1950) was one of the most widely recognized Hindu mystics of our age. He discovered Advaita Vedānta through his own experiences without the help of books or teachers. His own method of teaching consisted in relentlessly asking everyone who visited him: "Who are you?"

The world is real for the ignorant as well as for the wise; for the ignorant the Real is measured by the world, for one who knows the Real has no limits and is the foundation of the world. Both say "I" referring to themselves – the ignorant and the one who knows. For the ignorant the self is defined by the body, the wise knows that within the body the unlimited Self shines with its own splendour.[3]

Is the world real? Is it an illusion? With form? Without form? Conscious or unconscious? Is it joy or pain? Why worry about it! Search for your self! When you wake up, the world wakes up for you; when you fall asleep, where is it? First find out who it is through whom the world exists for you. Who is the knower? Who is ignorant? The one who knows? The one who knows not? What does it mean to know the self? Not to know the self? Knowledge and ignorance are only known in relation to each other. Knowledge of whom? Ignorance of what? This is the real question. No one is bound except by the ideas of "bound" and "unbound." Find out who is bound; if no one is bound, what then is liberation? Is liberation formless or with form? Or both with and without form? Thus discuss the pandits. When the "I," that discusses it, is no more to be found, what has happened to "liberation?"[4]

SATHYA SĀĪ BĀBĀ

Sathya Sāī Bābā (b. 1926) is probably the best known living Hindu charismatic teacher today. He is credited with having worked many miraculous healings, and people in their thousands come to have his *darśan* and to listen to his words. There are thousands of Sāī Bābā communities all over the world, prominently of course in India. Many of his utterances have been published.

Just as you seek the udder of the cow for the milk it gives, seek the Lord and His Glory only in nature. As a matter of fact, Nature is useful only when it adds to the wonder and awe that it is able to provoke and sustain. Everything is an image of the Lord. Krishna revelled in seeing His own images in the Mani Mantapa of His house, when He was a child. Just as the Lord is pleased when He sees Himself in His manifestations called Nature. That is why there is such a joy welling up in all when they hear the story of the Lord and how He calls all to Himself. It is the call of the *bimba* [image] for the *pratibimba* [original], to merge in it. So all are entitled to the merging, all finally have to attain it. Otherwise there is no meaning for the yearning to become greater and greater.[5]

Experience of the Divine must be sought in the company of good people. It is an illusion to imagine that you can see God in some temple or shrine or in some kind of meditation. Only in the Divine manifesting in a human form can you experience the Divine. If one cannot experience the Divine in a living human being, how can one experience it in an inanimate stone? It is only when one perceives with love that one realises one's true nature.[6]

Life is only relatively real; until death, it appears to be real, that is all. For the procession of the bride and groom, the father of the bride had brought an elephant, or rather the model of an elephant, correct to the minutest detail. The model was taken by all who saw it to be alive. Then, while all were admiring the wonderful work of art and arguing that it was alive, it

> exploded, shooting forth lovely little stars and snakes of light that gleamed through the sky. It was filled with fireworks, and when it was lit, the entire stock filling the inside emerged, with a burst of noise and a brilliant riot of light and colour.
>
> Man is like that elephant, true, until the explosion. Before the explosion happens, man must realise himself. The fireworks are *kāma* [lust], *krodha* [anger], *moha* [delusion], *mada* [intoxication] etc. and they now fill this artificial animal, useful only for the show. Man is saved from such calamity by Vedānta. Vedānta is like the roar of the lion, it gives courage and enterprise, it makes man a hero.[7]

> Make four resolutions about your life. Purity: desist from wicked thoughts, bad habits, low activities that weaken your self-respect. Service: serve others, for they are the reflections of the same Entity of which you are yourself a reflection. No one of you has any authenticity, except with reference to the One Original. Mutuality: feel always kinship with all creation. See the same current flowing through all the objects in the universe. Truth: do not deceive yourself or others, by distorting your experience.[8]

> Take Hanuman as your example in *seva* [service]. He served Rāma, the Prince of Righteousness, regardless of obstacles of all types. Though he was strong, learned and virtuous, he had no trace of pride. When asked who he was by the Rakṣasas in Laṅka into which he had entered so daringly, he described himself, in all humility, as "the servant of Rāma." That is a fine example of uprooting of the ego, which *seva* must bring about in us. No one can serve another while his ego is rampant. The attitudes of mutual help and selfless service develop the "humanness" of man and help the unfoldment of the divinity latent in him.[9]

ĀNANADAMAYĪ MĀ

Ānanadamayī Mā (1896–1983) was probably the best known female *guru* and religious leader in her time. Virtually illiterate and growing up in a small village in Bengal, she intuitively grasped profound religious notions and after initiating herself started teaching a large number of men and women what had been revealed to her. There are many Ānanadamayī Centres in India and abroad.

> Be it the perusal of Sacred texts, listening to religious disourses, engaging in *kīrtan* – God must be the alpha and omega of whatever is done. When reading, read about Him, when talking, talk of Him and when singing, sing His praises. These three practices are intrinsically the same; but because people respond differently, the same is expressed in three different

ways to suit each person's temperament and capacity for assimilation. Essentially there is only He and He alone, although everyone has his own spiritual path that leads to Him. What is the right path for each, depends on his personal predilection, based on the specific character of his inner qualifications.

Take for instance the study of Vedānta. Some seekers become completely drowned in it. Just as others may so lose themselves in *kīrtan* as to fall into a trance, a student of Vedānta may become wholly absorbed in his texts, even more so than the one who gets carried away by *kīrtan*. According to one's specific line of approach, one will be able to achieve full concentration through the study of a particular Scripture, or by some other means.[10]

A man's belief is greatly influenced by his environment; therefore he should choose the company of the Holy and Wise. Belief means to believe in one's Self, disbelief to mistake the non-Self for one's Self.

There are instances of Self-realization occurring by the Grace of God, whereas at other times it can be seen that he awakens in some feverish yearning after Truth. In the first case, attainment comes spontaneously, in the second it is brought about by trials. But all is wrought solely by His mercy.

Man thinks he is the doer of his actions, while actually everything is managed from "There;" the connection is "There," as well as the powerhouse – yet people say: "I do." How wonderful it is![11]

Always bear in mind: everything is in God's hands, and you are His tool to be used by Him as He pleases. Try to grasp the significance of "all is His," and you will immediately feel free from all burdens. What will be the result of your surrender to Him? None will seem alien, all will be your very own, your Self.[12]

By virtue of the Guru's power everything becomes possible; therefore seek a Guru. Meanwhile, since all names are His Name, all forms His Form, select one of them and keep it with you as your constant companion. At the same time he is also nameless and formless; for the Supreme it is possible to be everything and yet nothing. So long as you have not found a Guru, adhere to the Name or Form of Him that appeals to you most, and ceaselessly pray that He may reveal Himself to you as the *sadguru*. In very truth the Guru dwells within, and unless you discover the inner Guru, nothing can be achieved. If you feel no desire to turn to God, bind yourself by a daily routine of *sādhana*, as school children do, whose duty it is to follow a fixed time-table.[13]

Within the twenty-four hours of the day, some time must be definitely dedicated to God. Resolve, if possible, to engage regularly in *japa* of a particular name or *mantra* while sitting in a special posture, and gradually add to the time or the number of repetitions. In this way try to bind yourself to the Quest of God; wherever you may be, take refuge in Him, let Him be your goal. When by virtue of this endeavour you become deeply immersed in that current and devote ever more time to it, you will be transformed and your appetite for sense-enjoyment will grow feeble; thus you will reap the fruit of your accumulated effort. You may also come to feel that the body is liable to depart at any time, that death may arrive at any moment.[14]

A stage does exist in meditation where intense joy is felt, where one is as if submerged in it. But what is it that gets submerged? The mind, of course. At a certain level and under certain circumstances this experience may prove an obstacle. If repeated time and again, one may stagnate at its particular level and thereby be prevented from getting a taste of the Essence of Things.

Once genuine contemplation has been established, worldly attractions lose all their appeal. In the event of an experience pertaining to Supreme Reality or to the Self, one does not say: "Where have I been? I did not know anything for the time being." There can be no such thing as "not knowing." If it is possible to describe in words the bliss one has experienced, it is still enjoyment and therefore a hindrance. One must be fully conscious, wide awake. To fall into stupor or into yogic sleep will not take one anywhere. After real meditation worldly pleasures become unalluring, dull, entirely savourless.

What does *vairāgya* [renunciation] signify? When every single object of the world kindles, as it were, the fire of renunciation, so as to make one recoil as from a shock, then there is inward and outward awakening. This, however, does not mean that *vairāgya* implies aversion or contempt for anything in the world – it simply is unacceptable, the body refuses it. Neither dislike nor anger will arise. When *vairāgya* becomes a living inspiration, one begins to discriminate as to the true nature of the world, until finally, with the glowing certainty of direct perception, the knowledge of its illusoriness arises. Each and everything belonging to the world seems to burn; one cannot touch it. This also is a state that may ensue at a particular time.[15]

CONCLUSION

The reader who has completed this guided tour through the many exhibits that illustrate the long and rich history of Hinduism will have discovered recurring images and themes and also new and surprising developments at every stage. Throughout its very long history Hinduism has demonstrated amazing resilience against outside influences and at the same time a great power of assimilation of new elements. It has preserved precious insights of ancient seers and has produced bold minds that help shape the present. Becoming familiar with Hinduism makes us not only learn about its many expressions but also learn from them for our own benefit.

NOTES

CHAPTER 1

1. *Ṛgveda* I, 32. The first complete metric English translation was published by R. T. H. Griffith, a former principal of Benares Sanskrit College, in 1889. Reprinted in the Chowkhamba Sanskrit Studies vols XXXV, XXXVI, Varanasi 1963. The most scholarly complete translation of the *Ṛgveda* into a modern European language is deemed to be the German translation (with ample notes) by H. F. Geldner, *Der Ṛgveda*, (Harvard Oriental Series, vols 33, 34, 35, Cambridge, MA, 1955–57) which is in the process of being translated into English.
2. *Bṛhaddevatā* VI, 109–129. English trans. (with notes) by A. A. MacDonell, Harvard Oriental Series vol. V, 1904. Reprinted by Motilal Banarsidass, Varanasi 1965.
3. Ibid., I, 121.
4. *Śatapatha Brāhmaṇa* I, 6, 3, 1–17. English trans. by J. Eggeling (5 vols) in *Sacred Books of the East*, 1882–1900. Reprinted by Motilal Banarsidass, Delhi 1963.
5. *Chāndogya Upaniṣad* VIII, 7, 1 ff. English trans. of *The Principal Upaniṣads* by S. Radhakrishnan, Allen & Unwin, London, 1951. Also by R. Hume, Oxford University Press, 1921.
6. Ibid.
7. Ibid.
8. Ibid.
9. *Bhāgavata Purāṇa* VI, 7 ff. English trans. published by the Gita Press, Gorakhpur, 1952–60.
10. Ibid.
11. Ibid.
12. Ibid.
13. Ibid.

14. Ibid.
15. *Ṛgveda* X, 90.
16. *Ṛgveda* I, 163, 3.
17. *Śatapatha Brāhmaṇa* I, 6, 4, 5.
18. *Ṛgveda* VIII, 48, 3.
19. *Ṛgveda* IV, 23, 8 ff.

CHAPTER 2

1. *Ṛgveda* VII, 100, 1–4.
2. *Ṛgveda* I, 154, 5; I, 22, 20.
3. *Bṛhaddevatā* II, 66.
4. *Ṛgveda* X, 121.
5. *Śatapatha Brāhmaṇa* VII, 11.
6. *Viṣṇu Purāṇa* VI, 7. English trans. by H. H. Wilson, 1840. Reprinted by Punthi Pustak, Calcutta, 1961.
7. *Rāmāyaṇa* I, 28, 19–22. English (metrical) trans. by R. T. H. Griffith (5 vols) 1870–75. Reprinted in the Chawkhamba Sanskrit Series, vol. XXIX, Varanasi 1963. Prose translation by the Gita Press, Gorakhpur 1960–70. Translation of the Baroda Critical Edition (7 vols) by various authors (ed. R Goldmann) Princeton University Press 1984–98.
8. *Bhāgavata Purāṇa* VIII, 20.
9. *Mahābhārata* XII, 312 f. English trans. by P. C. Roy (12 vols), Calcutta, 1884–96. Reprinted by Oriental Publishing, Calcutta, n.d. Translation of the Pune critical Edition was begun by J. A. B. van Buitenen. It is incomplete to date. Five volumes were published by Chicago University Press, 1973–78.
10. *Agni Purāṇa* II. English trans. by M. N. Dutt (2 vols) in 1893. Reprinted in the Chowkhamba Sanskrit Studies vols LIV, LV, Varanasi 1967.
11. *Viṣṇu Purāṇa* I, 9.
12. Ibid., I, 20.
13. *Bhāgavata Purāṇa* IX, 16.
14. Vālmīki, *Rāmāyaṇa*, Yuddhakanda 128, 98–106.
15. *Adhyātma Rāmāyaṇa*, Balakanda I, 1. English trans. by Rai Bahadur Lala Baiji Nath in *Sacred Books of the Hindus* (extra vol. I), 1913. Reprinted by AMS Press, New York 1974.
16. *Viṣṇu Purāṇa* V, 25.
17. *Bhagavadgītā* II, 56–57. There are numerous English translations of the *Bhagavadgītā*, for example by F. Edgerton, S. Radhakrishnan, Juan Mascaro, R. C. Zaehner.
18. Ibid., II, 71.
19. Ibid., II, 14–15.
20. Ibid., II, 62–65.
21. Ibid., II, 6–11.
22. Ibid., IV, 16–22.

23. Ibid., II, 47–48.
24. Ibid., II, 22–25.
25. Ibid., VI, 5–7.
26. Ibid., IX, 4–11.
27. Ibid., XI, 15–20.
28. Ibid., XI, 32–33.
29. Ibid., XVIII, 64–66.
30. *Bhāgavata Purāṇa* X, 2.
31. *Viṣṇu Purāṇa* III, 18, 15–22.
32. Ibid., IV, 24, 73–102.
33. *Bhāgavata Purāṇa* III, 24 f.
34. Śrīnivasādāsa, *Yatīndramatadīpikā* IX, 19–21. English trans. by Swami Adidevananda, Ramakrishna Math, Mysore 1949.
35. *Siddhitraya* III. English trans. by R. Ramanujachari and K. Srinivasacarya, 1942. Reprinted by Ubhaya Vedanta Granthamala Book Trust, Madras 1972.
36. Ibid., II, 2, 41.
37. Ibid., II, 3.
38. *Vedārthasaṅgraha* no. 126. English trans. by S. S. Raghavachar, Ramakrishna Ashram, Mysore 1956.
39. Ibid., no. 242 f.
40. Vaikuntha Gadya 6.
41. *Vedārthasaṅgraha* no. 217.
42. Vedānta Deśika, *Rahasyatrayasāra* II. English trans. by M. R. Rajagopala Ayyangar, Agnihotram Ramanuja Thathachariar, Kumbakonam 1956.
43. Ibid., III.
44. Ibid., IV.
45. Ibid., IV.
46. Rāmānuja, *Śrībhāṣya* I, 1, 4. English trans. by G. Thibaut in *Sacred Books of the East*, vol. XLVIII, 1904. Reprinted by Motilal Banarsidass, Delhi 1962.
47. Vedānta Deśika, *Nyāsa Viṃśati*, 1–4. English trans. by D. Ramaswamy Aiyangar, Ubhaya Vedanta Granthamala, Madras 1979.
48. Ibid.
49. *Śrībhāṣya* IV, 4, 22.
50. Pillai Lokācārya, *Tattvatraya*. English trans. by N. B. Narasimha Iyengar, M. C. Krishnan, Madras 1974.
51. *Rahasyatrayasāra* XIII.
52. Pillai Lokācārya, *Arthapancaka*.
53. *Anuvyākhyāna* I.
54. *Mahābhārata Tātparya Nirṇaya* I, 86.
55. *Anuvyākhyāna* III, 3.
56. Madhva, *Bṛhadāraṇyaka Upaniṣad Bhāṣya* XIV. English trans. in *Sacred Books of the Hindus* (vol. 14) by Bahadur Sri Chand Vasu, 1916. Reprinted by AMS Press, New York 1974.
57. Madhva, *Brahmasūtrabhāṣya* IV, 4, 5.19. English trans. by S. Subba Rau, Minerva Press, Madras 1904.

58. *Subhodinī,* introduction to Chapter 1. English trans. by J. D. Redington, Motilal Banarsidass, Delhi 1983.
59. Ibid., I, 16.
60. Sundarabhaṭṭa, *Mantrārtha Rahasya Ṣoḍasi* I.
61. *Prapannakalpāvalī.*
62. *Prabhā on Brahmasūtra* IV, 3, 5. English trans. of *Vedānta Parijāta Saurabha of Nimbārka* and *Vedānta Kaustubha of Śrīnivāsa* by Roma Bose, Bibliotheca Indica no. 259 (3 vols), Calcutta 1940–43.
63. *Sri Caitanya Caritāmṛta* III, 20, 3–45 (*Śikṣāṣṭaka*). English trans. (17 vols) by Swami A. C. Bhaktivedanta, The Bhaktivedanta Book Trust, New York 1973–75.
64. Ibid., II, 9; III, 20.
65. Viśvanātha Cakravartti, *Bhaktirāsamṛtasindhubiṇḍu* (extracts). English trans. by K. Klostermaier in *Journal of the American Oriental Society* 94/1 (1974), pp. 96–107.
66. The following poems were translated by K. Klostermaier from a collection edited by R. D. Ranade, *Paramārtha Sopāna: Sourcebook of Pathway to God in Hindi Literature*, Adhyatma Vidya Mandir, Allahabad 1954.
67. Ibid., I, 6.
68. Ibid., I, 5.
69. Ibid., I, 14.
70. Ibid., I, 1.
71. Ibid., I, 4.
72. Ibid., I, 8.
73. Ibid., I, 3.
74. Ibid., I, 11.
75. Ibid., I, 2.
76. Ibid., I, 15.

CHAPTER 3

1. Two are reproduced below, the third hymn can be found in *Ṛgveda* II, 33.
2. *Ṛgveda* I, 114.
3. Ibid., VII, 46.
4. *Śatapatha Brāhmaṇa* IX, 1, 1, 1.
5. *Yajurveda* ch. 16 (selections). English trans. by R. T. H. Griffiths, Benares 1889. Reprinted by Lazarus & Co, Varanasi 1957.
6. *Atharvaveda* XI, 2. English trans. (2 vols) by W. D. Whitney, Berlin 1905. Reprinted by Motilal Banarsidass, Delhi 1962.
7. *Śatapatha Brāhmaṇa* IX, 1, 1, 6.
8. *Śvetāśvatara Upaniṣad* (extracts).
9. *Atharvaśira Upaniṣad*, (extracts). English trans. in *Śaiva Upaniṣads* by T. R. Srinivasa Ayyangar and G. Srinivasa Murti, Adyar Library 1953.
10. *Vāyu Purāṇa* I, 30. English trans. by G. V. Tagare, Motilal Banarsidass, Delhi 1987.

11. *Bhāgavata Purāṇa* IV, 2–6.
12. *Vāyu Purāṇa* 30.
13. The Śiva sahasranāma is also found in *Mahābhārata* XII, 284.
14. *Bhāgavata Purāṇa* VIII, 7.
15. *Śiva Purāṇa*, Rudrasaṃhitā: Yuddhakhaṇḍa 1–12. English trans. (4 vols) by J. L. Shastri in *Ancient Indian Tradition and Mythology*, Motilal Banarsidass, Delhi 1970–73.
16. Ibid., Pārvatīkhaṇḍa 18 f.
17. *Liṅga Purāṇa* I, 160. English trans. (2 vols) by J. L. Shastri in *Ancient Indian Tradition and Mythology*, Motilal Banarsidass, Delhi 1982.
18. *Śiva Purāṇa*, Rudrasaṃhitā: Pārvatīkhaṇḍa 30.
19. A. K. Coomaraswamy, *The Dance of Śiva*, pp. 85 ff.
20. Mādhava, *Sarvadarśanasaṁgraha* ch. 6. English trans. (except ch. 16) by E. B. Cowell and A. E. Gough, 1982. Reprinted by Chowkhamba Sanskrit Studies vol. X, Varanasi 1961.
21. Ibid., ch. 7.
22. *Śrīkaṇṭha Bhāṣya* IV, 2, 16. English trans. by R. Chaudhuri, Pracyavani Research Series vol. XI, Calcutta 1959.
23. Ibid., IV, 4, 1.
24. Ibid., IV, 4, 9.
25. Ibid., IV, 4, 15.
26. Ibid., IV, 4, 22.
27. Ibid., end.
28. Kṣemarāja, *Pratyabhijñāhṛdaya* (extracts). English trans. by J. Singh, Motilal Banarsidass, Benares 1963.
29. *Śrīkarabhāṣya* IV, 4, 14.
30. *Sarvadarśanasaṁgraha* ch. 9.
31. Quoted in T. M. P. Mahaderah, "Saivism" III, p. 438 of *The History and Culture of the Indian People* ed. R. C. Majumdar, 2nd edn Bharatiya Vidya Bhavan, Bombay, 1962.
32. *Hymns of the Tamil Śaivite Saints*, pp. 13 ff. English trans. by F. Kingsbury and G. E. Phillips. Association Press, Calcutta, and Oxford University Press, London, 1921.
33. Ibid., p. 17.
34. Ibid.
35. Ibid., p. 19.
36. Ibid., p. 23.
37. Ibid., pp. 43 ff.
38. Ibid., p. 47.
39. Ibid., p. 65.
40. Ibid., pp. 75 ff.
41. Ibid., p. 83.
42. Ibid., pp. 73 f.
43. *The Tiruvācakam* or "Sacred Utterances" of the Tamil poet, saint and sage Manikka-Vācagar. The Tamil text with the Fifty-one Poems, with English trans., introductions and notes by The Revd G. U. Pope, Clarendon Press, Oxford, 1990.

44. Ibid., I, 26–48.
45. Ibid., II, 1–12.
46. Ibid., III, 13–28.
47. Ibid., X 21–24.
48. Ibid., XLV, 5–12.
49. *Tiruvachakam: The Hindu Testament of Love* XXV, 8–10. English trans. by Ratna Navaratnam, Bharatiya Vidya Bhavan, Bombay 1963.
50. *Śivastotras*. Text and English trans. in *Altar Flowers*, Advaita Ashrama, Almora 1934.

CHAPTER 4

1. *Ṛgveda* V, 84.
2. Ibid., V, 84, 1–2.
3. *Nirukta* IV, 22. English trans. of *The Nighaṇṭu and the Nirukta* by L. Sarup, 1926. Reprinted by Motilal Banarsidass, Delhi 1967.
4. *Ṛgveda* X, 125. Based on Griffith trans.
5. *Mahābhārata*, Sauptikaparvan 8, 64 ff.
6. Ibid.
7. Ibid., 8, 82.
8. *Mahābhārata*, Bhismaparvan 23, 4–16.
9. Ibid.
10. Raghu Vira, editor of the *Virāṭaparvan*, relegates the entire Durgā-*stotra* of the Vulgate (6) to Appendix I, 4, D.
11. *Mahābhārata*, Virātaparvan 6, 2–4 (Vulgate edn).
12. Ibid., 17–21.
13. Ibid., 30–32.
14. *Mahābhārata*, Salyaparvan, 45.
15. *Mārkaṇḍeya Purāṇa* LXXXI–XCIII. Complete English trans. by F. E. Pargiter, Bibliotheca Indica, 1904. Reprinted by Indological Book House, Delhi 1969.
16. Ibid.
17. Ibid.
18. *Mārkaṇḍeya Purāṇa*, Devīmahātmya
19. Ibid.
20. Ibid.
21. Ibid.
22. Ibid.
23. *Devī Bhāgavata Purāṇa* V, 21. English trans. of *The Śrīmad Devī Bhāgavatam* by Swami Vijnanananda, in *Sacred Books of the Hindus* vol. XXVI, Allahabad 1923. Reprinted by AMS Press, New York 1974.
24. *Bhaviṣya Purāṇa* IV, 138.
25. Arthur Avalon, *Introduction to Tantra Śāstra*, quoting *Yoginī Tantra* I. 10.
26. *Ānandalāharī*. English trans. (*Wave of Bliss)* by Arthur Avalon, Ganesh & Co., Madras 1953.
27. *Annapurnastotra* 1–6. *Altar Flowers*.

28. *Tripurā-Rahasyā (Jñānakhaṇḍa)* XXII (last section, condensed). English trans. by A. U. Vasavada, in Chowkhamba Sanskrit Studies, Varanasi 1965.
29. *Mahānirvāna Tantra (The Great Liberation)* X, 209 f. English trans. by Arthur Avalon, Ganesh & Co., Madras 1913.
30. *Brahmasūtrabhāṣya* I, 3, 30.
31. *Viṣṇu Purāṇa* IV, 7, 61–63.
32. *Śrībhāṣya* I, 1, 1.
33. Ibid.
34. *Prameyaratnāvalī* I, 14–18. English trans. in Appendix to *The Vedānta Sūtras of Bādarāyaṇa with the Commentary of Baladeva* by Rai Bahadur Srisa Chandra Vasu Vidyarnava, *Sacred Books of the Hindus*, Allahabad 1934.
35. *Sri Caitanya Caritāmṛta* I, 4; II, 8.
36. *Sayings of Śri Rāmakrishna. The most exhaustive collection of them their number being 1120*, no. 441. Śri Rāmakrishna Math, Mylapore, Madras 1960.
37. *Śrī Aurobindo on Himself and on the Mother*, pp. 501–503. Śri Aurobindo International University Centre Collection vol. I, Śri Aurobindo Ashram, Pondicherry 1953.
38. V. S. Agrawala, "Mother Earth," *Nehru Abhinandan Granth*, pp. 490–496

CHAPTER 5

1. *Manusmṛti* I, 87–94, 98–101. English trans. of *The Laws of Manu* by G. Bühler, *Sacred Books of the East* vol. XXV, 1886. Reprinted by Motilal Banarsidass, Delhi 1962.
2. Ibid., I, 107–110.

CHAPTER 6

1. *Ṛgveda* X, 129.
2. *Chāndogya Upaniṣad* VI, 2.
3. *Bṛhadāraṇyaka Upaniṣad* VI, 4.
4. *Chāndogya Upaniṣad* VIII, 7, 1 ff.
5. *Kaṭha Upaniṣad* III, 12; IV, 14–15.
6. *Chāndogya Upaniṣad* VII, XV, 1.
7. Ibid., VIII, VII, 1.
8. *Bṛahadāraṇyaka Upaniṣad* III, VII, 15.23.
9. Ibid., IV, IV, 5.
10. *Kaṭha Upaniṣad* III, 15.
11. *Muṇḍaka Upaniṣad* III, 2, 3–4.
12. Kaṇāda, *Vaiśeṣikasūtras* 1 f. English trans. of *Vaiśeṣikadarśana* by N. Sinha, *Sacred Books of the Hindus*, Allahabad 1911.
13. *The Padārthadharmasaṅgraha of Prāśāstapāda*, no. 156. English trans. by G. Jha, Lazarus, Allahabad 1916.

14. *The Vaiśesika Philosophy according to the Daśapadārtha Sastra.* English trans. by H. Ui, Chowkhamba Sanskrit Studies, Varanasi 1917.
15. *Gautama's Nyāysūtras (A System of Indian Logic with Vatsyāyana Bhāṣya).* English trans. by G. Jha, Oriental Book Agency, Poona 1939.
16. Udayanācārya *Nyāyakusumāñjali.* English trans. by E. B. Cowell, Calcutta 1864.
17. *Nyāya-bhāṣya* IV, 1, 21 f. From *Gautama's Nyāysūtra's 1939.*
18. *The Sāṁkhyakārikā of Īśvara Kṛṣṇa.* English trans. by S. S. Suryanarayana Sastry, University of Madras 1935.
19. Ibid.
20. Ibid.
21. Patañjali *Yogasūtras* I, 2; IV, 3–5. English trans. in *The Science of Yoga* by I. K. Taimni, Theosophical Publishing house, Adyar 1961.
22. *Jaimini Sūtras* I, I, 1.2.4.5; I, II, 1; IV, III, 15.
23. *Śābarabhāṣya* I, I, 1. English trans. (3 vols) by G. Jha, Oriental Institute, Baroda 1933–36. Reprinted 1973–74.
24. *Ślokavārttika* II, 117–122. English trans. by G. Jha, Bibliotheca Indica, Calcutta 1909.
25. Parthasārathi Miśra, *Śāstradīpikā (Tarkapada)*, p. 21. English trans. by D. Venkataramiah, Oriental Institute, Baroda 1940.
26. *Śarīrakarabhāṣya*, Introduction. English trans. of *The Vedānta-Sūtras with the Commentary by Śaṅkarācārya* (2 vols) by G. Thibaut, *Sacred Books of the East* vols XXXIV and XXXVIII, 1904. Reprinted by Motilal Banarsidass, Delhi 1962.
27. *Sarvavedāntasiddhāntasaṅgraha*, 16–21. English trans. of *The Quintessence of Vedānta* by Swami Tattwananda, Ramakrishna Advaita Ashrama, Kaladi 1970.
28. Ibid., 297–309.
29. Ibid., 310–317.
30. *Aṣṭāvakra Saṃhitā* I, 2.3.6. English trans. by Swami Nityaswarupananda, Advaita Ashrama, Almora 1940.
31. Ibid., I, 20.
32. Ibid., VII.
33. Ibid., VIII.
34. *Religion and Society*, p. 49. London: George Allen & Unwin, 2nd edn (6th impression) 1969.
35. *East and West in Religion*, p. 209. London: George Allen & Unwin, (3rd impression) 1954.
36. *Religion and Society*, pp. 42, 48.
37. *East and West in Religion*, p. 105.
38. Ibid., p. 124.

CHAPTER 7

1. In *The English Works of Rājā Rām Mohan Roy*, Allahabad 1905.
2. *The Precepts of Jesus*, Introduction. In *The English Works.*

3. In *The English Works.*
4. Debendranath Tagore, *Autobiography of Maharsi*, p. 57. Calcutta 1909.
5. Ibid., p. 101.
6. Ibid., p. 190
7. Keshub Chandra Sen, *Lectures in India*, p. 25 (2 vols), Calcutta 1901–04.
8. Ibid., p. 169.
9. Keshub Chandra Sen, *The New Dispensation*, pp. 215 f. (2 vols), 2nd edn, Calcutta 1915.
10. They form the last part of Dāyananda's *Satyārthaprakāśa.*
11. *The Gospel of Rāmakrishna*, p. 41 f. English trans. by Swami Nikhalananḍa, Mylapore 1951.
12. *Sayings of Śri Rāmakrishna*, no. 828. Śri Rāmakrishna Math, Mylapore, Madras 1960.
13. Ibid., no. 462.
14. Ibid., no. 688.
15. Ibid., no. 474.
16. *The Gospel of Rāmakrishna*, p. 72.
17. *Sayings of Shri Rāmakrishna*, no. 506.
18. *The Gospel of Rāmakrishna*, pp. 641 f.
19. Ibid.
20. Ibid., pp. 287 f.
21. *The Complete Works of Swami Vivekānanda* II, 279. (7 vols), 6th edn, Advaita Ashram, Mayavati-Almora 1950.
22. Ibid., III, 204. V, 322.
23. Ibid., V, 144 f.
24. Ibid., III, 213.
25. Ibid., V, 153.
26. Ibid., V, 2 f.
27. "Inspired Talks" June 26, 1895. In *Selections from Swami Vivekananda*, Advaita Ashrama, Calcutta 1953, pp. 394 ff.
28. Ibid., June 25, 1895, pp. 390 f.

CHAPTER 8

1. D. V. Tahmankar, *Lokamanya Tilak: Father of Indian Unrest and Maker of Modern India*, p. 59.
2. *Indian Social Reformer 20* (1919), p. 423.
3. Reproduced in Tendulkar, *Mahatma* I, 1958, pp. 88–89.
4. *Gītāñjalī*, no. 36; quoted from a Facsimile. English trans. 1912.
5. *The Religion of Man*, pp. 18 f. McMillan & Co, London and Calcutta 1950.
6. Ibid., pp. 118 ff.
7. Prospectus of Viśva-Bhāratī University.
8. Ibid.

9. *The Ideal of Human Unity*, pp. 252 f. All the works of Aurobindo Ghose appeared in the Sri Aurobindo International University Centre Collection, Sri Aurobindo Ashram, Pondicherry 1953 ff.
10. Ibid., p. 254.
11. *The Human Cycle*, pp. 192 ff.
12. *The Ideal of Human Unity*, pp. 322 ff.
13. *The Renaissance of India*, 1950, p. 56.
14. Ibid., pp. 71 f.
15. *Congress Presidential Addresses*, pp. 732–755. In the *Collected Works of Mahatma Gandhi*, published by the Government of India 1969.
16. Address to Missionary Conference, Madras, 14 February 1916.
17. *Young India*, 27 October 1927.
18. *Autobiography*, pp. 286 f.
19. *Harijan*, 12 November 1932.
20. *Young India*, 11 September 1924.
21. *Harijan*, 28 November 1936.
22. Ibid., 2 March 1940.
23. Ibid., 1 May 1937.
24. *Young India*, 31 December 1931.
25. Ibid., 25 May 1921.
26. Facsimile note reproduced in Tendulkar, *Mahatma* VIII, 288.
27. *The Leader*, 25 December 1916.
28. *Young India*, 4 August 1920.
29. *Sarvodaya – Principles and Programme*, Navajivan 1951, pp. 55 ff.
30. Speech given on 19 September 1958 in Navapur/Maharashtra in *Sarvodaya*, p. 230.
31. Ibid., p. 396.
32. Ibid., p. 429.
33. Introduction to K. Mashruwala, *Gandhi and Marx*, p.34.
34. Suresh Ram, *Vinoba Bhave and His Mission*, p. 407. Published by Akhil Bharat Sarva Seva Sangh, 2nd edn, Rajghat, Kasi 1958.
35. Ibid., p. 134.
36. Ibid., p. 511.
37. In M. Pattabhiram, *General Elections in India 1967*, pp. 207–226. Allied Publishers; Bombay, New Delhi, Calcutta, Madras 1967.
38. *Bunch of Thoughts*, 1954. Vikrama Prakashan, 2nd edn, Bangalore 1966.
39. *The Concept of Hindu Nation*, pp. 2 ff. Voice of India, New Delhi 1995.
40. Ibid., pp. 28 ff.
41. 1993 White Paper.
42. Lantusinha Gautamī, in *Kalyāṇ*, 40/187–9.
43. Foreword to Chaturvedi Badrinath *Dharma, India, and the World Order*, St Andrew Press, Edinburgh, 1993, p. XV.
44. Ibid., p. 1.
45. Ibid., p. 3.
46. Ibid., p. 5.

CHAPTER 9

1. *Dalit Voice*, vol. 16/24, pp. 3 f., November 1–15, 1997.
2. *India Perspectives*, August 1989, pp. 4 f.
3. Ibid.

CHAPTER 10

1. *In Woods of God-Realization* V, 141. Rama Tirtha Pratisthan, Lucknow 1956.
2. Ibid., V, 3.
3. *Uḷḷadu Nāṛpadu*.
4. Ibid.
5. *Sathya Sāī Speaks* III, 170. Sri Sathya Sai Books and Publications trust, Prasanthinilayam (Ananthapur District,) Andhra Pradesh 1988.
6. Ibid., XI, 61.
7. Ibid., III, 172.
8. Ibid., II, 213 f.
9. Ibid., XI, 192.
10. *Words of Śrī Ānandamayī Mā*, pp. 1 f. Translated and compiled by Atmananda. Published by Shree Shree Annadamayee Sangha, Bhadaini, Varanasi 1961.
11. Ibid., p. 5.
12. Ibid., p. 6.
13. Ibid.
14. Ibid., p. 10.
15. Ibid., p. 11.

GLOSSARY

abhāva	Nonperception (in the Nyāya-system); nonbeing (in the Vaiśeṣika-system).
abhaya	fearlessness; in iconology: *abhaya mudrā* is the hand pose of a deity, inspiring confidence and trust.
abhiniveśa	desire; in the *yoga*-system: craving for life.
abhiṣeka	annointment, part of installation ceremony of a king and an image of the deity.
abhyāsa	exercise, practice, exertion.
acāra	immobile; attribute of the Supreme Being.
ācāra	way of life; mode of behaviour.
ācārya	master; (also used as equivalent to Master of Arts).
acetana	without consciousness (an attribute of matter).
acintya	beyond intellectual understanding.
adbhūta	marvellous, miraculous.
adharma	unrighteousness, evil.
adhikāra	qualification (especially of students of religion).
adhyāsa	superimposition; misidentification.
adhyātma	supreme; spiritual; relating to the Supreme Being.
Aditi	Vedic Goddess, 'Mother Earth', mother of *ādityas*.
adṛṣṭa	invisible; technical term in Nyāya and Vaiseṣika.
advaita	nonduality; name of a school of Vedānta.
ādya prakṛti	primeval matter.
ādya śakti	primeval power, title of the Goddess.
āgama	source, beginning, scriptures; name of a class of writings which are considered revealed.
aghora	horrible; name of a sect of Śaivites.
agni	fire; one of the foremost Vedic gods.
agnicayana	a particular kind of Vedic fire sacrifice.

agnihotra	a Vedic fire sacrifice.
agniṣṭoma	fire sacrifice.
ahaṁkāra	principle of individuation; egotism.
ahiṃsā	not killing; nonviolence.
ahi	snake.
ahita	improper, unwholesome, not propitious.
aikya	unity, oneness.
aiśvarya	Lordliness.
aja	unborn (masc.); attribute of the Supreme Being; billygoat.
ajā	unborn (fem.), attribute of Primordial Matter; nannygoat.
ajñāna	ignorance; absence of (redeeming) knowledge.
akala	without parts; attribute of Supreme Being.
ākāśa	ether (one of the five elements of Indian cosmology); space.
akhila	undivided, complete.
akṛti	uncreated; eternal principle underlying words etc.
akṣa-mālā	rosary made of beads from a shrub sacred to Śiva.
akṣara	imperishable; syllable (letter); name of Supreme Being.
aṃbikā	mother; Mother Goddess.
amṛta	nectar; draught of immortality.
aṃśa	part, fragment.
anādhāra	without support.
anādi	without beginning; eternal.
anahaṭa	"unstruck," mystical sound arising from within the body, signifiying divine grace.
ānanda	bliss; used as last part of the proper name of many *samnyāsins*.
ananta	without end; proper name of the world-snake upon which Viṣṇu rests.
aṇava	veil; congenital ignorance concerning the ultimate;
anga	member, constituent part, e.g., of a major work.
aṇimā	smallness; in *yoga*: faculty to diminish one's size.
aniruddha	free, without hindrance; proper name of one of the *vyūhas* of Viṣṇu.
anitya	not permanent; transient.
aṅkuśa	goad; one of the divine attributes.
anṛta	against the (moral) law.
anta	end, death.
antarātman	conscience.
antaryāmī	the 'inner ruler', the Supreme Being as present in the human heart (literally understood).
aṇu	atom.
anubhava	experience.
anugraha	attraction; grace of God.
anumāna	inference.

apara	unsurpassed; attribute of the Supreme Being.
aparigraha	without having (or wanting) possessions.
aparokṣa	immediate, present.
apas	water.
apāśraya	supportless.
apauruṣeya	not man-made; technical term for the supernatural origin of the Veda in Mīmāṁsā.
apsara	nymph.
apūrva	technical term in the Mīmāṁsā system to denote the not-yet realized effect of a sacrifice.
araṇya	forest.
arcā	rites of worship of an image.
arcāvatāra	image of God, who took on this form in order to become an object of worship for the devotees.
ardha	half.
ardhanārīśvara	figurative representation of Śiva, in which one half shows a male figure, the other half a female one.
arjuna	bright; proper name of the hero of the *Bhagavadgītā*.
arka	sun.
artha	object; meaning; wealth.
arthavāda	"eulogy," mere description (without authority).
ārya	noble (man); self-designation of the "Āryans".
āsana	seat, sitting posture.
asat	not true; "not real".
āśirvādam	(ritual) blessing.
asmitā	egoism; from *asmi*, "I am".
āśrama	hermitage; stage in life; proper name of a group of *samnyāsis*.
aṣṭachāp(a)	"eight seals"; group of eight medieval poets of Northern India who inserted their own proper names into the last stanza of their poems as "signature".
aṣṭamūrti	"eightfold embodiment," eight proper names of Śiva.
asteya	not stealing.
āstika	someone who accepts the authority of the Veda; orthodox.
aśubha	inauspicious.
aśuddha	impure.
asuras	demons; class of superhuman beings.
aśvamedha	horse sacrifice.
aśvatha	a tree (*ficus sacra*).
aśvins	Vedic gods, a pair of brothers; in astronomy: Castor and Pollux.
ātmakūṭa	self-deceit.
ātman	self.
ātmanivedana	self-surrender (as part of religious initiation).

avatāra	descent (of god in a bodily form).
avidyā	ignorance (of reality).
avyakta	unmanifest.
āyurveda	traditional Indian medicine; literally, "life-knowledge".
baddha	bound (into *saṃsāra*).
bala	strength, power.
bāṇa	arrow; attribute of images of deities.
bandha	bondage.
bhadra	well, happy; blessing.
bhaga	luck, fortune.
bhagavān	lord; most general title of God.
Bhagavadgītā	"Song of the Lord," celebrated epic poem, a dialogue between Kṛṣṇa and Arjuna, part of the *Mahābhārata*.
bhajana	devotional recitation.
bhakta	devotee.
bhakti	love, devotion.
bhasma	(sacred) ashes.
bhāṣya	commentary.
bhāva	condition; emotion; nature.
bhaviṣya	future.
bhaya	fear, terror.
bheda	difference.
bhoga	enjoyment.
bhū, bhūmī	earth; proper name of Viṣṇu's second consort.
bhukti	enjoyment.
bhūta	a being, a spirit.
bibhatsa	trembling.
bīja	seed.
bīja-mantra	"seed-spell," mystical syllables identified with the Goddess, used by Śāktas.
bindu	"drop," crescent.
brahmā	(personal) creator-god.
brahmacarin	student; celibate.
brahmacarya	first period in life, celibate studenthood.
brahmaloka	world of Brahma; highest abode.
brahman	(impersonal) absolute.
brāhmaṇa	member of the highest caste; class of ritual texts.
brahmārandra	the place from where the soul departs at death (the rear of the cranium).
buddhi	intelligence; in the Sāṁkhya system name of the first product of the union of *puruṣa* and *prakṛti*.
caitanya	spirit, consciousness, also proper name for the Supreme; proper name of a Bengali saint of the sixteenth century.
caitta	consciousness.

cakra	circle, disc; centres in body; one of Viṣṇu's weapons; discus.
cakravartin	universal ruler.
caṇḍa	moon; silver.
caṇḍāla	wild; bad; proper name of lowest caste; outcaste.
candana	sandalwood.
caṇḍī	fierce woman; proper name of Devī.
carita	biography.
caryā	activity; mode of behavior.
caturmukha	four-faced; proper name of Brahmā.
caturvarṇāśrama	the four *varṇas* ("castes") and stages of life.
chāyā	shadow.
cit	consciousness; spirit.
citta	thought.
daitya	a goblin, a slave, a demon.
dakṣina	sacrificial fees.
dakṣinācāra	right-handed path.
dāna	gift; charity.
Dānava	member of a group hostile to Vedic Āryans.
darśana	view; audience; theory; philosophical system.
dāsa	servant; often part of proper name.
dāsa-mārga	"way of the servant," lowest rank in Śaiva-siddhānta.
daśanāmī	ten-named; proper name of a religious order.
dasyu	slave; name for non-Āryan in *Ṛg Veda*.
dayā	compassion.
deva, devatā	divine (superior) being.
devayāna	path of the gods.
devī	goddess.
dhairya	firmness.
dhama	area; body.
dhāraṇa	support.
dharma	"law," religion, support
dharmaśāśtra	law book.
dharmakṣetra	"the field of righteousness".
dhatṛ	giver; proper name for God.
dhyāna	meditation; concentration in Yoga.
dig-vijaya	conquest of the four quarters; appellation of the successful competition of a religious teacher.
dīkṣā	initiation.
dīpā	lamp.
divya-mārga	"way of the deities," highest rank in Śaiva-siddhānta.
duḥkha	sorrow, suffering.
dvaita	duality; name of a school of Vedānta.
dvaitādvaita vivarjita	beyond duality and non-duality.

dvandva	pair of opposites (hot-cold, etc.).
dvāpara yuga	second era of each *kalpa.*
dveṣa	hatred.
dvijati	twice-born; appellation of the three upper castes whose initiation is considered a second birth.
dvīpa	island; continent.
dyaus	resplendent; sky; Vedic high god.
ekādaśī	eleventh day (of each half-month); sacred to Vaiṣṇavas.
ekāgratā	one-pointedness, single-mindedness.
ekaśṛṅga	one-horn (unicorn); the fish-descent (of Viṣṇu) with one horn, on which Manu fastened his raft and thus was saved in the great flood.
gaddi	throne, seat, headship (as of a *maṭha*).
gandharva	celestial musician.
Gaṇeśa	lord of the celestial armies; elephant-headed son of Śiva and Pārvatī.
garbha	womb; *garbha-gṛha*; innermost santuary of the temples.
Garuḍa	Viṣṇu's vehicle; gryphius.
ghāṭ(a)	steps; especially flight of steps leading to a river or tank.
gopa	cowherd.
gopī	milk maid.
gosvāmī	lord of cows; title for high-ranking Vaiṣṇavas of certain communities.
grāma-devatās	village deities.
guṇa	quality.
guru	elder; spiritual master; teacher in general.
gurūpāsati	surrender to the master (as part of initiation).
guru-paraṃparā	lineage of gurus, succession of guru and disciple.
hala	plough, attribute of Bālarāma.
halāhala	poison churned up from the Milk Ocean, consumed by Śiva in order to save the world.
hara	literally, the one who takes away; name of Śiva.
hari	literally, the yellowish green one; name of Viṣṇu.
harṣa	joy.
hasyā	laughter.
Hayaśirṣa	"horse-head," an *avatāra* of Viṣṇu.
hetu	cause.
hiṃsā	violence, killing.
hindūtva	"hindu-dom," Hinduism as a cultural and political entity.
hiraṇyagarbha	literally "golden womb"; in Hindu cosmology the first being.
hita	beneficial, good.
hitavācana	well-intentioned speech.
hlādinī	enjoyment.

hlādinī-śakti	"power of enjoyment," one of the three *śaktis* of Kṛṣṇa.
homa	fire oblation.
hotṛ	class of Vedic priests.
hṛdaya	heart; core of something.
icchā	wish, desire.
indriya	sense organs.
īrṣyā	envy, jealousy.
iṣṭa	preferred, wished for.
iṣṭa-deva(tā)	the god of one's choice.
īśvara	Lord; God.
itihāsa	history; technical term for the Hindu epics.
japa	repetition of the name of God or a *mantra*.
jātī	birth; race, family, "sub-caste".
jaya	victory; also as greeting; "hail".
jīva(-ātman)	life; individual living being.
jñāna	knowledge.
jñānaniṣṭha	state of being firmly and irrevocably established in ultimate knowledge.
jñāni	a knower (of the absolute).
jyotis	light.
jyotir-liṅga	"liṅga formed of light," twelve famous Śiva-*liṅgas* which are not made by human hands.
jyotiṣa	one of the auxiliary sciences of the Veda: astronomy and astrology.
jyotiṣṭoma	a seasonal sacrifice for the departed.
kaiṁkārya	"service," used in connection with service of God in heaven as ultimate aim (*kaiṁkārya-prāpti*).
kaivalya	"aloneness"; ultimate aim of *yoga*.
kāla	time; black colour; fate; death.
kālamukha	black-mouth; name of Śiva; name of a Śaivite sect.
kālī	the "black one"; name of the terrible form of the goddess.
kali-yuga	age of strife; last period in each world-era (*kalpa*).
kalkin	the future (last) *avatāra* of Viṣṇu in the form of a white horse.
kalpa	world-era, day of Brahmā (432 million years); ritual; one of the auxiliary sciences of Veda.
kalpa-sūtras	texts describing sacrificial rituals.
kāma	desire, lust, love; name of god of love.
kāmadhenu	wish-fulfilling cow.
kāmya-karma	ritual performed to fulfill a particular wish.
kāṇḍa	part (of a text).
kāpalī	literally one with a skull; name of followers of certain Śaivite groups.
kāraṇa	cause; title of the Supreme Being; God.

karma	work; action; result of an action.
kārya	worship of an image through various acts.
kavaca	armour, protection; designation of certain prayers invoking the protection of a deity.
kavi	poet, wise man, omniscient.
keyura	earring, attribute of images of deities.
khadga	sword, attribute of images of deities.
kīrtaṇa	congregational religious singing.
kleśa	suffering; pain.
kośa	sheath; cover; treasury; lexicon.
krīya	activity; skill; exercises.
krodha	anger.
kṛpā	favor; grace.
Kṛṣṇa	black; proper name of the most famous *avatāra* of Viṣṇu.
kṛta-yuga	the first part of each world era; the golden age.
Kubera	god of wealth, king of the *yakṣas*, friend of Śiva.
kumbha	waterpot; astronomically, sign of Aquarius.
kuṃbha-melā	a great gathering at specific holy places every twelfth year.
kuṇḍalinī	serpent; in Tantricism, life-energy.
Kūrma	tortoise; one of the *avatāras* of Viṣṇu.
lakṣana	characteristic; attribute; sign.
līlā	play.
liṅga	characteristic sign; subtle nature; phallic symbol of Śiva.
lobha	greed.
loka	world; sphere.
loka-nātha	Lord of the world.
loka-pāla	guardian of the world.
mada	intoxication; dementia.
mādhava	sweet like honey (*madhu*); proper name of Kṛṣṇa; proper name of several famous philosophers.
madhurasa	literally, honey sentiment; highest love and affection.
mādhurya bhāva	"feeling of sweetness," highest degree of *bhakti*.
madhya deśa	"middle country," Central (Northern) India, the best place for brahmins to live in.
mahā	great.
Mahābhārata	"The Great Bhārata (Narrative)"; a huge epic and a veritable encyclopedia of Hinduism.
mahā-pāpa	"great sin," unforgivable action.
mahant(a)	head of a monastic establishment.
maharṣi	great sage; honorific title.
mahat	great; in the Samkhya system, first evolute (intellect).
mahātmā	great soul; honorific title.
māhātmya	eulogy, text praising a particular place.
maheśvara	great lord; proper name of Śiva.

mahiṣa	buffalo; proper name of a demon killed by Devī.
maithuṇa	pair; astronomically: Gemini.
makara	crocodile; alligator.
mala	stain.
mālā	garland; chain; "rosary" of beads.
maṃsa	meat.
māna	pride; idea, concept; honour.
manas	mind.
mānava	relating to Manu; human.
mānava-dharma	laws given by Manu (for humankind).
maṇḍala	circle; section of *Ṛgveda*.
maṇḍapa	covered hall; tent.
maṇḍira	palace; temple.
maṅgala	auspicious, lucky.
maṅgala-śloka	an opening verse or prayer to ensure that the undertaking is auspicious.
maṇi	jewel.
mantra	word, formula (especially from scriptures).
Manu	ancestor and lawgiver of humankind.
manvantara	an age of one (of fourteen) Manu; according to Hindu tradition we live now in the seventh *manvantara* (seven more are to follow before the end).
mārga	way; street; especially in metaphor, path of salvation.
marjāra	cat, *marjāra-mārga*, "the cat's way".
markaṭa	monkey, *markaṭa-mārga*, "the monkey's way".
Marut	wind; wind god.
maṭha	monastic establishment.
matsya	fish; one of the *avatāras* of Viṣṇu.
māyā	fiction, delusion.
melā	fair, assembly.
mīmāṃsā	inquisition; system; proper name of one *darśana*.
mithyā	futility; false; e.g. *mithyā-jñāna* is false knowledge.
mleccha	"barbarian," somebody who does not belong to Hindu culture.
moha	delusion.
mokṣa	liberation.
mṛtyu	death.
mudra	(hand) pose.
mukta	one who is liberated; e.g. *jīvan-mukta* is one liberated while still living in the body.
mukti	liberation.
mukti-dātā	giver of liberation, title of Viṣṇu.
mūla	root.
mūla-prakṛti	primary matter.

mulayahan	name of demon, personification of evil, subdued by Śiva.
mumukṣu	one who desires liberation.
muni	literally one who keeps silence; ascetic; "monk".
mūrti	literally, embodiment; figure; image.
muśala	hammer, attribute of images of deities.
nādī	river, (body) vessel, nerve.
naga	superior being; snake; naked, heretic.
naimittika karma	non-obligatory ritual for the purpose of obtaining a particular object.
nāma-japa	repetition of name(s) of God.
nāmakīrtaṇa	congregational singing of the name(s) of God.
nāma-rūpa	name and form; individuality.
nāmaskāra	greeting in a spirit of worship.
Nandi	Śiva's vehicle; a bull.
nāraka	hell.
nāsadīya	title of a famous Ṛgvedic hymn beginning with *na asad* ("there was not").
nāstika	heretic; someone who denies the authority of the Veda.
nāstikya	irreligiosity.
nāṭarāja	"King of Dance," title of Śiva.
nātha	lord. *Viśvanātha*, "Lord of the Universe".
nigama	*Veda*; authoritative scripture.
nīla	dark blue. *Śiva nīlakaṇṭha*: Śiva with a dark-blue throat.
nirguṇa	without qualities or attributes.
Nirukta	classical work of etymology.
niṣkala	without part; undivided, complete.
nitya	eternal.
nivṛtti	withdrawal.
Nṛsinha	man-lion; one of the *avatāras* of Viṣṇu.
nyāya	rule, method; motto; logics; syllogism.
pāda	foot; verse, part of a text.
padārtha	category (in Vaiśeṣika system).
padma	lotus.
pañca	five; e.g. *pañcāgni*: five fires.
pañcāṅga	the traditional Indian astrological almanac.
Pāñcarātra	branch of Vaiṣṇavism.
pañcāyātana-pūjā	worship of five gods.
paṇḍit(a)	learned man; honorific title.
pantha	path, way; e.g. *Kabīr-pantha*: the religious sect founded by Kabīr.
pāpa	sin.
para	beyond; supreme; liberation.
paramārthika	that which concerns ultimate reality.
paraṃparā	tradition.

Paraśurāma	Rāma with the battle-ax; one of the *avatāras* of Viṣṇu.
Pārvatī	daughter of the mountains; name of Śiva's consort.
pāśa	fetter.
paśu	animal; cattle; in Śaivasiddhānta: unliberated person.
paśupati	"lord of the cattle," name of Śiva.
piṇḍa	small ball of rice which is offered to ancestors as an oblation.
piśāca	imp; ogre.
pīṭha	place sacred to Śāktas.
pitṛ	ancestor, forefather; *pitṛyāna:* the path of the ancestors.
prabhā	splendor.
pradakṣinā	respect shown to a person or image through certain actions, such as circumambulation.
pradhāna	head; source; in the Sāṁkhya system: material principle from which everything develops.
prajāpati	Lord of creatures; creator.
prakāśa	splendor.
prakṛti	matter; nature.
pralaya	dissolution of the world.
pramāda	error.
pramāṇa	logical proof; means of cognition.
prāṇa	life breath.
prāṇava	the mantra OM.
prāṇāyāma	breath-control.
prapanna	one who has surrendered to God.
prapatti	(formal) act of surrender to God.
prārabdha	remainder of karma from former births.
prārthana	prayer.
prasāda	grace, share of food offered to deity.
prasthāna trayī	triad of authorities (*Upaniṣads, Bhagavadgītā*, *Brahmasūtras*).
pratibiṃba	reflection; mirror-image.
pratijñā	recognition; proposition.
pratisarga	dissolution of the universe.
pratisiddha karma	forbidden action or ritual.
pratyabhijñā	recognition.
pratyahāra	withdrawal of the senses.
pratyakṣa	immediate (sense) perception.
pravṛtti	inclination; active liberation.
prāyaścitta	atonement (through certain prescribed acts).
prayatna	effort.
prema	love; used as technical term for spiritual love.
preta	soul of a deceased who has not (yet) received offerings.
prīti	amity; love.
pṛthivī	earth.
pūjā	(image) worship.

punarjanma	rebirth.
punarmṛtyu	re-death.
puṇya	merit.
purāṇa	old; proper name of class of authoritative scriptures.
purohita	class of Vedic priests.
puruṣa	man; person; supreme being; spirit.
puruṣārtha	aim of human life.
puruṣottama	supreme person.
puṣpa	flower.
puṣṭimārga	special form of *bhakti*.
putra	son.
putra-mārga	way of the son; third rank in Śaiva-siddhānta.
rāga	passion; in music; basic tune.
rāgānuga bhakti	"passionate love"; special form of devotion.
rajas	excitement; one of the basic three *guṇas*.
rājayoga	"royal way"; name of Patañjali's *yoga* system.
rajñī	splendor.
rakṣasa	goblin.
Rāma	main hero of the *Rāmāyaṇa*; general name for God.
Rāmarājya	Rāma's rule; "kingdom of God".
Rāmāyaṇa	"Rāma's Adventures," a large epic poem, ascribed to Vālmīki. There are many vernacular re-creations of this original work like Tulsīdās' *Rāmcaritmānas*.
rasa	juice; sentiment.
rasa-līlā	theatrical re-enactment of scenes from the life of Kṛṣṇa.
rati	pleasure; proper name of consort of god of Love.
ratna	jewel; pearl; often used as honorific title.
ratrī	night.
ṛk	hymn.
ṛṣi	seer; wise man.
ṛta	(Vedic) law of the world (moral and cosmic).
rudra	reddish; name of Vedic god; name of Śiva especially in his frightful aspect.
rudrākṣa	"Rudra's eye"; rough-round seed of an Indian shrub, used in garlands by Śaivites.
Rukminī	Kṛṣṇa's spouse.
śabda	sound; word; scriptural authority.
saccidānanda	the Supreme Being (being, consciousness, bliss).
sadācāra	morality; good behavior.
ṣaḍdarśana	the six orthodox systems.
sādhana	means (to gain liberation).
sādhaka	one who practices a *sādhana*.
sadhāraṇa dharma	common law; religion common to humankind.

sādhu	"holy man"; mendicant.
sādhvī	a female ascetic.
sāgara	sea; great mass of things.
saguṇa	with qualities.
saguṇa brahman	*brahman* with attributes.
sahajā	natural; in-born.
sahāmārga	the way of the companion; the second rank in Śaiva-siddhānta.
sahasra-nāma	"thousand names," litany with a thousand names and titles of a deity.
śākhā	branch; a school of thought or practice.
sākṣātkāra	bodily vision of the supreme.
sākṣī	witness; the Supreme as present in humans.
śākta	follower of Śakti cult.
śakti	power; name of Śiva's consort.
śālagrāma	ammonite; symbol under which Viṣṇu is present.
sālokya	sharing the same world; one of the stages of liberation.
samādhi	deep concentration; death; memorial.
sāman	Vedic tune.
sāmānya	equality; category in *Vaiśeṣika*.
samāvāya	similarity.
samāveśa	togetherness.
saṃbhoga	enjoyment.
saṃdhya	twilight; dusk and dawn; prayers recited at dawn.
saṃdhya-bhāṣa	words with double meaning.
saṃhitā	collection; name of class of authoritative scriptures.
samīpa	nearness; stage of liberation.
samjñā	understanding.
sāṁkhya	figure, number; proper name of philosophical system.
saṁkīrtaṇa	congregational singing.
saṃnyāsa	renunciation.
saṃnyāsin	ascetic, homeless mendicant.
saṃpradāya	a religious order or sect.
saṃsāra	world; connoting constant cyclic change.
saṃskāra	rites; "sacraments".
saṃskṛta	artfully composed, refined, name of ancient Indian high language.
samyama	concentration.
sanātana dharma	eternal law; self-designation of Hinduism.
śaṅkha	conch shell.
sanmārga	"the true way"; highest stage in Śaivasiddhānta.
śānti	peace.
santoṣa	contentment.
śaraṇā-gati	seeking refuge.
sarga	creation; emanation.

sāraṇga	bow-string.
śarīra	body.
sārūpa	of equal form.
śāstra	doctrine; treatise, authoritative teaching.
śāstri	one who knows the traditional doctrine; Bachelor of Arts.
sat	being, truth.
satī	"faithful," wife who (voluntarily) dies with deceased husband.
satsaṅg	"gathering of the righteous," religious meeting.
sattva	being; nature; virtue; one of the three *guṇas*.
satya	truth; reality.
sauca	purity.
saulabhyam	benevolence.
sauśilya	kindness.
savitṛ	Vedic sun-god.
sāyujya	togetherness.
śeṣa	"endless," world-serpent upon which Viṣṇu rests.
seva	service.
siddha	accomplished; saint.
siddhi	accomplishment; in *yoga*, extraordinary faculties.
śikhā	tuft on the crown of the head.
śikhara	spirelike elevation over central sanctuary in a Hindu temple.
śīkṣā	instruction.
śīlā	good behavior; morality.
Sītā	furrow; proper name of Rāma's consort.
Śiva	"propitious," proper name of major Hindu deity.
śloka	double verse.
smāsana	cremation ground.
smṛti	what has been committed to memory; proper name for a certain class of scriptures.
soma	intoxicating drink used in vedic sacrifices.
Soma	God.
spaṇḍa-śāstra	treatise of vibrations, branch of Kaśmīr Śaivism.
sphoṭa	boil; idea; connection between letter and meaning.
śraddhā	faith.
śrāddha	last rites.
śrautasūtras	ritual texts dealing with public Vedic sacrifices.
śravaṇa	listening to the recitation of religious texts.
Śrī	fortune; proper name of Viṣṇu's consort; Sir.
śrīvatsa	mark on Viṣṇu's body signifying Lakṣmī's presence.
śṛṅgāra	feeling of erotic love.
sṛṣṭhi	creation; emanation.
śruti	what has been revealed and heard, "scripture".
Sthala Purāṇa	collection of legends about a holy place.

sthūla	gross, material.
stithi	maintenance (of the world).
stotra	hymn in praise of God.
śubha	auspicious.
śuddha	pure.
śuddhi	ritual of purification (for readmission into caste).
śudra	member of the lowest caste.
sūkṣma	subtle.
sūkta	Vedic hymn.
śūnya	zero; nothing; emptiness.
sura	divine being.
surā	intoxicating drink.
sūrya	sun.
sūta	bard; charioteer.
sūtra	aphoristic textbook; thread.
svadharma	one's own duties.
svādhyāya	study of Vedic texts.
svahā	invocation at offering to *devas*.
svāmī	Lord; religious honorific: "Reverend".
svarga	heaven.
svayambhu	being of itself; name for Supreme Being.
Śyāma	black; name of Kṛṣṇa.
tamas	darkness; dullness; one of the three *guṇas*.
tantra	loom; system of practices; main branch of Hinduism.
tapas	heat; energy.
tapasvī	ascetic; one who has accumulated much merit through self-mortification.
tarka	formal logic; argument.
tattva	principle; nature; reality, element.
tejas	splendor; light; heat.
ṭīkā	subcommentary.
tilaka	mark on forehead.
tirobhāva	disappearance.
ṭippaṇī	gloss.
tīrtha	fording place; place of pilgrimage (on holy river).
tīrthayātra	pilgrimage.
tiru (Tamil)	holy; "Mr.".
tithi	moon day.
traividyā	knowledge of the three *Vedas*.
tretāyuga	third world age.
trilocana	three-eyed; name of Śiva.
triloka	the three worlds.
trimārga	literally, "three ways"; the collective name for the paths of works, devotion, knowledge.

tripuṇḍra	Śiva's trident; sign of the forehead.
tristhalī	the three most important places of pilgrimage viz. Prāyāga (Allahabad), Kāśī (Benares) and Gāyā.
trivarga	the triad of *dharma*, *artha*, *kāma*.
tulasī	a small tree (holy basil), sacred to Viṣṇu.
turīya	the fourth; designation of highest stage of consciousness.
turyātīta	beyond the fourth; highest stage in some Hindu schools who claim to transcend the Vedāntic *turīya*.
tyāgi	renouncer; ascetic.
udāhāraṇa	example, illustration; part of Nyāya syllogism.
udbhava	appearance.
udaṃbara	Indian fig-tree, sacred to Śiva.
udyama	exertion; rising or lifting up.
upadeśa	advice; religious instruction.
upādhi	attribute; title; deceit.
Upa-Gītā	"lesser Gītā".
upamāna	analogy.
upaṃśū	prayer uttered in a whisper.
upanayana	initiation; investiture with sacred thread.
upāṅga	auxiliary sciences or texts to Vedāṅgas.
upaniṣad	class of authoritative scriptures; secret doctrine.
Upa-purāṇa	lesser *Purāṇa*.
upāsana	worship.
upavāsa	(religious) fasting.
vācya śakti	power of speech.
vāhana	conveyance.
vaicitriya	manifoldness; distraction.
vaidhi-bhakti	devotion expressing itself through ritual worship.
vaidika dharma	"Vedic religion," self designation of Hinduism.
Vaikuṇṭha	Viṣṇu's heaven.
vairāgi(nī)	ascetic (fem.).
vairāgya	renunciation.
vaiśeṣika	name of a philosophical system.
vaiśya	member of third caste; businessman, artisan.
vajra	diamond; thunderbolt.
vāk	voice; word.
vālmīka	an ant's hill.
vāmācāra	left-handed way (in Tantra).
vāmana	dwarf; one of the *avatāras* of Viṣṇu.
vaṃśa	genealogy.
vānaprastha	forest dweller; third stage in a Brahmin's life.
varāha	boar; one of the *avatāras* of Viṣṇu.
varṇāśramadharma	social system of Hinduism based on a partition into four classes and four stages of life.

vātsalya	love toward a child, one of the stages of *bhakti*.
vāyu	wind; wind god.
Veda	sacred knowledge: revelation; scripture.
vedāṅga	limb of *Veda*; auxiliary sciences.
vedānta	end of *Veda*; *Upaniṣads*; name of a system.
vedī	altar for Vedic sacrifices.
vibhava	emanation.
vibhuti	supernatural power.
videha	without a body.
vidhi	ritual.
vidyā	knowledge.
vijñānamaya	made of knowledge.
vinaya	discipline.
vipra	Brahmin.
vīra	hero.
virajā	purity; name of river separating the world of mortals from Viṣṇu's heaven.
virāṭ	first product of Brahman; universe.
vīrya	heroism.
viṣāda	despair.
viśeṣa	propriety.
viśiṣṭa	qualification.
viśva-rūpa	all form; Kṛṣṇa appearing as cosmic person.
vitarka	debate; logical argument.
viveka	descrimination.
vrata	vow; celebration.
vratya	mendicant; class of people; Supreme Being.
vṛddhi	growth.
vṛtti	being; condition; fluctuation; activity, means of subsistence.
vyākaraṇa	grammar.
vyakta	manifest; revealed.
vyāpāra	function.
Vyāsa	arranger; proper name of Vedic sage, compiler of the *Vedas*, the *Mahābhārata* and the *Purāṇas*.
vyavahāra	livelihood; the world of senses.
vyūha	part; special manifestation of Viṣṇu.
yajña	Vedic sacrifice.
yajñopavita	sacred thread.
yajus	rites.
yakṣa	goblin; tree-spirit.
yama	god of the netherworld; restraint (yoga).
yantra	machine; meditational device.
yati	wandering ascetic.
yatidharma	rules for ascetics.

yātrā	pilgrimage.
yoga	yoke; name of a system.
yojana	"mile" (either four, five or nine miles).
yoni	source; womb.
yuga	world era.

INDEX